Talking Up
a Storm

Voices of
the New
West

Gregory
L. Morris

University of
Nebraska Press
Lincoln and London

© 1994 by the University
of Nebraska Press. All
rights reserved. Manufac-
tured in the United States
of America.⊗The paper
in this book meets the
minimum requirements of
American National
Standard for Information
Sciences – Permanence of
Paper for Printed Library
Materials, ANSI Z39.48-
1984. First Bison Books
Printing: 1995. Most
recent printing indicated
by the last digit below:
10 9 8 7 6 5 4 3 2 1
Library of Congress
Cataloging in Publication
Data. Morris, Gregory L.
(Gregory Lynn), 1950–
Talking up a Storm :
voices of the new West /
Gregory L. Morris.
p.   cm. Includes biblio-
graphical references (p.)
ISBN 0-8032-3169-5 (cl. :
alk. paper) ISBN 0-8032-
8224-9 (pa.) 1. American
literature – West (U.S.) –
History and criticism –
Theory, etc. 2. West
(U.S.) – Intellectual life –
20th century. 3. Authors,
American – 20th century
– Interviews. 4. Authors,
American – West (U.S.) –
Interviews. 5. West (U.S.)
– In literature. I. Title.
PS271.M67 1994
813'.54093278 – dc20
93-46326 CIP

For my parents,
Lois and Leon Morris;
and for their grandchildren,
Katherine and Benjamin

CONTENTS

ACKNOWLEDGMENTS

A project of this sort accumulates a sizable list of folks who need to be thanked, but I can think of a few who deserve special mention. First of all, I very much appreciate the support of Penn State–Erie, The Behrend College, whose awarding of a Behrend Faculty Research Initiation Grant made possible much of the travel required by this project. From Behrend I would also like to thank Michael Piotrowski, a student who in the early stages of this collection helped formulate directions the interviews might take; and Norma Hartner, who in the later stages worked her magic in transforming data-on-disk to actual words-on-paper.

For her constancy, for her goodness of heart and patience of ear, I give my thanks and my love to my wife, Gayle. She has heard more than she ever expected to hear of and from these writers, and has helped shape the spirit of this book more than she might ever know.

Finally, of course, I offer my deepest thanks to the writers whose voices fill this book. Were it not for their generosities of time and effort, were it not for their insight and eloquence, this collection would never have seen daylight. For those gifts, I am truly and forever grateful.

All photographs are by the author unless otherwise noted.

INTRODUCTION

These are flush and wondrous times, if not for the American West, then at least for its fiction. Its writers throw wide the "doors to their houses," and what we find upon entering is a literature that (as William Kittredge suggests) "is no longer what we think it should be,"[1] a literature that surprises us and upsets our expectations of what we have come to define and know as Western American fiction.

In fact one of the most significant developments in recent American fiction has been the emergence of distinctive and *new* Western voices, voices that are at once literary and political, that seek both to demolish myth and to create myth anew. Though bound by geography – at least by a *gross* geography – these voices speak from a variety of ethnic and aesthetic origins, and inhabit a variety of landscapes.

These are not the voices, now, of the pulp Western, of Zane Grey and Max Brand and Louis L'Amour, who spoke to preserve the persistent and cherished mythos of our American West. Nor are they the voices of an older generation of Western writers, figures whom John Milton once described as the "upper crust"[2] among Western fiction writers, such as Wallace Stegner and Frederick Manfred, A. B. Guthrie and Dorothy Johnson, Walter Van Tilburg Clark and Wright Morris, Frank Waters and Larry McMurtry. These are the writers who have established the several tones of Western American fiction in the first half or so of this century and who have defined our expectations for that fiction – Western fiction as "we think it should be." These writers shared more or less the same vision of the West, that of a region whose splendid and varied past was slowly catching up to its present; a region whose historical identity spawned a pervasive and generally accepted mythos, one eagerly fed upon by a hungry national imagination; a region whose material and spiritual wealth had not yet quite been exhausted.

The writers I am talking about (and to) are born of a new generation and of a new aesthetic. Generally born after 1940, many of them (but not all)

xi

grew up under the artistic influence of the Stegner-Guthrie tradition, and are now seeking to redirect that tradition. They are writers *born* both in and out of the American West, writers who now *live* both in and out of the American West, but who write primarily of that American West in their fiction. And they are now gaining a national hearing, their work demanding and gaining the critical attention it has long been denied.

Of the many reasons for this increased attention, most important I think is the fact that these are writers who have struck certain chords within the national consciousness, whose concerns extend well beyond the region from which or of which they write. They write of the West because it is their West and our West, and because they recognize the significance of that landscape to both the artistic and the national imaginations. Yet they also write problematically of the West, a land caught up in the anguish of its own transition. Their visions are clouded by ambivalence, their voices hesitant and frequently skeptical. They stand in new and tense relation to the place of which they write, and to the writers who have written of that place before them.

Certainly, this younger generation of writers acknowledges its indebtedness to the established tradition of modern Western fiction; indeed, many of these newer authors studied with members of that older generation and cut their artistic teeth upon their mentors' work. They openly and generously acknowledge their respect (but not their reverence) for these writers; they acknowledge their inheritance of certain elements of that tradition (elements of style, of vision). Indeed, many are just as fiercely protective and proprietary as their predecessors; literary range wars are not uncommon these days out West, and much creative time and energy is spent fencing off aesthetic territory. Outsiders, like homesteaders and sheepmen in the early days, are often suspect. But this younger generation enjoys a less coherent vision of both what the West and the Western writer should be. These writers are, in fact, what might be described as postmodernist and post-regionalist writers.

For one thing, these men and women partake of a particularly ambiguous and ambivalent attitude toward *place*. They are much less concerned with the historical value of place, much less concerned, too, with what Max Westbrook called the "sacrality" of place.[3] The historical and spiritual significance of the West, while still a vital part of the vision of some contemporary Western fiction writers, has suffered too much reduction, too much dilution, too much profanation to exert the kind of pervasive influence it once did in the literature of the West. The West, too, is less often seen as a specific *region*, its writers now pushing the West beyond regionalism and toward integration. The geographic and imaginative vision of the West has broadened itself, it seems, in its slow, often reluctant evolution ("America as region," Tom McGuane remarks). Finally, the impulse among the characters of this New Western fiction is more often to escape *from* the West than to escape *to* the West, an impulse that reflects a rejection rather than an embracing of the long-prevailing mythos.

These New Western fiction writers also stand in a slightly different relation to *time* than did the previous generation. They are less obsessed with the past, particularly the distant and the not-so-distant pasts, of the American West (historical stages defined by Richard Etulain as the "frontier West" and the "regional West") and are more concerned with the present and future Wests.[4] To be sure, our best Western writers (and our best writers, period) have always explored the moral complexity of our own peculiar history in our own peculiar geography. Jon Tuska remarks that the finest of our Western fiction writers

> have recognized . . . in the depths of their being that the past does have something to teach us, if we are willing to learn from it, and that the Western novel and story are the ideal literary form through which our American past can be evoked vividly and painfully – painfully because it was mostly painful. The story of the American West is not romance; it is very often tragedy. But even in tragedy, as writers since Aeschylus have known, there can be human nobility. Most of all fiction about the American West is about *man in nature*, not the denatured, mechanical, sterile world that increasingly has come to serve as a backdrop for human activity in other kinds of fiction. In this sense, the West is just what the Indians always thought it was, the land beyond the setting sun, the Spiritland.[5]

And the "historical reconstruction" that Tuska describes in his work, a kind of fiction that casts a backward glance upon the West, is still an important part of our best Western writing. Ron Hansen, Molly Gloss, and Ivan Doig, among others, work to reinterpret the historical circumstance of the West and, thereby, the nation. The national conscience (or the lack thereof) exerted itself heavily upon the West, and these writers study the effects (so often tragic, as Tuska notes) of such influence upon the people and the landscape they inhabit.

But what takes place in this particularly historically minded fiction is a very clear refiguring of the mythology of the Old West, which fiction writers and historians alike are beginning to see as worn and frayed and ultimately debilitating. Thus, while revisionist historians such as Patricia Limerick, Donald Worster, and others redraw the history and historiography of the American West, writers such as Ron Hansen (in his novels *Desperadoes* and *The Assassination of Jesse James by the Coward Robert Ford*) and William Kittredge (in his story "Phantom Silver," an irreverent and powerful rehandling of the Lone Ranger legend) work to reimagine the West, to demythologize the West, to disturb and alter forever that filmy, nostalgic national dreamscape. Such demythification and, perhaps, remythification is necessary, beneficial, as Patricia Limerick notes in her revisionist study of the West, *The Legacy of Conquest:* "Acknowledging the moral complexity of Western history does not require us to surrender the mythic power traditionally associated with the region's story. On the contrary, moral complexity provides the base for parables and tales of greater and deeper meaning."[6]

What is also being altered is our perception of the *New* West, as writers seek to describe it in terms that will defy time and place and accurately portray the social and historical conditions of that place. For one thing, the New West which they are busy imagining is politically underempowered, managed and mismanaged by outside (usually Eastern) interests. They feel – indeed, they witness – the exertion of such forces in their political backyards, and in their fictions they write to reveal the condition of the West as American colony. Parochialism, often a fault of regional art, gives way here to a concern with the national political vision, and even with the international (multinational) political vision. What we are witnessing is a very real politicization of these writers. Thus, John Keeble, in his novels *Yellowfish* and *Broken Ground* and in his nonfiction (*Out of the Channel,* his study of the 1989 Alaskan oil spill), makes his central concern the relationship between the individual, the government, and the corporation, and the nature of corporate evil. James Crumley, in his novel *Dancing Bear,* examines the exploitation of the West through corporate and governmental collusion; and in other novels he notes the colonialization of the West (a view held by many of the writers interviewed here, and certainly by many of the people living in the West). The West is held hostage to "national priorities," so that it becomes a dumping ground for our various national wastes: toxic chemicals, nuclear tailings, Eastern tourists, crackpot religious and political groups.

Yet these writers are politically astute realists, and so are careful to note the inherent paradoxes of the region: the incorrigibly "independent" West dependent upon federal support, Westerners' inherent suspiciousness of outsiders in a region all-too-well known for its exploitation of outsiders and foreigners, the insistence upon the openness of a landscape that is historically and morally not theirs to open and close. At times, one detects traces of the old populism, but what really is at the heart of these fictions is an intense and unidealized concern with the activity – human, corporate, political, spiritual – upon a specific, significant landscape, the consequences of which they see as potentially (if not already) tragic.

Perhaps the most dramatic shift in contemporary Western fiction has been in the viewpoints taken by its women writers, who are significantly reenvisioning the West and the roles played by women. We are now beginning to see how the Western woman historically functioned apart from the myth; and the women writers who have imaginatively inherited that experience seek to capture both the historical and the modern essence of that experience, and to understand what it means to live a life in the West as a woman. Gretel Ehrlich, in her novel *Heart Mountain*, takes the landscape of Wyoming during World War II and at once politicizes and eroticizes that landscape. Molly Gloss, in her novel *The Jump-Off Creek*, reaches into the imagined life of a lone Oregon ranchwoman settling, establishing her place within that singular portion of the Western geography. And Mary Clearman Blew, in her collection of stories, *Runaway*, explains what it is like "growing up female in Charlie Russell country."

Interestingly enough, where these newer writers of the West stand in greatest proximity to the region's older writers is in the matter of style. As I mentioned earlier, many of these new writers studied with the older generation – indeed, many of the younger writers studied with other members of the new generation (Beer and Long, for example, worked with Kittredge). They may not have adopted the aesthetic or political visions of their teachers, yet these New Westerners often have come around to a stylistic position closely akin to that of their predecessors. First of all, many of these writers (though certainly not all) are responding to, and rebelling against, what is fashionably called the postmodern aesthetic; they seek a fiction grounded in responsibility, in human crisis and thought and eventual action. Ivan Doig's comment on "what fiction should do" is, I think, representative of the stance taken by many interviewed here:

I want my characters to exist within historical laws of gravity. That's how people *do* exist, after all. Irony and angst are not the only things –

or even the main things – that operate on people. . . . The market forces in agriculture, the weather – those are big things to the people I write about, the cosmos they live in. Now, within that cosmos . . . happen a lot of personal complications for my characters – but unlike much of modern "canonical" fiction, those personal complications don't constitute the whole of my characters and plotlines. I just think there's bigger game than that.

Again, not all of the authors included in this collection would agree with Doig; certainly not all would agree even to be in pursuit of the same "game." But many do seem to work from an aesthetic that is conservative, traditional, and set against the prevailing winds.

Still, there is a problem of style among these writers, and part of that problem lies in their need to find a language compatible with their own shifting attitudes toward landscape. Many of them *want* to believe in the sacred and meaningful relationship between language and the land, because the Old West writers believed in that relationship – it is their link to that tradition, and their means to the source of that tradition's power; but the radical and profound changes worked upon the Western landscape now make such belief difficult. So the New West writers settle for a style that allows a compromise, one that perhaps provides a new rhythm for an altered, abused landscape.

The West and its literature, then, clearly are not dead issues. Those interviewed here, through their work, through their commentary upon that work and upon that place they take as their subject, speak with eloquence and force of the West's vitality and jeopardy. The Western vision, as described in its current fictions, is expansive, various, often breathtaking. We no longer know what to expect from these writers – and that is a sure sign of good health.

There are times when actual event and circumstance explain matters more persuasively than does simple analysis. And I cannot think of a more expressive and poignant emblem of the transition taking place in Western American fiction than one particular event that occurred in the process of conducting these interviews.

In October 1990, I traveled to Dutton, Montana, to talk with Richard Ford. During my three-day visit, I accompanied Ford and his wife Kristina to a conference celebrating the life and work of A. B. Guthrie held outside of Choteau ("My favorite Montana city," claimed Ford), on the grounds of the Pine Butte Swamp Conservatory. Ford was to sit on a panel with Mary Clearman Blew, the two of them to talk generally about writers and writing. As it happened, Ford's appearance coincided with the first day of pheasant season, and we spent the early morning hours lucklessly combing the stubble fields outside of Dutton. Ford, an avid pheasant hunter, was not eager to give up the rest of the day to a trip to Choteau and to an almost predictable series of questions and answers about the writing life.

Still, we made the drive, and for part of the trip Ford cracked wise about Guthrie and his work, admitting even to never having read *The Big Sky*. Once at Pine Butte, we gathered with teachers and with other authors (William Kittredge, Annick Smith, and James Welch were in attendance that day), and listened as Ford and Blew talked colorfully of being writers, of being Montana writers (a designation Blew was more ready to admit to than was Ford). Afterward, Ford reluctantly agreed to accept Guthrie's invitation to visit him at his home on the conservatory grounds (Guthrie, because of his age and his extremely poor health, had not appeared yet at the conference).

Inside Guthrie's log-cabin home, the writer rested, tubes running from a nearby oxygen tank to his nostrils. Guthrie had become a ninety-year-old man beleaguered by emphysema, tugging his life about wherever he so slowly walked. While we all gathered around the same table, Ford and Guthrie paired off in dialogue, settling in to a quiet, patient, admiring discussion of each other's work. Again and again, Guthrie's near-native Montana burr would trail off into painful whisper, allowing Ford's Mississippi drawl to retrieve the thread of conversation and narrative. Here were two writers whose work was as distinct and distant as the nearly half-century of years that separated their births. No clear legacy was handed down that afternoon, no inheritance was granted or acknowledged. But on the drive back to Dutton, Ford spoke with new and sincere respect (not reverence or adulation, but respect) for this writer and his particular, private vision of the West, tacitly admitting his own place in that westering tradition. Within the year, Guthrie would be dead and Ford would be resettled in New Orleans.

The interviews collected here all were conducted between 1988 and 1992, and were carried out in one of two ways, depending upon the preference of the writer. Many authors wished to be interviewed in person (not to be so, thought Gretel Ehrlich, would be "cheating"), while others opted to respond in writing to my written questions. In both cases, I have tried to edit in the sorts of elements that would make these interviews as conversational and as fluid as possible. In all cases, I am thankful for the inherent grace and poetry of the writers' words themselves, and to their own efforts (in the in-person interviews) in editing out the rough spots.

In selecting the writers to be interviewed, I aimed for as great a creative and geographical range as practical limits would allow. I wanted to represent the various Wests as well as possible, and have tried not to shortchange any particular region of the West. The more voices, the better. If this collection does tilt in any one direction, however, it is toward the state of Montana, and this is because so much of the late "renaissance" in Western fiction can be traced to that locale. The nurturing over time of Western writers (and readers) at the University of Montana in Missoula by Richard Hugo, Leslie Fiedler, and William Kittredge, and the publication of *The Last Best Place: A Montana Anthology*, have combined to shape a very real community of writers within the state.[7] Perhaps only in the West could one even speak of a statewide "community" of writers that might compare to more localized coteries such as those that gathered around Taos or Big Sur. Perhaps this is another function of Western fiction itself: the reduction and management of space by language.

I have also certainly omitted many voices that should be heard; such omission is (as I have already noted) a function both of time and space, and of the wish to avoid duplication; for example, I saw no need to try to improve upon the comments of writers included in Laura Coltelli's collec-tion of interviews with Native American writers, *Winged Words* (Lincoln: University of Nebraska Press, 1990), though I did see fit to include one writer not interviewed in Coltelli's work. Some writers, too, simply declined to be interviewed.

As for the questions themselves, I sought to fashion questions that fit the work of the individual authors and to avoid stock, uniform questions that might be answered by all (though specific recurring themes certainly emerge from the interviews). My aim was to persuade these writers to talk about *their* lives and *their* work and to define their private and artistic relationship with the West.

I restricted the scope of this collection to fiction writers, largely because of my own sense that some of the most exciting creative work being done these days is in this area. Obviously, the writers here are not strictly fiction writers, either. Most labor in other realms as well; some are poets, some are film-

makers and screenwriters, most are essayists. Indeed, one of the most remarkable developments among these writers of fiction is their work in
nonfiction. A great many of these men and women are busy writing essays
about place, about literature, and about the historical, often autobiographical Self in relation to that place and that literature.

All of the writers collected here write with a wonderful and abundant
variety of voices. What I have tried to capture is the voice-within-the-voice,
the writer in self-reflection, the writer speaking directly, purposefully, and (I
hope) truthfully of a tradition and of his or her place in that tradition. As we
listen, we learn something of where that tradition is headed, we make out
the lineaments of what will one day be a significant portion of our literary
heritage.

NOTES

1. William Kittredge, "Doors to Our House," *Owning It All* (St. Paul, Minn.:
Graywolf Press, 1987), p.176.
2. John Milton, "The Novel in the American West," in *Critical Essays on the Western
American Novel*, ed. William T. Pilkington (Boston: G. K. Hall, 1980), p.4.
3. Max Westbrook, "The Western Esthetic," in *Critical Essays on the Western American Novel*, ed. Pilkington, p.77.
4. Richard W. Etulain, "Frontier and Region in Western Literature," in *Critical
Essays on the Western American Novel*, ed. Pilkington, p.86.
5. Jon Tuska, *The American West in Fiction* (1982; repr. Lincoln: University of Nebraska Press, 1988), pp.25–26.
6. Patricia Nelson Limerick, *The Legacy of Conquest: The Unbroken Past of the American West* (New York: W. W. Norton & Company, 1987), p.54.
7. William Kittredge and Annick Smith, eds., *The Last Best Place: A Montana
Anthology* (Helena: Montana Historical Society, 1988).

Talking Up a Storm

Ralph Beer

Ralph Beer, born in 1947, was raised on a ranch near Clancy, Montana – the same ranch homesteaded by his grandfather – and today still lives on and works that ranch. While a member of the graduate writing program at the University of Montana Beer edited the literary magazine *Cutbank,* and he has been a contributing editor of *Harper's.* Beer's novel *The Blind Corral* was awarded the 1986 Silver Spur Award as that year's best Western novel. Beer is also the author of several short stories and a frequent essayist on the West.

Beer himself is a large man with a bounteous mustache and a deep-voiced laugh and a real sense of the "physical" about him. He and his wife Margaret built the new log house in which they live; both the original bunkhouse and homestead cabin still exist, just a few hundred yards away from the new house. Before we conducted the interview (in June 1990), we walked the ranch and rested upon a large rock outcropping overlooking the Prickly Pear Valley; as we talked, Beer made no bones about feeling closed-in-upon by commuter subdivisions, about inhabiting the "last best place" in the valley.

GREGORY MORRIS: *You are one of what seems to be a rare breed: a native Montanan – and a native Montanan writer – who has stayed in Montana to live and work. What has that been like, growing up in Montana, remaining in and seemingly putting down roots here?*

RALPH BEER: I don't think my experience – of growing up in Montana and making the decision to come back to Montana (actually, I had other plans when I got out of the Army, I was headed for Canada and Alaska) – I don't think my experience on this place has been a typical Montana-ranchboy-growing-up-on-the-farm experience. It's been somewhat different in that this place has been the kind of place that never, ever really supported itself. We always had to bring money into the place to support it. And yet, until just two or three years ago, I never stopped hoping that someday it would get to that point, that we could acquire more land without getting heavily leveraged. In the last couple of years, I saw that this was not going to happen, that the ranch was never going to get to that point. I realized that if I wanted a better place, I would have to *find* a better place. At the same time, the way we did things up here and the influence of my dad and his dad, who subscribed to the hillbilly ethics of "Don't borrow any money!" and "Do it by hand!" have kept this ranch out of debt and led me to feel about this place in ways that are not typical emotional responses to places from people who grew up on them and who try to make a living on them. Because they often end up doing battle with those places, they also end up trying to take more out of the place than the place ought to give in order to make their interest payments.

You mentioned Canada, and your intention to head that way once you left the Army; and you did eventually make it up there, doing "a stint as a cowboy in British Columbia." Were you, like your novel's hero, Jackson Heckethorn, riding rodeo?

No, I wasn't rodeoing. I ran off – I fell in love and I ran off with a beautiful girl in 1971 before I was drafted. I ended up working for a horsebreaker up there named Kenneth Glaze; he was an old cowboy from Colorado, and he was the real deal. He had a little place tucked up in the bush up by Hixon, British Columbia. I rode horses for him, fenced for him, put up hay for him with the teams; there was no electricity, no refrigeration. I worked later on another ranch there that was a little more modern operation. These people ran a cow-calf operation in 80 or so square miles of bush. There was nothing out there, not even a road, so you'd get on a saddle horse and go find the cows. While I was up there, the lady and I built a log cabin, which was one of the high points of my life.

Then I was drafted. I came back to the States and did my hitch, with all of the intention in the world of going right back up there as soon as I got out of the Army. But when I got home, my granddad was sick, and I looked around and said, "Canada? *This* is where I ought to be."

Sounds similar to Jackson Heckethorn's situation in The Blind Corral.

Sure, though I think Jackson's decision is a lot tougher than mine.

What eventually convinced you that you could become a writer, having spent all your life as a Montana rancher?

I *still* don't think I'm convinced that I can be a writer. I think that I was very lucky, largely because of friendships with people like Neil McMahon, who writes under the name Daniel Rhodes; he was in the writing program in Missoula in 1977 and we were pals. He kept dragging me into bars where there were these other writers, and I liked them – they were funny and interesting and told good stories – writers like Bill Kittredge and Dick Hugo and Jim Crumley and Jim Welch, and lots of interesting graduate students who I thought were terrifically smart people. I surely wasn't convinced at that time – 1977, 1978, 1979 – that I could join their ranks. I had no intention of even trying.

Finally, because I liked these people so much (and after my dad said he'd cover for me here at the ranch), I decided to go to Missoula and take some graduate courses. My buddy Neil and I bought a house together there, in 1978, and I took one of Bill Kittredge's graduate workshops. I wrote a story for that course that ended up being published in *TriQuarterly*, and that became the first six chapters of my novel. It was my very first story! Everybody was supportive and encouraging, and good enough to say, "No, no, Ralph, you don't want to do this. Take this out of here because . . ." They were teaching me things, and it accumulated finally to the point where I could write another story and write another story and four or five years later take on writing a novel.

So you began as a short story writer?

Yes, just groping around. The simplest things would stop me, though. Point of view, for example, would stop me: "I've read hundreds of novels in the third person, but how can you possibly write that way? 'He did this, he did that, he picked up his shovel and went down to the creek.'" It sounded flat as hell when I tried to do it, so it took me a long time to learn how to manage those things. Voice – I found voice to be the key to the whole damned thing, because if you get the narrative voice right you're in business. If you had a story and a couple of characters who somehow came to life in your imagination, and you could find the voice, then away you went. If you didn't have those – next story! Which has always been the hardest thing for me, trying to find the story; I don't get very many good ideas for stories, although I do get a lot of *bad* ideas for stories. A story that has some kind of leaping-off point where the characters jump off the edge of the world at the beginning and come to some kind of recognition of emotional change at the end of the story? It's hard for me to discover those stories. They just do not come often. And without that idea, I'm better off fixing the baler than trying to write.

Do you feel you're at an early stage in your development as a writer?

I think, if I can get going again, if I can start writing hard again the way I wrote when I was working on my novel, that whatever I write next will be different from what I've written before. Because there's a two-year gap in there and I'm not the person I was when I wrote *The Blind Corral* – I'm much humbler, much wiser!

I can feel it when I'm doing handwork down at the barn. There's nothing like handwork to let your imagination loose; I start digging a hole of some kind, and whatever those voices are going to be and whatever those situations and storylines are going to be, they're going to be different from what I imagined and visualized before.

You think there's that kind of imaginative release in work itself?

Absolutely, absolutely – at least for me, personally; I surely can't speak for anybody else. I know an awful lot of writers who go soft. Writing's hard on people, it takes all your energy; if you start at eight in the morning and work until one or two in the afternoon, it takes everything out of you. I just don't see how people do anything else when they're writing, and a lot of people don't and so they get soft. I stumbled onto this business of thinking while

6

working years ago, splitting wood by hand. Since last September, my wife Margaret and I have cut and split and stacked 30 cord of wood, which is a *lot* of wood; and I've found that there's nothing like going out there and getting in the woodpile for about four hours and just splitting a block of wood and putting it in a pile, splitting a block of wood and putting it in a pile, to let my mind start to work on altogether other levels because the work is so simple and dull. What tipped me off was I realized that when I was splitting wood I referred to myself in my mind as "you"; it was as if I was talking to me, but there were two of me – "I" was talking to "you." I got curious about that, it just kept happening and happening; it took me a long time even to discover it, I would guess. But I think that business of "I" addressing "You" has something to do with telling stories or wanting to write stories. Of course I had no social life at all when this started, so maybe I just needed to talk to the only "you" available.

In your case, those stories seemed connected to kinship and place, to the sort of familial and communal "membership" Wendell Berry describes in his fiction (and you quote Berry in an epigraph to The Blind Corral*). Do you think such a membership exists, that sort of spiritual connection usually among male members of a family or a community?*

I think if we're real lucky we'll grow up in a situation where one generation leaves some kind of place or at least a remembered experience to the next generation that involves love. It did here. I used to have a photograph, which I've lost, of my granddad standing on the front porch of his old log house over there, and on the back he'd written, in ballpoint pen: "Howard I. Beer and the ranch I love." He was an old man, seventy-five or so, and solitary and tough, and I thought: Yeah. He would *never* say that to me, but it's the absolute truth. My dad felt that way about this place and I feel that way about this place, and it's a feeling that has been handed from one to the other. And I think that much of that love hinged on working together and telling stories connected to *where* that work was done.

When I was a little kid, we'd go out and cut wood in the wintertime; we'd work hard, then come in, build a big fire in the stove, and my granddad would throw some deer steaks in a frying pan. It was always men. My dad's mother died in 1937, and my wife Margaret is the first woman to live on this place *since* 1937. So it's over fifty years since there's been a woman on this ranch. My folks had a house in town and a little place out in the Helena

Valley, and my mom really didn't want to have anything to do with the ranch. She very seldom ever came up here, and if she did she'd just come up and look around; she didn't have any real connection to the place; we certainly didn't try to exclude her – she just wasn't very interested in the place. I grew up with that, and it didn't seem to bother anybody, it wasn't a cause of strife.

But my granddad and my dad and I would work together, cut wood, say, during the wintertime, and then come in and fire up the kitchen range and cook up some deer steaks and potatoes, and they would start telling stories: "Do you remember that stud that Clyde Burgess had?" "Yeah, I remember that stud!" Some kind of little story would develop that had some kind of a point to it – something to do with courage or facing things or dumb luck good or bad or the way things were. Like I was telling you yesterday, when my grandmother died, in the middle of winter, my dad had to walk home, get a team of horses and go down to the highway and pull the car home after the funeral – and then they milked the cows. Forty cows. By hand. Well, that's a little story I heard; maybe it's not a complete story, but those kinds of events and episodes in the lives of my kin used to leave me with a feeling about this place, which grew and deepened with time into love and a sense of kinship for this home place.

I once felt that this country was a lot bigger than it seems to me now, and was still populated with all those people who had at one time or another inhabited it, although some of those people had gone broke and left in the 1920s. In my imagination, as a little boy, they were all still here and somehow still alive; and a lot of those people end up in the things I write. Those stories gave me a sense of this being a wonderful place, a place that was alive and inhabited, even though it was only really inhabited most of the time by one old man and a handful of neighbors. That was the major impetus for me writing that novel: I wanted to go back and live in that wonderful place of imagination and memory again.

That sense of place is certainly central to your work. You said yesterday that if there's anything that connects you with a tradition, or even creates a tradition, among Western writers, it's that sense of place. And for you, that's a very personal, very intimate relation to place.

My granddad was an expert horseman, he was a horseman's horseman. He was also the ringleader among all these homesteaders who lived around here. A lot of people have the idea of homesteaders as being these "honyockers or grow broke" type people who may have been up there on the plains north of Great Falls, on 160 acres, turning over sod. But in this particular country, farming was just a joke. On a lot of these places they had to haul in their drinking water in barrels because there *was* no water, and not much hope of water. So these guys would try to turn a dollar any way they could. They'd go get a bunch of horses that weren't branded, second- and third- and fourth-generation colts – the original horses had belonged to some homesteader who *had* gone broke and they'd turned them out and they'd bred and bred and bred – and they'd go out and catch a bunch of those big three- or four-year-old colts and bring them in, try to break them and turn a dollar.

Out there on the porch there's the hood off my granddad's whiskey still; he made a lot of money making and selling whiskey, he made enough money that while most everyone else was going broke and leaving the country, he managed to raise five kids on this place. But it took a lot of guts to do it. My dad, when he was six years old, one day opened the gate for a big black Cadillac car that drove in with six men in it looking for my grandfather, and they were all wearing suits and topcoats; but they didn't get him with any whiskey. It took a lot of courage to do what he did. This country right in here, this pocket of, say, a 100-mile radius, was full of people like him, people who were tough and who didn't have very far to fall, because they were so close to the bottom already.

So they did these things that in my imagination, as a child and as a young man, seemed pretty interesting and wild and adventuresome. A lot of the stories that I heard were told by one or more of the original participants; my dad and my granddad would sit over in my granddad's cabin and tell these stories back and forth, but it'd be like father telling son and son telling back to the father these stories that had been told many, many times. So, for me, those stories were valid, and if they were amplified in any way it was proba-bly in *my* imagination and in *my* memory. In my novel, there's a story about a guy who's a drunk named Bill Hirsch, and Bill Hirsch gets drunk one night and falls asleep in a snowdrift and freezes his feet: that was written just as exactly faithful to the story as I heard it as a boy as I could make it; I didn't amplify it at all, I hope. It happened, and yes, he filed his own toes off and kept those toes around his cabin in a mustard jar full of alcohol.

But I think we're going to have to find new stories to tell ourselves, because the old stories don't have much weight anymore. The old stories keep getting people into trouble around here, in fact; the old stories of going off to wilderness and living in wilderness, in isolation, seeing civilization as corrupt and the wilderness as pure, keep getting people killed in Montana. Three or four years ago, these bad hillbillies snatched a woman, a world-class athlete, and ended up killing a man; they got into all kinds of trouble, they made some bad mistakes, yet I think one of the reasons they did those things is that they simply weren't able to adapt their lives to the rapidly changing scene down in the Gallatin Valley country. The older man had grown up in those mountains, and the next thing he knew there was a big ski resort and all kinds of development, lots of rich people and a golf course – an Arnold Palmer golf course, for Christ's sake! Being overrun by money and moneyed people tends to make some folks mean, especially if they cling to that old mythology: We'll move West, we'll go to higher country, we'll run off to territory – and there's no more territory to run off to, really. If you want to run off to territory now, you'd better think about going to Nebraska!

Since we're talking about stories, let's talk a bit about your story "The Harder They Come." In that story you examine what happens when a choice is made between land and community. Gregor MacIvers is the isolated rancher – divorced, solitary, insular – who in his isolation and withdrawal opts for "land over community," a choice that "isolated him from good," and which eventually kills him. How do you reconcile that need to distance oneself from what's going on in the West – "the people problem," as you call it in The Blind Corral *– with the need for community?*

That story was not an attempt to reconcile anything. It was an attempt to show how that kind of isolation happens to people, and how one little mistake will lead to another little mistake and then lead to another little mistake. I know that kind of story is true. It is a masculine story, in that most of the things MacIvers is obsessed with are outdoor or masculine pursuits. In some circles, that's a strike against him. He's also angry and upset about being divorced. Between the lines, he misses his wife a lot. He is not going to admit it to himself; he's going to be angry about it and blame her for his choices so that he *doesn't have to* admit his mistakes to himself. The things he reflects on as he's down there with a broken neck, dying in that haybarn, are the mistakes that he made that led him to that point; and some of his mistakes involve the mistake of not admitting things to yourself: if you'd just sit yourself down for a while and say, Okay, I fucked up here; I'd better straighten this out. Or I'd better not do that anymore. I'd better go talk to these people and straighten this all out. I'd better go talk to my *wife* and straighten *that* out. But he made this little chain of choices. If anything, that story is about the dark side of isolation, the dark side of making those kinds of choices, about how isolation feeds on itself, and how you can damned near justify anything if you try to be real "Western." If you're living alone, with a head full of Western mythology, you *can* justify almost anything; you can even justify yourself.

I wrote that story right after I finished my novel, about three months after I finished my novel. I sat down and wrote that story in a fairly short – short, for me – period of time; I worked on it every day, and got it done in two or three months. In spite of what I just said, I like old MacIvers, the main character, and I like the story, even though it's a pretty grim one. I like the reflective business that he's forced into finally, where he does start thinking about the death of his father, about pushing too hard, working too hard so that he *doesn't* have to think about things, staying tired all the time and putting all his energy into acquiring more land. I like the business where he finally has to grope his way to the point where he can laugh at his own greed and his own life. One of the things that tickles me about that story is how much of it I stole from other writers; I stole the idea from the Jack London story, "To Build a Fire," where the lone man does the same thing: he makes a small series of mistakes until he finally ends up freezing to death. And Bill Kittredge's story, "A Breaker of Horses," where the guy's finally immobilized and has to deal with things – I stole that too, but don't tell Bill. There are also lines in the story that are either stolen directly from or just slightly altered from other writers I admire, like Jim Welch and Jim Crumley. I engage in this thievery to pay homage to writers I love and respect. It seems a better way of recognizing their good work than to say, "Gee, I like your book."

I'm curious about your friendship with Crumley, who seems to appear – under the name of Duncan Carlisle – in The Blind Corral. *Is there a history to that friendship? Are you one of the Dumpp Family Singers?*

The first thing I have to say about the Dumpp Family Singers is that when I wrote the first draft of my book, I already had the first six chapters, as well as some chapters that ended up in the middle of the book, chapters about Harley dying. In that first attempt to get through the draft, I realized I was in trouble somewhere; it seemed like Jackson Heckethorn was on this long, gradual decline and that things were getting grayer and grayer and grayer for poor old Jack. On some level, I realized that I had to get him out of there, had to get him off that ranch, take him someplace else and let something else happen to him. I wrote a bunch of nonsense – he ended up going to Missoula in pursuit of the girl who's in Canada. None of that made it into the book, thank goodness, but the instinct was right, and when I went back to revise the first draft, I realized I had to get him out of there but I didn't have to take him very far. So I just took Jackson to Clancy – a very funky little town about 5 miles from here – and let him run into these people, whom I think an awful lot of; and I let those people jack Jackson around the way those people used to jack *me* around!

I lived in pretty severe isolation up here for much of the fifteen years after I got home from the Army, and I would go to Missoula on a Friday night and end up in the Eastgate Liquor Store and Lounge; there were a bunch of people there I wanted to see, I wanted to talk to them and I wanted to listen to them – I *especially* wanted to listen to them. So I would find myself standing next to Crumley down by the telephone at the end of the bar, listening to him. The guy who got me going to Missoula and the Eastgate in the first place – and who helped me build my haybarn – was, again, Neil McMahon; Neil introduced me to all of those people. So these friendships were formed very gradually, but these people would draw me in and socialize me and humanize me; and that was very important to me. I needed it and I wanted it, and they were kind enough to provide it. There was a guy in the graduate program, when I got in, named Carl Clatterbuck – he could be a great short story writer, I think – he has a terrific voice, that unique kind of storytelling voice that's mean and funny at the same time. It's an odd sort of voice, it's a voice that when you read his stories stands out and pulls you along, like Ray Carver's voice.

Anyway, Clatterbuck and McMahon were buddies, so the four of us – Clatterbuck, McMahon, Crumley, and I – gradually, over a period of two to three years, got to be pretty close friends. One day we went up to the Missoula landfill to haul some garbage for Rick DeMarinis, who was too broke at the time to pay for garbage service; we loaded up my pick-up with about two months' worth of Rick's garbage and took it up to the landfill and ended up having a lot of fun up there, watching the machinery and goofing around, picking through the garbage and chasing the seagulls – real adolescent behavior that seemed to be a lot of fun. Hell, it *was* a lot of fun! On the way home from the dump, we started making up the mythology of this imaginary family and we groped our way toward some kind of title for this group. Finally I said, "Let's call ourselves the Dumpp Family Singers." (It was *my* idea – Crumley will dispute this for sure!) Then we gave each other names: Crumley was Pa, of course, because he was the old fart; Neil became Neilon, you know, the more hillbilly the better; Carl became Young Eugene; and I became Orris Dumpp.

Then Crumley dedicated *Dancing Bear* to the Dumpp Family Singers, so I picked that up and tried to roll it over one more time in my book, because the Dumpp Family Singers, by that point, had become fairly well known in Missoula – most of the people over there were probably tired of the Dumpp Family Singers by then, tired of our little jokes. I called them the Von Trash Family Singers, and I had to change a couple of the people. I tried to do Crumley, as Duncan Carlisle, pretty straight; I just tried to do Crumley, because Crumley as Crumley is plenty good enough. But I had trouble with my buddy Neil; he read my novel manuscript and he was the first one to tell me, You're going to have to do something here, because this is flat. And he was right. So I turned Neil into a midget, and away we went again. It was a good move for me – it was one of those things that you don't think out very clearly but just do instinctively because you don't know what else to do – but it really helped me write that book because the grayness would start to come and you could see that Jackson was going to get bogged down at the ranch. Then he goes to Clancy, and something happens to him that confuses him even more. But *I* had a lot of fun – every time I'd get to the Dumpp Family sequence when I was working on the book – fifth draft, sixth draft – I'd start having fun; I'd tune the dialogue and worry about the individual movements of the characters. So it helped me get through the book, because I knew that on the other side of that Jackson was going to start facing reality again. The Dumpp Family helped me write my book in several ways, not the least of which was by simply being *in* it.

Since we're talking about The Blind Corral, *let's talk about it in some detail. That novel seems very much in the realistic tradition, particularly in the amount and the depth of the work detail you offer there. There seems a very strong sense of the physical, of the physically real in the book – ranchwork is very carefully and very rigorously described. Do you see yourself as a realist fiction writer, as part of that tradition?*

Fifteen years ago, I kept reading Hemingway over and over and over. Up here, working on the ranch, I used to treat myself at lunch: I'd come in and fix myself lunch and read one Hemingway short story. Then I'd go back down to the corrals and go back to work and think about that story. So I don't know if I'm part of any tradition at all, but those stories, that kind of writing had an effect on me, and I think it's the only way I *could* write back at the stage I was in when I wrote the first chapters of *Blind Corral.* I didn't know any other way to write, and that way was hard enough. But I didn't consciously make a decision to walk in the footsteps of the realists, no.

There are a couple of scenes in my book that aren't realistic scenes. You know the movie *Aguirre, The Wrath of God?* There's a scene near the end of the movie where Aguirre is down on the floodplain of the Amazon, and there are monkeys all over his raft; he looks up in this tree and there's a Spanish galleon up there. Well, there's a scene in my novel that's like that, and that's certainly not realism. There's a scene where Jackson is hunting deer and he's getting ready to shoot this little buck. He's waiting for the buck to turn its head away from him, because he knows the buck can see him, if he moves, out of the corner of his eye; he's got an old 30-40 Craig rifle and he's got the bead on the end of the barrel right on the buck's eye, and he's just waiting for him to turn so he can shoot him back of the ear. Between Jackson and the deer there's a little road cut through the woods, and in the trees all around Jackson and all around the deer, there's hemp bailer twine blowing in the wind, and it's been in there so long it's all rotten. Between Jack and the deer, on this road, Harley and Jack as a boy and his brother Summerfield go by with a hayboat and cattle following the hayboat – and he sees them pass between him and the deer. His brother, Summerfield, has been dead for several years. After this vision passes into the storm, Jackson shoots the deer. That's not realism!

And I like that little scene; I wasn't trying to put a Spanish galleon in a tree when I wrote it, but it happened that way. And I think it's some reflection of the way I occasionally think up here, not that I have visions or anything but that occasionally I do get to where I'll be looking at something and remembering, pretty intensely, something else that happened twenty-five years ago *in that place, in that spot.* That, I think more than anything else, sucks me into this place; that is why it would be hard to leave this place. I am the fourth one here, and this place very truly is in my blood, perhaps *almost* to the point where I can remember life here before I was born.

But the way you describe place in the novel doesn't seem intensely subjective, doesn't tend to romanticize place. The images aren't lyrical or passionate. Is that part of the distancing effort, with Jackson trying to distance himself from that geography of the ranch?

I'm not sure I can answer that question because I think several things are involved. For one, it's a function of Jackson Heckethorn's character. For most of the book you're looking right through Jackson's eyes and he's scrambled in a way; he has a way of looking dead at things and seeing things just directly. For example, the old haybarn's fallen down into this big pile of boards and lumber, and he just looks at it and reports what he sees. On the other hand, he's confused because he's been badly injured and he's hiding, too; he's been making pretty hard efforts not to see the girl in Canada – it was probably just as easy to stay in the hospital as it was to come home. But my point is that when he's not reporting the actual, he is sometimes overcome by what he remembers and what he imagines.

This combination of things is Jackson's character, which isn't exactly *my* character; Jack Heckethorn and I are different people. I groped my way to him and to that voice and to that perspective gradually, over the course of several years, until I was comfortable thinking, Yes, this is a good way to get at these different things, by having him look at things straight on at times and be an unreliable reporter at other times. Whenever he's around Annie, he's drifty, almost adolescent; Annie's always telling him, Do this, do that, don't talk like that. But when he's by himself, or when he's confronting Harley and arguing with Harley, Jack's usually dead-on. That flexibility in his character shows up in the way he sees and the way he describes what he sees.

The hard part about writing that book was finding a story that would allow Jackson Heckethorn to live a long enough period of time and act a long enough period of time, so that I could say what was on *my* mind. I wasn't even sure what that was at first, and I had to grope my way toward that, too. But writing plainly about a man who sees his home place and kin plainly doesn't mean that we, author and character, don't see them as beautiful and lyrical and capable of filling us occasionally with passion. Home and kin and memories save us both.

The book seems very specifically structured. You divide it into four parts, and in each part there's something that ties Jackson ever more strongly to the ranch, something that checks his impulse to leave and that keeps him there just a little bit longer. So that, despite what you say, you seemed to have a strong sense of where the story was headed.

A lot of that is rewriting, a lot of that is getting to the end of the book and then going from the end back to the front and saying, What do I have to do here to get to the end in better ways? Some of that is just artificial structuring of plot, so you can keep the reader turning pages. And I had to keep myself interested.

One thing I can't help but notice is the portrayal of women in The Blind Corral. *With the exception of Annie and Amy, the women in this novel do not come off very well. Women are defined quite narrowly, and are valued either for their labor or their sexual skills; they must prove themselves of worth to the* men *in their world before assuming any individual identity of their own. Those women who do not prove themselves remain in the background, nameless, anonymous – the Canadian girl, Jackson's mother. Is this a personal vision of women? A Western vision? How would you respond to such a criticism?*

Well, I'm sorry to hear that you think the women characters are defined narrowly, but I disagree that they must (or think they must) prove themselves of worth to men. As characters, they are too busy trying to take care of themselves, their cattle, their place, and their neighbors. And God I love them for that. They are family because they are good neighbors. They just happen to be women, mother and daughter. They aren't a damned bit concerned with working out their sexuality – which would be an incredibly silly idea for 99 percent of real ranchwomen. And they don't suffer from free-floating anxiety about whether or not they are accepted by men as equals because they are so obviously up to being anybody's equal. They are, these women, good hands.

Like I said, there wasn't a woman on *this* place for fifty years. There was never a woman here when I was a kid. But Amy Stevens was a real person who neighbored here. I used to put up hay for her when I was in my teens. I was scared of her; I liked her a lot, and I tried to be faithful to her when I wrote that character based on her. The real Amy Stevens I knew was, I'm damned sure, comfortable with her "role" as a woman – probably never crossed her mind to worry about it. And I tried to be faithful to her because she *was* a strong reflection of a real person living in this country, country which is hard on all people and animals, not just, as the saying goes, women and horses. Matter of fact, I thought that Amy as real person and Amy as character both came off pretty well: the kind of *person* I like to be around. The same goes for Annie, based again faithfully on a real person, a real woman.

The other women characters you mentioned are minor characters who take up very little space in the book the way some people, male and female, take up little space in our actual lives.

But let me get this off my chest. I've heard this talk, mostly from women writers and would-be writers who live in town, about us male writers writing badly about women in the rural West, until, frankly, I'm growing bored with it. Maybe women writers ought to get busy and create a literature that satisfies their requirements instead of harping on us poor macho types. There *are* some awfully good women writers doing the real thing right now: Gretel Ehrlich, Teresa Jordan, Mary Clearman Blew, a Native American woman, Debra Earling, and more. We need more. Battalions, maybe. But let them worry about women. I'll worry about men and horses and Harleys.

One of the things of special importance to Jackson is the rodeo – his "rodeo dreams" and the girl who represents the possibility of those dreams. How would you describe the particular quality of rodeo and of those dreams? What is the lure held by those dreams?

I've never rodeoed, never been in a rodeo. I know some people who do rodeo – Paul Zarzyski, Kim Zupan, for example – and I talk to them. I am terrifically interested in what they have done; I think it's a brave and wonderful thing to do, and I'm a fan. But when I was a kid growing up here, we always started cutting hay about the Fourth of July, which was also just about the same time that the big local rodeo in Helena was on, so I was always up there on the hill in those rocks going around and around in little circles with the mowing machine, while everybody else in the country was at the rodeo. I didn't really start going to rodeos – going as a spectator – until I was out of college.

I just read my book again for the first time in several years, getting ready for this interview, and one of the things I was astonished to find in there was how much that book really is about an attempt to leave. It's just hammered all over the place in that novel, and I wasn't aware of the extent of it, of the importance of leaving. I think that's what rodeo dreams, for native Montanans, is largely all about: it's a way to get away from the damned place; it's a way to go out and meet the world; it's a way to get in a car and drive from one town to another, be fairly anonymous until you get on your horse or get on your bull; it's a way to win a little money; it's a way to fraternize with other people who are more or less interested in the things you're interested in; it's not a team sport, you don't have to go to practice every night. If you're good enough, if you've got the inclination and you're tough, you can go do it. It's a way for a lot of young men to get off the place occasionally, go compete, and be a hero for a little while. Rodeo dreams are about the things you maybe can't have at home: miles of highway, cold beer, strange and sexy women, thrills, and the chance to wear a new white shirt and a good hat on the Fourth of July. I *can* tell you this: Rodeo dreams beat the hell out of bowling dreams.

And yet Jackson stays, isn't able to get away, at least at this point. And your central metaphor of the blind corral seems to play to that inability to escape. Could you explain that metaphor a bit, and its source in your world?

Blind corrals were commonly used when everything was done with horses. This country is so rough, though, that still the best way to get around a lot of it is on a saddle horse, unless you want to put lots of money into four-wheel drives. There is an old abandoned corral up between Jack Mountain and Sheep Mountain, and it was called locally the "Blind Corral." When I was working on the first draft of my novel, I kept a manilla folder of miscellaneous sheets, and one of the sheets listed possible titles for the book; I had a different working title on the book. At some point, when I was maybe 200 pages into the book, I went back and looked at the page of titles, and there it was: The Blind Corral. I couldn't even remember writing it down, yet I saw then immediately that it made complete sense as a metaphor because what a blind corral is, is a corral that's hidden in trees or in rocks or in brush; it usually has some kind of wings, either a canyon or barbed wire fences or brush fences. There used to be big brush fences through here when my dad was a kid, they were built by a man named Cutler, who broke horses for the Army; he'd cut a tree almost all the way off and bend it over, leaving enough of the tree so that it'd stay green for a long time. Then another tree and another in rows. A lot of work. There are remnants, still, around the countryside. They were a way of managing these absolutely wild, unbroken horses; if you were lucky enough, you could run the horses into these wing fences that gradually funnel down, smaller and smaller and smaller, into a gate. You'd have somebody there, waiting to close that gate.

This is a blind corral right here; you can see the two wing fences coming down, that's the lane. Out there by the road we came in on yesterday the lane is about a quarter-mile wide. My granddad and his cowboy buddies would come in off the bald hills with these horses, and it was tough just to hit the lane, just to get them started. Then, when you got 'em coming down through those trees, you had to really pour it to them, you had to be right on their ass. You had to have a kid there to close the gate, because the horses would come in, make one circle, and come right back out. My dad used to go over there and hide in the rocks and close the gate for them.

It seemed like a good metaphor to me in this respect, that you sometimes finally find yourself getting narrowed down and narrowed down and narrowed down until you're trapped. That's what happens to Jack. That book is about his desire, and other people's desire, to leave: going, and finding some other better place. There's a line in that book that really struck me when I reread it recently; Jack asks his mother over in Butte – who's this rough old gal with suspect morals, a pretty awful old lady – "Why did you leave?" And she says, "Because I couldn't stay." It's on Jack's mind, all the time, this business of leaving. But during the months he lingers, he rediscovers not only that he loves this place but in that discovery, he begins to rediscover *himself. That* is what matters most.

Another bit of physical detail that plays a major role in the novel is the Veracruz mine. It's there that Jackson seems to make the final decision to stay on, to keep the familial line intact. Is there a history to that site?

Well, there's an actual mine that we passed coming in yesterday, there's a big dump out there – that's all that's left of it now, that dirt – and it was called the Veracruz. My granddad worked in it when he was twelve, thirteen years old. Two hundred and ten feet deep, it was. And when I was a boy, the gallus frame – a hoist frame, made of big square timbers – was still standing. The timbers eventually rotted and the hoist collapsed on itself with the bull wheels and everything, and fell down the hole. When I was a kid, I would stand there and throw rocks down that hole, and I'd wait for a *long* while before they hit bottom.

That's where I put Jack; he climbs to the top and sits up there on that gallus frame. The whole thing is pretty wobbly – chunks of it are falling off and down into the hole – and what he hears down in that hole is what I think makes it possible to get out of the book with some sense of hope. He hears water down there; he starts dropping shell casings and keeps hearing them splash. The whole problem of their dry land range was that there wasn't any water out there for stock; if the Heckethorns fenced the range, which is what they were going to have to do, they had to get water – and there it *is,* it's in that old mine.

Like you say, there is a darkness to that novel that is relentless at times – the shooting of the horse, for example – and there's even the suggestion of suicide as Jackson sits up there on that frame –

Yes, he's thinking about leaning into it. . . . That was another case of being lucky. I think I've been very lucky: lucky to have friends in Missoula who helped me, and lucky to have these actual things right here that I grew up with, that eventually I could use – I could go right out there, a quarter of a mile away, and say to myself: There it is. Use that. The same principle applies to some more personal, less physical aspects of my life, too, I'm sure.

But I think that's made it real tough for me in attempting to write my second novel. I wanted to get away from this place and write a novel that *isn't* set here. And I've discovered that I don't have the ability to go to some new place and assume the identity of that place and be arrogant enough to think that I can inhabit the lives and imaginations and dreams of the people who live there. I just can't do that.

So it's a matter of arrogance?

What else *could* it be? A lack of imagination, perhaps?

But are you arguing that for a person to write successfully about a place, that person must be rooted in that place?

Yes. You'd better know the place, and you'd better know the people who live there, and you'd better have some commitment to that place and those people or else what you write is not going to bear up under time or scrutiny. It will ultimately be rejected not only by the people who inhabit that place but by other wise readers as well.

Oddly enough, I don't mean to say that some writers shouldn't try to move to Nebraska, say, and write the great Nebraska novel. Hell, Jim Harrison did something very close to that in *Dalva*. But I am ill at ease with writers who seem to blow through a farming community, for example, and not only name that place in their title, but try to convince the reader of an intimate understanding of that place and its inhabitants through the thoughts and actions of fictional characters, when, in fact, there has been no long apprenticeship of residence, no long period of time and observation put in to *learn* what that place and its people really are. That's phony. Period. It takes a long time to sort out the complexities of life in *any* particular town or community or rural neighborhood. To get it halfway right, you'd better make a long-term commitment to living there and to becoming part of that town and part of that life and all that is particular to that place. How else do we get true books about place like Harry Crews's wonderful book, *A Childhood, The Biography of a Place*, or Wendell Berry's heartbreaking novel, *The Memory of Old Jack?* Not, I suspect, by blowing through Bacon County, Georgia, or Port Royal, Kentucky, and using those places as *backdrops* for fiction that might otherwise be set elsewhere.

Tom McGuane is a good example of a writer who has come to Montana and made that kind of commitment. McGuane has been here twenty years, and I admire the way he has learned the place, the skills that go with that place, the lingo, and the *ways*.

There are others, however, writers I won't name (but they know who they are) who have come here and tried to do it on the cheap, quick and easy. Do a little fishing, rent a place, write a novel set here. Their work, I *know*, is not respected, nor will it be long remembered.

The writer's responsibility – or one of the writer's responsibilities – then, is to stay and to describe the chaos? I think of your essay "In Spite of Distance," in which you place part of the blame for what you call the "Western chaos" on the region's writers. Do you see writers as now finding sense in that chaos and pointing ways out of that disorder – or are they simply pointing up the chaos now?

I don't have a dead-certain answer to that, but I think the situation might be changing. I think the balance may be going like this: in the 1970s, writers like Crumley were pointing out that chaos and how sometimes it's funny: like the purse snatcher, at the beginning of *The Wrong Case*, who gets hit by a car and is dragged down the street. And Milo, who is up in his office watching says, "Well, I guess crime *doesn't* pay." It's a wonderful scene, and it's all about this chaotic stuff going on in this little Western town, all this cheap crime that really shouldn't be there in that little town. So I think in the '70s that was enough of a job right there, just seeing it, recognizing it, and writing about it.

Now, the scales may be tipping to where writers are trying seriously to sort through some of that chaos, to point to some of its roots. I think Tom McGuane is out there on the edge of this; I admire McGuane a lot – I haven't always admired him, I've had to come to it slowly – but I do, I can't help myself. He came here from somewhere else, from *several* somewhere elses, and made a place for himself and turned into a horseman and became a hand and became well liked by his neighbors, and became good at living in Montana in a way that most of us don't. I think McGuane went through a phase where he was pointing to this kind of craziness – in *Rancho Deluxe*, for example, there's a lot of it. But in his last couple of books he's obviously trying to sort it out through characters who are attempting to make some sense of it and themselves and yet be able to stay. Either come and stay, or at least come and make an attempt to stay before they finally throw up their hands and say, Gee, there really wasn't a painting in that frame at all, it was just the paint on the wall – and all this time I thought they were hills! It's all been an illusion, it's all been a dream, it's all been imagination and memory, flawed memory.

In my book, where I do attempt that kind of sorting out, I usually do it in those scenes where Jackson goes to town. Every time he goes to town he gets into trouble; most of the things he runs into in town are confusing to him. He ends up on Last Chance Gulch and it's gone, all the buildings are gone; all the bums are saying, I'm not coming back here anymore. When he goes to town with the Von Trash Family Singers, he gets beat up and too drunk and wakes up in a house where he doesn't know anyone.

So I think I was taking it up to a point, and I think that writers like McGuane are taking it *beyond* that point, and that's good. But I think it's tough. You can live out here on the Beer Ranch, and in fifteen minutes you can be in Helena driving by Burger King: it's always a shock, at least to me.

Do you think that there is a way the Westerner ought to act now, with the myths wearing thin?

I think we're going to have to work hard at discovering new ways to act. There isn't any formula for it; we're individuals, and we're all facing different situations. We're going to have to adapt and accommodate ourselves to change, or we're going to go under, in our heads and in our hearts, if not physically or financially.

The change is inevitable?

It has been up to this point. The changes here in my lifetime have been staggering. We didn't get electricity until 1962, and we got running water last summer. We still heat everything with wood. And I'm all for change – I'm glad to have electricity and hot water. Who in their right mind would say that outhouses are uplifting?

But we're going to have to adapt internally. We can make all sorts of external accommodations: we can get a job in town or we can get a job at a sawmill or we can learn computer skills. It's the internal changes, though, that are the tough ones, coming to a point where you're willing to live with the new without being unhappy about it. That isn't an overnight process; it comes and goes in waves. You can end up being unhappy most of your life with what's coming, you'd rather have the open country back so you can get on a saddle horse and ride to Helena without running into gates and fences, like it was twenty years ago. I just hate what I see now in Montana City, all that junk down there – restaurants and housing developments and storage garages and gas stations – the worst kind of trash on what was native grass ten or twelve years ago.

You can't help but feel some sense of loss at that kind of change. It's not pretty and it's not nice to live next to, and it seems that more and more of America is becoming like that. Our towns in Montana are coming to look alike: Billings, Great Falls, Butte, Bozeman, Missoula, they all have a strip that's a four-lane street with car dealerships and chicken joints and all that American *junk!* And I don't like it. It's not enhancing the quality of life here in Montana, and people who move here for a better quality of life are simply leaving behind places where this sort of change has already occurred, to come here where it's going to come again in the next ten, fifteen, twenty years.

That's something we're all going to have to deal with. Maybe that's the business of sorting our way through this chaos; we all find our lives chaotic at some point, and we have to sort our way through, whether we're Western writers or Eastern readers or whatnot. Out here it does seem squirrely because the rural is suddenly so close to the urban.

Ultimately, it's our responsibility, as Montana writers, to do our *best* to tell the *truth* about this place. That's our big job, and a tough one it is, sur-rounded as we are by the pressures of modern American materialism in our regional culture *and* in the publishing industry. To tell the truth about where we live, we must be very good writers (artists) or willing to pass up monetary rewards and popular acclaim, or, more likely, *both*. Like the man run to the outhouse roof by a bull, this can seem very "lonely at the top."

WORKS

The Blind Corral. New York: Viking Penguin, 1986. Fiction.

Mary Clearman Blew

Born in 1939, Mary Clearman Blew spent a large part of her girlhood on a ranch on northern Montana's "highline," on the site of her great-grandfather's original homestead. After working in educational administration in Havre, Montana, Blew left her native state for Idaho, where she took a teaching job at Lewis-Clark State College, in Lewiston. Blew continues to teach fiction writing and Renaissance literature there today. Blew's short fiction has been widely anthologized; and her essays about the West – and about growing up female in the West – have established her as a leading voice among the new community of Western writers.

Blew and I first met in Coeur d'Alene, Idaho, where she agreed to participate in this project. Like some other writers in this collection, however, Blew preferred to respond in writing to questions rather than to speak directly to those questions. Although we have talked about her work in subsequent meetings – in Choteau, Montana, in Estes Park, Colorado – what appears here is only what Blew included in her original written responses, completed in 1991.

GREGORY MORRIS: *Like so many writers from the West, you have a strong familial connection to this region, a connection you've described both in your fiction and your nonfiction. In your case, that link seems particularly to be made with your mother and your grandmothers, a link you write about in the essay, "January 1922." Could you describe this sort of female inheritance as you see it descending through your family?*

MARY CLEARMAN BLEW: In my family, the men were glamorous and the women persevered. My mother and grandmothers led hard lives, but they handed down solace in the form of family tales. My grandmother on my father's side used to tell about my great-grandmother's brush with a mass murderer who, in June of 1889, stopped at her cabin in central Montana and asked her the way to the Judith River, where he subsequently buried the five bodies he was carrying in his wagon. Years later I researched the story and learned many details my grandmother never told, that the murderer was captured and hanged himself in his jail cell, and that his body disappeared from the cemetery where it was buried, and also that my great-grandfather had been the foreman of the coroner's jury. The story as my grandmother told it had focused only on Great-grandmother's brush with death and the reassurance of her living to tell about it. Like many of her stories, it testified to an alternate current, and I think I am always aware of being part of that current.

Could you describe what it means, personally, "to grow up female in Charlie Russell country" (as you've titled one of your essays)? When you write of the experience, in a story like "College Bound 1957," you seem to write with bitterness and regret.

When I read this essay aloud to a group in central Montana, where the cowboy artist Charles M. Russell lived as a young man and where many of his paintings are set, my audience immediately understood what I meant. Outside Montana, apparently, the reference is obscure. Russell's paintings celebrate the last stand of the plains Indians, the twilight of the open range, the lonely heroics of the frontier. To grow up female in Charlie Russell country is to grow up in the context of a myth of the West in which women are idealized, if they exist at all. The woman who grows up in Charlie Russell country is going to have to hack her way to space of her own.

I went to high school during that period of low expectations for women fostered by the 1950s. Many of the younger teachers had absorbed a self-fulfilling determinism and thought they were being only realistic: town girls go to college for their MRS degrees, ranchgirls stay home and marry ranch-boys. Luckily my mother and grandmothers had survived the Depression and believed that girls should be able to support themselves. They raised hell and high water to send me off for my teaching credentials, and I took it from there.

I am surprised at the number of readers who find "bitterness and regret" in "College Bound," and I think they may be bringing their own feelings to the story. I was interested in Margaret's comic energy, her naïve and un-deflectable purpose, as she bumbles after a fantasy that is more vivid to her than the everyday world she conquers even though, or perhaps because, she misunderstands it.

And was it different on the highline?

I didn't grow up on the highline, though I lived there twenty years. The most important single facet of the highline is its isolation. The Army cleared out the Indians in the waning years of the nineteenth century and estab-lished what was at that time the most heavily fortified outpost in the United States. Fort Assiniboine was like a self-contained bubble on the edge of the world. Havre continues to be self-contained, remote, separated from the rest of the world by ill-maintained roads and undependable airlinks. People live in fear there without knowing it. I remember how, after a fatal knifing at a high school kegger on the reservation in the 1980s, rumors flashed around on CB radios that the Indians had risen and were killing white children. There is a sense in Havre of barely contained hysteria.

You described (in a previous interview) your leaving Montana "with a broken heart" – why? Are you, yourself, a "runaway"?

More of an exile. I still get passionate letters from people who ask how I can write about Havre in anything less than encomium. But I didn't leave volun-tarily. Montana's economy had faltered, and the liberal arts programs at Northern Montana College had been slashed, and after twenty years I no longer had a job. I was only one of many, particularly in the arts and the humanities, who left Montana in the late 1980s. But these were very difficult years for me personally because my husband was dying of pulmonary fibrosis.

Do you see Idaho as a homeplace now? Do you have any difficulty reconciling the industrial/corporate presence there – the lumber industry, the paper mills – with your personal political vision of the contemporary West?

I don't see myself as a political writer at all, except in the respect that I try to write honestly. I dislike the stench of the pulp mills as much as anyone. Idaho has welcomed the industrial/corporate presence that Montana designed its tax structure to keep out. And yet one result is that Montana is in danger of becoming a preserve for the very rich, while I have a job and can live in Idaho at least in part because of those very pulp mills. To try to live as though we can wall ourselves off from the rest of the planet, to pretend we are totally self-contained, seems to me the most ruthless kind of self-deception.

Common in your stories are those girl-women protagonists caught between the expectations of place and personal desire. I'm thinking particularly of the Juley stories – "Granddaughter" and "Kissing My Elbow" and "Sample's Crossing" and "Last Night As I Lay On the Prairie" – which seem a coherent series of stories centering on one such girl-woman. First, did you intend these stories originally as something longer and more unified? Was there a novel planned for Juley?

For awhile I cherished the idea of a "Juley" novel, and the short stories probably are sidelong glances at an imagined longer narrative about Juley's exile and reconciliation with the past.

How, then, do these women go about fashioning that identity and reconciling that past in a world so largely determined by place and gender and history?

Women like Juley are less troubled, I think, by a need to prove themselves or to take over men's work than by the need to find their own space to breathe. In "Kissing My Elbow," Juley does imagine herself as a kind of third sex in that her self is no longer a reflection of other people's expectations.

A sense of place and past seems to me double-edged. On the one hand, it provides continuity and connections; on the other, it is a powerful trap. In my story "Album," Jean doesn't want to believe she will experience the old sorrows. In breaking with the past, she persuades herself that she can evade the human condition until, reluctantly, her aunts tell her more than she wants to know. In this respect the original title of the story ("Paths Unto the Dead") is probably the better.

While I am not a social historian, my impression is that, for many women, the importance of the family circle, the counsel and love of older women relatives, has been fading since the mid-nineteenth century. I have cherished my storytelling grandmothers and aunts who kept the family legends alive for me. On the other hand, I have often felt stifled by tradition. It's hard to be a link in a genetic/cultural chain and still be yourself.

You also write of the older Western woman – Alberta, Kate. What is their situation, their predicament? Is a complete peace ever made with the opposed impulses of escape and surrender?

Well, thank God we never stop kicking over the traces. Complete peace??? My mother and aunts are seventy-six, eighty, and eighty-two. They still are intensely engaged with past and present and the stories through which they understand their lives.

Though you write powerfully of the women in your West, many of your stories are told from a male perspective and shed light on what it's like to "grow up male in Charlie Russell country." Quite often those men – or sometimes boys – speak in voices twisted by anger, by rage. Are there specific, peculiar pressures upon these men within that place?

I think rage lies close to the surface in many Westerners, men and women. Often it has to do with intolerable circumstances. During the years of drought and rising interest rates on the highline, some of the veterinaries said they suddenly were seeing an increase in farm dogs with broken ribs. But often the rage has to do with a more pervasive disappointment. In "Sample's Crossing," I think that the young man's disengagement is the opposite face of rage, and that he seeks for love with as much hunger if less passion than Jimmy in "I Beat the Midget." Pressures on young men in the West? Living up to the myth may be harder on men, in the long run, than on women. And the strictures of the Western code of silence apply specifically to men.

Some of your stories, like "Stall Warning" and "On the Hellgate," describe men facing their various fears and inadequacies, men who do not necessarily overcome those fears and inadequacies.

I guess many of us fail to overcome our fears and inadequacies. The narrator in "Stall Warning" learns that he is not invulnerable. He knows the young woman he is teaching to fly will eventually learn the same lesson. What he finally understands – and what I like about him – is that he can feel fearful and inadequate and still keep flying.

As a writer dealing with the prevailing mythos of the West, do you see any particularly significant effect of the recent revisionist historiography of the West upon the fiction of that West?

The most important thing about the revisionist historiography is its willingness to listen to many voices and see the many different facets of the West. And one characteristic of contemporary writers in the West is their diversity. I can't think of any writer who claims that hers (or his) is *the* West. Certainly any stereotype is dangerous, but diversity, and the willingness to accept diversity, would seem to be as far from stereotype as we can get.

Part of this revisionist process involves reconciling the Old West with the New West, and many of your characters engage themselves with that process, with reconciling the "anachronisms" – the remnants of the Old West – with the facts of the New West. In "Reining Patterns," for example, the girl, Johnnie, feels the connection with her grandfather and her great-grandfather, imagines even "with power wires crisscrossing the sky and the faint hum of traffic from the state highway . . . how it must have been." Can these elements of the past be reconciled with elements of the present?

The past is always with us. We are what we are. We are what we are becoming. But to idealize the past, as Johnnie does, is to stifle part of what we are. Johnnie doesn't reconcile Old West and New West, she dedicates herself like a Vestal to a flame that never really burned as bright as she wants to believe it did. She seems to me a much sorrier woman than Alberta, who (in "Alberta's Story") sells the family ranch to buy herself some comforts and help send her young friend Debbie to college. If Johnnie is lucky, she will grow up to be Alberta.

Let's talk specifically a bit about the two collections, Lambing Out *(1977) and* Runaway *(1990). How did those two collections come together? Is there an intended coherence to the two books?*

When I put *Lambing Out* together in 1977, I hadn't heard much about coherent or thematic collections of short stories. I wanted a pleasing juxtaposition of stories, and I wanted a progression from innocence to disillusionment, hence the two birthing stories, "Lambing Out" and "Monsters," at the beginning and the end. *Runaway*, on the other hand, started out as a collection of stories of retrospection. I think now that I was exploring the direction I've taken in the essays, where I drop the screen of character. Jim Hepworth at Confluence Press looked at my arrangement and preferred the stories that looked ahead: "Alberta's Story," "The Snowies, the Judiths," and "Runaway" itself. The result was a rearrangement and a change of title (from "Sample's Crossing," which has a private meaning for me but which, I finally was convinced, was too private to carry the weight of the collection).

Between the two collections spans a thirteen-year gap. Why was the second collection so long in coming to print?

I wasn't able to write during the years I spent in higher education administration, though I pretended to myself that I could. I don't suppose that the isolation of the highline was a help, either, but coming back to teaching after ten years feels as though a weight has been lifted. And I have been very fortunate in my colleagues and students at Lewis-Clark State College.

As a writer of fiction, you've stuck pretty closely to the short story. But like many other new writers of the West, you've felt compelled to work in the essay form as well. One of the reasons you've given for working with the essays is that you've "felt impatient with the traditional accoutrements of fiction." This is an interesting remark: are you moved to try a fiction fitted out with nontraditional accoutrements? Are your essays, perhaps, examples of fiction written in nontraditional ways? Of your stories, I think of "Last Night As I Lay On the Prairie," with its narrative shifts between stories-within-the-story, as perhaps your most technically experimental story.

I hadn't thought much about the essays as experimental fiction, with "Last Night As I Lay On the Prairie" as a transition, until you suggested it. I would have said no, I am very traditional, anything but experimental. But writing the essays has been surprising. They've poured out, for one thing. And they have been a way to confront the multiple voices, the stories within stories, the sense of past and present as simultaneous. I don't quite know where this form will lead next, but I'm eager to follow.

You seem to have found it more compelling to write of the Native American presence, and of its specific historical and spiritual influence upon your Montana,

31

in your essays – in "Fort Assiniboine" and "Wahkpa Chu'gn," for example – than in your fiction. In the two stories that do feature a Native American element, "Monsters" and "Bare Trees," what emerges is a portrait tinged with rage and a certain dark quirkiness. Do you see a difference in the nature of those expressions, and in the color of those visions?

I am a white woman, born and bred in the West, loaded with the baggage of my upbringing, which includes an unforgiving work ethic, a prairie stoicism, and a suspicion of all that is manicured, polished, decorated, or mannered. What I see and hear, I must see and hear through these blinders, I hope in spite of my blinders. Gradually I am trying to write in full acknowledgment of who I am. Rage? Dark quirkiness? One reason I feel impatient with traditional characterization is the deceptive shelter it gives. Gary in "Monsters" and June in "Bare Trees" are probably closer personae of my own than some of the more obvious characters that readers single out. Maybe the result is the unassimilated rage that I have since found new ways of writing about, or with.

WORKS

All but the Waltz: Essays on a Montana Family. New York: Viking, 1991. Essays.

Lambing Out and Other Stories. Published under the name Mary Clearman. Columbia: University of Missouri, 1977. Short fiction.

Runaway: A Collection of Stories. Lewiston, Id.: Confluence Press, 1990. Short fiction.

Elizabeth Cook-Lynn

Elizabeth Cook-Lynn was born in the Government Hospital at Fort Thompson, South Dakota, in 1930, and grew up on the Crow Creek, a tributary of the Missouri River. She is a member of the Crow Creek Sioux Tribe. (While the Dakota and Lakota are both members of the Sioux people, they maintain a significant linguistic difference; Cook-Lynn is a Dakota Sioux, and all translations included here are therefore rendered from their meanings in Dakota.) An avid reader as a child, Cook-Lynn later studied at South Dakota State College, where she was dismayed to discover the absence of any Native American presence in the history and the literature of her country. Cook-Lynn began to write and to establish such a presence.

Her work has taken many forms, from poetry and fiction to critical and social essays. She is an outspoken woman, a strong and commanding Native American voice heard in many quarters and in many shapes. She has taught in several universities and edits the *Wicazo Sa Review*. This interview was written by Cook-Lynn in the summer of 1992, from her permanent home in Rapid City, South Dakota.

GREGORY MORRIS: *You grew up, of course, on the Crow Creek Reservation in South Dakota. Could you describe the effects of that life upon your relationship to the American West? How did it shape that relationship?*

ELIZABETH COOK-LYNN: A great question for starting this discussion! The short answer to that is it probably helped me to understand that Indians have no relationship to what America calls the West at all. Indian reservations in those days, and perhaps nowadays as well, are the homelands to people who were/are subjected to various outside influences and, certainly, in my time the cowboy and Indian stuff was only in the movies. "The American West," as is talked by the moviemakers, as Louis L'Amour, Guthrie, Stegner, and all the rest talk of it here simply leaves Indians out of it as any kind of ongoing contributors. Fictionally, we simply weren't real if you were looking at it from my life on the Crow Creek Reservation in South Dakota.

One of the central conflicts in your fiction (and one that must be related to your own upbringing) is that between the various spiritual attitudes within American Indian culture: the tension, for example, between traditional native belief and the imported (imposed?) Christian/Catholic belief. Could you characterize that tension and its impact upon your fiction? Is any sort of resolution possible in that conflict?

I would characterize that tension as the colonialist/indigenist conflict which exists, perhaps, everywhere in the modern world: Russia, South Africa, the Middle East. It cannot be characterized as just a religious matter, more it is an ethical matter. The resolution, then, must be between equals. Ethical solutions do not rise out of the inferior/superior paradigm so inherent in white/Indian relations in America.

I am interested in your relationship with the literature of the American West, as well. You have commented that you "cannot read" Wallace Stegner and other white writers of the West. What do you mean by that? What difficulties do they present to you as a reader and as a writer?

It is true I don't read the literature of the "American West" either for pleasure or instruction. If I read it at all it is out of obligation, that is, as a scholar I *must* read certain texts, and the works of many writers and thinkers who influence our times. The difficulties which they present to me as a reader and as a writer are enormous. Aesthetics. History. James Welch may have put it as appropriately as anybody I can think of when he said something like this: "White writers must adopt a stance vis-à-vis the American Indian. Indians just have a stance." There are some Indian writers, however, whose work I also don't read. Perhaps for different reasons. There are "real" stories, you know. And, then, there are "contrived" ones. I try to write/read stories with characters who behave as though they might resemble real people, the old Mark Twain admonition. The truth is I don't see many real Indians in the works of American Western fiction writers, even today.

Do you feel yourself a part of any particular American Indian written tradition? Are the varied strains of Western American Indian writing too discrete for such tradition-formation? You speak elsewhere of your "responsibility in the creative process," and of the dichotomy that exists in your function as a modern Dakota writer. You also speak of the "self-absorption" in your work, and of the crucial necessity of such self-absorption. Could you elaborate on those matters?

And are there problems inherent in the situation of the American Indian woman writer? Vine Deloria, Sr., has commented that modesty most characterized the Indian woman – does such modesty inhibit the woman writer and discourage the finding of a voice?

I've always thought of the Sioux as eloquent people. I grew up with relatives who were great talkers; one of my grandfathers, Joe Irving, was a wonderful "bullshitter," to use one of his son's descriptions of him. And a successful politician. He represented Crow Creek Indians at the Rapid City Councils in the early 1930s, about the time of the Indian Reorganization Act. He talked all three dialects of the Sioux language; was expressive, too, in English. He had a great sense of humor and thought he was God's gift to women. We all knew then and we know now that we come from a region that has been – since the end of the Indian/white wars – in a state of cultural conflict. In spite of what you may think after watching the movie *Dances with Wolves*, the country of the Dakota since the white immigrants came to power there a century ago is a place of cultural conflict as oppressive as any place in the world. My "responsibility" is to that reality. Women as well as men, writers as well as nonwriters, we all continue to be ourselves. "The situation of the American Indian *woman* writer," as you put it, should not be distinctive from the American Indian *male* writer. And, among the people, I think that is true. For white publishers, scholars, perhaps there is something else going on, but I try to refrain from commenting too much on the male/female "thing." Right now, I have a literary agency looking at my next fiction called *Circle of Dancers,* and they want to talk about it as a "woman's" story. The female partner of the agency likes the story *because,* she says, it is Aurelia's continuing story, and it is, therefore, a woman's story. I'm very, very, very happy that she likes the story though I think of it as a *tribal* story.

I don't know about Vine Delora, Sr.'s comment concerning "modesty" as a primary virtue of Dakota/Lakota womanhood. Perhaps, if they had asked a woman, they would have gotten a different answer. Ah! therein lies the mystery! In Sioux language, you know, there are gender usages but I wouldn't call them differences, exactly. It's just that the speaker must always be known. I'm not any kind of linguistic authority, so you'll have to ask someone else what it all means.

What about your own relationship to your own reader? What is the nature of the relationship between the American Indian writer and her reader or readers? Do you write for a reader "inside the circle" – in other words, for an Indian reader? Are there ways for the non-native reader to enter the circle? Do you see any danger in the "rush to understand" Native American culture and writing?

I often wonder about this question because as I write I have no notion of who the reader might be. I simply concentrate on telling the story. But, beyond that, let me ask you a question: Why must "non-native readers enter the circle"? I guess the truth of the matter must be that I don't write for the same reasons that most writers write. A creative writing professor and fiction writer at the University of Arizona trashed my novel *From the River's Edge* in the *New York Times* when the book first came out, for several reasons that are probably shared by others in his profession: one was the novel's "inability to maintain the 'vivid and continuous dream,' that the novelist John Gardner rightly named as the special reality of fiction." I'm quite sure that it is possible to "teach" the techniques that absorb the reader in this "vivid and continuous dream," but the dream, itself, is a personal thing which cannot be taught or learned, so the best I can do is tell you about my dream and hope that you find it a real retelling. I don't really believe that "the continuous dream" is the function of the novel, but, of course, John Gardner said many other things which might be taken up.

As for "entering the circle," as you name it here, this is so hard because the metaphor cannot be taken lightly as it is a familial as well as a tribal matter. It is important to explore this question, perhaps more fully than you had intended. Briefly, let me tell you of an incident that occurred when I taught a native woman's literature course at a western university recently. It was a course which had been taught for at least a decade and for much of that time, one of the final activities was to take the students to a nearby Indian university for a "sweat." When I recoiled from this "requirement," saying that in my tribal upbringing the sweatlodge (the *inipi, uwipi*) is either religious or familial, and that this particular college course met neither description, thus, we would schedule the usual two-hour writing examination as the final "experience" of the course, I nearly had an uprising of students in the class. Current intellectual discourse seems to include an outrageous "invasion" of native expressions (such as rituals, ceremonials, religions, customs), and I am not at all sure to what extent I as a writer or a teacher can be involved in it. We must, I think, develop respect for one another through our study of literature; instead, everybody wants to seek temporal pleasures, invade privacies.

You have remarked that one of the criticisms of your fiction has been of its polemical nature – for example, your novel The River's Edge *deals outrightly with political and social issues and takes a clearly defined stance on the matter of white justice. At the same time, you have noted that polemicism is part of the Dakota storytelling tradition. Could you describe that tradition a bit, and the way in which polemics figures in to that tradition?*

"Polemics" might not be the right word. What does it mean? "The art or practice of disputation or controversy"? Well, I certainly don't mean that in the sense of theological dispute, or anything of that sort. Perhaps I mean to use it in the political sense. Example: there is a little story about the mud-hen, and how she gets red eyes. That is what the story is about, as it was told, perhaps, by my grandparents' generation. Later on, during reservation days, it really became a story about how the little mud-hen "looked" and "saw" the agency superintendent acting "*unktomi*" [spider or trickster]. She warned the others and they saved themselves. So, don't you see, the stories have always been "useful" for understanding the present danger, namely political dilemma. Remember that our own intellectual and moral control of our lives as a people is under severe attack. If you don't believe that, live in South Dakota for a while as an Indian. What we have in defense of our lives is a concept of self, related to the specific geography of our origins and we have continued to achieve that defense . . . not by building great cities, not by mining gold and uranium, not by plowing up the earth for profit. The achievement of our defense of self-concept is in our narrative art which is concerned with morality, learning how to live as a Dakota, knowing and recalling the past. It is important, therefore, for storytellers to tell us about time and place, "useful" stuff for understanding the world and its present danger. Is that, in some way, "polemic"? Or does it just make us mud-hens? Ho-Ho. One of the problems with all this, from a European literary point of view, of course, is that, as Wallace Stevens has said, "The meanings given by others are sometimes meanings not intended by the poet or that were never present in his mind," and that's okay, too. Ambiguity, thy name is fiction. But, we must simply do the best we can, continue to be responsible, and not give in to madness or add to the confusion.

As a Dakota storyteller, you also frequently mix or combine forms, especially in Then Badger Said This. *Is there a particular cultural or aesthetic reason for this interweaving of forms?*

Similarly, the plotting of your fiction takes different forms or strategies. Is there, say, a difference in the technical structuring of From the River's Edge *(just as there is a difference in the narrative technique) that is related to American Indian storytelling technique? For example, in the novel, smack in the middle of the trial, John Tatekeya goes to Bismarck, North Dakota, with his brothers for the* wacipi *ceremony. That trip seems a real disruption of the narrative structure of the novel, but do you see it that way?*

I have no great notion about "form" in fiction writing. The experiment in *Badger* was to see what the examination of myth, history, and personal experience tells us about our present lives. How can we know who we are in some kind of literary way that might be related to ceremony? Is the function of such literature the same as ceremony? I found out, of course, that it is not. I found out, of course, that because written literature of the *Badger* sort is not a tribal art, in the traditional sense, and it is just my lonely voice, it can never become "useful" as the subversive oral art which has been at the core of our survival has been "useful." That does not make it, however, useless! What it did for me, personally, was it told me that though Indians for centuries did not want to write, as we have not wanted to do a lot of other things, we must move forward with our lives. Indians need to join the discourse which will go on with or without us to let them know we continue and to tell others that the spiritual conquest of the American Indian has never taken place. That's a hard thing to know, if you are an Indian living and going to school in the places where I have been, where the "westward movement" hardly mentions Indians, and Stegner says: "The Plains Indians are done."

I find your notion about Tatekeya's little trip to Bismarck as a "real disruption of the narrative structure" of the novel an important idea. And, perhaps, it points up the differences between the "oral subversive storytelling" idea versus the "literary narrative technique" in novel plot making. That important trip to *wacipi* follows what others have called the "low comedy chicken stealing" scene. One reviewer even called Tatekeya a "despairing drunk" after that scene. Such critics, if I may say so, are people who don't know the subversive stories. Nor do they even know much about history. The Mayan Indians, as you may recall, sometime in the 1500s, when they got fed up with the Conquistadors, decided that they would kill all the invaders and kill all the animals and plants brought to this continent by Europeans. Thus, they started to kill the pigs and chickens and this went on for some time. American storytellers get caught up in "who won?" and "who lost?" Indians, however, tell the story as part of the "resistance." It is "ongoing," the "resistance." And it is continual. Tatekeya's stealing/selling of the chickens is a "resistance" story. And it is no mere "wandering" when he heads to the largest gathering of Plains singers and dancers of the summer. The trial is not part of the storytelling. It is a "plot" structuring device and, ultimately, the trial is irrelevant. My point is, I suppose, that "plotting of fiction" is, also, irrelevant, because the function of plot is "conflict," and it implies a "resolution." In the colonialist/indigenists "conflict" as it exists today, there can be no "resolution." Not unless we want to kill all the pigs and chickens, yes?

What these technical questions boil down to, I suppose, is one more precise question about the ways in which you resolve the opposing impulses of the native oral tradition and the Anglo-European written tradition. Is this conflict problematic for you at all?

How would you describe your own development as a writer, as a teller of stories? In your story "A Good Chance" you examine one problematic (and tragic) case of an Indian poet – is this case symptomatic or representative of the dilemma of the native artist–writer?

The impulse of language is the same, whether it is written or oral, I think. So, I don't quite know what is meant here about opposing impulses of oral versus written. I think I got good at using English because I went to a boarding school (briefly, to be sure) where we studied Latin. I copied words, poems, kept notebooks even before I knew much about language. Dakota and English were both used in my homelife, a lot of singing, political and historical discussion by the Indian male politicians in my family, Latin usage in the Mass at Catholic schools. The Sioux are not called "the windbags of the Plains" for nothing, you know! I always knew the elegance of language, in prayer and in secular usage. We as children were not allowed to be careless in language, and we were taught the polite attention which was to be paid, always, to speakers, adults. In the story you mention here, there is irony in the title because the Indian poet does not have "a good chance" to do what he needs to do, or even what he would like to do, yet "chance" has everything to do with it. That is the point of the story, I suppose. Mostly, I was trying for a "real" story. In my mind, I dedicate this story to Sam Crow, a friend of my father's who lived out on the Crow Creek: a neighbor of ours, a man who was shot to death in the Chamberlain [South Dakota] city jail by a white policeman. It is also dedicated to a friend of mine, Melvin White Magpie, from Pine Ridge, South Dakota, who died in the Nebraska State Pen of stab wounds. The two killings were thirty years apart and I often think nothing has changed and I wonder if it ever will.

Let us move toward specific comments on your fiction, and some of the ideas in that fiction. In From the River's Edge, *you speak of the "transformation of Dakota values." You seem self-critical here, as harsh with the Dakota culture as with the white culture. Do you see this novel as a critique of both cultures? What elements of contemporary Sioux life do you feel need to be transformed? How much of this criticism of contemporary Sioux existence filters into your fiction?*

No, I don't often think of it as self-criticism. The all-consuming obsession of the Sioux is the control of our own lives and languages and literatures through our connection to the land. Throughout foreign domination, ancient hatreds, and the attempted genocide of our people, we have maintained a concept of the tribal way of life. This is a story about the loss of the land and the destruction of a river. At least, I hope that's what it is. The fear that we will no longer be Dakotas/Lakotas is real and I am not much interested in blame, just a clear understanding of what happened to us. I think white readers often think it is about blaming them, or about their guilt. But, they are quite mistaken. Literature functions, I'm told, to bring order to seemingly chaotic events. The destruction of rivers in this country seems chaotic to me, as does much else that goes on here in the name of profit. Yet, it is a deliberate act. One must try to make sense of it and its consequences in human terms as well as societal.

As for the separate conclusions reached in From the River's Edge *by John Tatekeya and by his lover Aurelia, are those conclusions compatible within modern native life? What does it mean to consider the "possibility of an honorable life" in the contemporary culture?*

I think the recovery of a moral world is no longer possible, but we still have the impulse to try to survive, don't we, as a species? John survives because he is a man who knows who he is, I suppose, thus he can continue to seek help, and that makes him simply a human being weeping for himself. For Aurelia, the existential questions about "who am I?" still elude her, therefore, she cannot weep nor can she believe. Almost all of us have been there at one time or another in our lives.

One of the central images in your novel, and in your stories in The Power of Horses, *is of the Missouri River; and one of the central political concerns connected with this image is the Missouri River Power Project, with its Oahe Dam and the subsequent flooding of tribal lands in South Dakota. I'm interested in the way you link the political fact of that project to the spiritual quality of the landscape – as I say, you seem to work that connection throughout your fiction. Could you describe your fictional and spiritual relationship to Western geography? (Perhaps this has something to do with your "relationship" to writers like Stegner and Manfred?)*

The Missouri River issue is, I suppose, both political and spiritual but more than anything, it is a tribal matter. These are treaty-protected lands all up and down the Missouri River and it is no accident that treaty language begins each segment of the story. It is not just a Tatekeya story. It is a tribal story. It is not just a matter of how an individual survives, unconnected to how a tribe survives. I cannot say how this has something to do with my "relationship" to writers like Stegner and Manfred since neither of them is concerned with tribal survival in the sense the Sioux know of it. Generally, I don't think in terms of my fictional and spiritual relationship to Western geography. Perhaps I must learn how to talk about that idea.

Of the stories in The Power of Horses, *"The Clearest Blue Day" seems especially significant, for it captures what might be described as your particular "vision": the confluence of the three separate impulses represented by Claude, the young native dancer; the black missionary woman; and the old Sioux singer. Does this story seem as central to you as it does to this reader?*

Yes, "The Clearest Blue Day" seems to be central. Indeed, I think I am telling the same story over and over. About "vision," I don't know. Perhaps "obsession" would be a better term. You know, Woody Allen's "obsession" is whether or not women are going to like him, or the size of his penis. Flannery O'Connor's "obsession" was Christian hypocrisy. Faulkner told about the fall of the Southern Aristocracy and its consequences over and over again. So, I suppose this might be a writer's dilemma.

The "blue day" story was written almost in one sitting after I'd gone back to Lower Brulee and danced with my daughters there. We were trying to camp there and it rained like hell that weekend and we spent half the time in the car and I didn't sleep much. It was probably in the late 1960s, early 1970s and I had not finished *Then Badger Said This*, though I was in the process of that experimentation. It was a real attempt at using the episodic plot structure which was being experimented with by Joyce Carol Oates and others at that time. The story is, again, about change. Enforced change. Of the river and the people. It suggests all sorts of things, I think, about the Missouri River Tribes of the Sioux and their homelands, people who have always lived along the tributaries. I've finally lived long enough to have some perspective about the enormous changes which have occurred in this century. Nothing helps like age in understanding your own obsessions.

At times you seem to veer toward a sort of story cycle in The Power of Horses, *with characters and landscapes recurring throughout the collection. And one central figure, Big Pipe (about whom I'm especially curious), appears in both the stories and the novel. Do you see yourself creating a "community of fiction" in your work at all?*

"A community of fiction"? There are recurring themes, the same people appear. One of the earliest and most frequent admonitions to writers is to write about something you know. And I know these people, including Harvey Big Pipe, and these places. They are fictional and the stories aren't "true," of course. But, they are real. An "imagined reality" seems a contradiction but I think it's not. In terms of "story cycles," all of the stories and narrative traditions I know are cyclical so it seems quite natural. Nothing that happens stands in isolation from anything else in Dakota life and thought. There are so many more stories about Big Pipe that I know, and Aurelia, too. About the *Then Badger Said This* piece, I've got shoeboxes full of that stuff. Once I start writing about these people I find they have more to say and give than I had thought. Jason Big Pipe is a good example. My treatment of him is, I think, quite realistic. It is possible for people to "get better" and, like Grace Paley, I want to see them do that. I want to believe so I keep on working with the story, keep on telling more and more. Though I'm thought to be a cynic by my friends, if I keep telling the story this cynical nature can be brought around, don't you see?

In a few of your stories – "Mahpiyato," "A Visit from Reverend Tileston," "A Family Matter," "The Power of Horses," "A Child's Story" – you focus on the American Indian woman, both young and old. Is there a particularly feminist strain to these portraits at all? Is there an intellectual and emotional conflict between the traditional tribal impulse and the contemporary political impulse for the American Indian woman?

I want to tell you something about Mahpiyato. You see, Mahpiyato is truly one of the creators but is not, in the telling of the myth, necessarily thought to be female. The grandmother storyteller simply makes Mahpiyato "female," for herself and the grandchild listener. What it means is that storytellers are fabricators, which is just another word for "liars." She is giving the grandchild an "imagined reality" and she is "very convincing" and she has that right, as she is the grandmother. What may give us hope against such vaguely fraudulent and dangerous business is that the child "watched cautiously, leaning to one side so as not to catch the full glare in her eyes."

As for my thoughts on the "intellectual and emotional conflict between the traditional tribal impulse and the contemporary political impulse for American Indian women," I feel that the change in tribal societies is as wrenching for all of us as it is for anyone in all of American life, and, yes, I think that the lives of women are very hard. I don't see women as victims any more than I see Indians as victims. But, we do have to take risks and help our children to a safer world. At a paper I presented at a meeting of Third World Writers which took place at Sacramento State a few years ago, I found myself disagreeing with the position native women were placed in by the gifted novelist Rudolfo Anaya; I hope to publish that essay which, I think, was called something like "Third World Writers and the Metaphors We Have Known." It was in response to a piece Anaya had published in the *Columbus Review,* in which he was taking up again the metaphor of the mother earth. Maybe I had just gotten fed up with metaphors and was being a little cranky, but I don't think so. I tell my three daughters and my *Chu(n)skay* [son] that the women of the Sioux were virtuous and know how to go to war. It is my fervent hope that this is still true.

Finally, you have recently returned to your native South Dakota after several years in Washington State. What has brought you back to this landscape, and how does your current work link itself to that landscape?

The question here really should be, "Why did you leave?" The answer to that is I could not find an intellectual life in South Dakota. I literally crawled around on my hands and knees looking for a higher ed teaching job (the community colleges here were not yet started), and I was a divorced mother of four children. I needed a good job, one that would give me some career choices and allow me to raise my children in a reasonably productive atmosphere. I have never left "this landscape," and I never intended to go away, let alone stay away. Yet, I lived in Rapid City a couple-three times and kept moving away. I have a Lakota friend who lives in California and every time I see him he says, "My heart is at home." I call him, and myself and others like us, "economic exiles." For some of us, making the kind of living we want in South Dakota is difficult. After I got my master's degree the only job response that I got that sounded like they really wanted me was in a clerk/typist position at the Fort Thompson Agency. There was one South Dakota university that even answered my inquiries. Things have changed *some* in twenty-five years, but let's count how many Sioux tenured faculty persons there are in South Dakota institutions. Just for the fun of it.

Let me end with a poem which I wrote when I was teaching at Eastern Washington University in Cheney, Washington.

My Flight

How can I know
what keeps me disengaged, fleeing
for my life? As émigré, I never meant
to stay here routinely professing

45

in this wordless, sad, New World.
Darkly, I meet others
in the hallway: those who
survive our lives
resist the market mentality
and believe the saving
of baby seals
is a reinvention
of Humanism.
I dreamed I locked the door
and left.

See you later!

No roadsigns to point me
in the right direction. When
Oyate gather to sing the songs
that Little Horse sang
I will be there.

WORKS

From the River's Edge. New York: Arcade/Little, Brown, 1991. Novel.

The Power of Horses and Other Stories. New York: Arcade/Little, Brown, 1990. Short fiction.

Seek the House of Relatives. Marvin, S.D.: Blue Cloud Press, 1983. Poetry.

Then Badger Said This. Fairfield, Wash.: Ye Galleon Press, 1983. Short fiction and poetry.

James Crumley

James Crumley was born in the Hill Country of Texas – in the small town of Three Rivers, to be precise – in 1939. He was schooled at Georgia Institute of Technology, Texas A&I University, the University of Iowa Writers Workshop – and by a two-year hitch in the U.S. Army (which provided much of the material for his first novel, about the Vietnam War). Having taught at Reed College in Oregon, Colorado State, the University of Texas at El Paso, and the University of Montana, Crumley has come to settle in Missoula, where he is at work on what he calls his "Texas novel." Crumley is also involved in writing screenplays for his detective novels, featuring their Montana-based heroes C. W. Sughrue and Milo Milodragovitch.

Evidence of Crumley's days as a collegiate football player are still evident in his physical frame, though these days he also sports a ponytail and an earring in his left ear. This interview was conducted in June 1990 in Crumley's Honda, as we drove around Missoula and the surrounding countryside, Crumley feeling most comfortable talking about himself as he drove. In the course of that driving, Crumley pointed out landmarks in his personal and literary lives, told stories and made remarks that did not find their way into this interview, and introduced me to Ripley Schemm, poet and widow of Richard Hugo. We also stopped mid-tour at the Milltown Union Bar, a site made almost mythical by a host of Montana writers in their work. Later in the day, the interview continued on a drive to a Mexican restaurant in Victor, Montana.

GREGORY MORRIS: *In your essay "Driving Around Houston," you end by declaring: "My exile has become permanent." From what have you exiled yourself – Texas? Southwest Texas? Houston? Why has such an exile become necessary? What defines (physically, emotionally) that landscape for you? Are you now at home, rooted in Missoula? Or is such rootedness impossible for you (as it is for many of your characters)?*

JAMES CRUMLEY: I grew up in south Texas in one of those small towns that's unfortunately located, in that it's not far enough down into south Texas to be comfortable about having 65 percent Chicano population. So what you have is a small, bigoted, white community surrounded by a sea of brown faces. It's kind of an unhappy place; it's more unhappy than any other small town I've been around. Nor was it a good place for a person who likes to read books to grow up. I had to fistfight on the bus every goddamn day.

I have to admit that I still retain a residual resentment of all those people who treated me badly. I didn't look back for a long time. That's probably why I have so much trouble with what I'm calling "my Texas novel," because it's difficult for me to write about things that I don't remember fondly.

At one point, in the Army, I wouldn't tell people I was from Texas – I'd tell them I was from New Mexico, where I did live for a while when I was young. Texas makes me really nervous, and it's only been in the last five years that I've been able to go home, so to speak (because my mother still lives in the same small town where I grew up), without it causing serious anxiety. My politics have never really fit in, nor has my way of life. I always felt much more affinity for the Mexican kids that I was growing up with, but at the same time there was that pressure to fit in.

It was really odd, then, to be in Houston when I was researching that essay. I had gone, somehow, from being a dope-smoking hippie (when I was teaching at Colorado State) to having to go to Houston to talk to businessmen and political people. It was the first piece of journalism I'd ever tried, and I didn't know what I was doing. So I found myself doing odd things like sitting in Herman Park Zoo watching the alligators and the cancer patients, and that became a metaphor for Houston. As it turned out, I was right about Houston. That boom *did* end, and office space *did* get soft. Going to Houston was a cathartic event for me, in lots of ways.

Texas just isn't home. *Missoula* is home. I've now lived here longer than I lived in south Texas. Essentially, I only lived in south Texas for ten years, and then three years when I got back from the Army and finished college. I have troubles with a place that is that self-conscious.

(This house, by the way, is the great old mansion which used to sit at the bottom of the park. They cut it up into three parts and moved it up here. That's where I got all that shit about the Milo Milodragovitch mansion. I don't know what I would have written if I hadn't moved here: where the hell can you find stories like that? A fucking third of that house was sitting on the Van Buren Street bridge, when I got to town, and it had broken the bridge. The bridge has never been used as a street again; it's a footbridge. You can't buy stuff like that. Missoula, itself, is an odd place. You know, David Lynch was born here; and after seeing *Blue Velvet*, Bill Kittredge said, "Gee, that's like a night in Missoula!")

I think storytelling has something to do with the West. Stories are as important here now as they used to be in the South, in the early post-Civil War South when there was a serious oral tradition. Dick Hugo used to say that the good thing about students, when you got them here, was that they knew how to tell stories. They might not be able to spell, they might not be able to read very well, but by God they could tell stories.

Was it difficult, growing up male in Texas? Your story "Three Cheers for Thomas J. Rabb" seems in some ways an indictment of that environment, an environment that makes it especially important to find "a place in a physical world."

Sure, though I didn't get too much of that, certainly not from my folks. I suspect that like anybody with a lot of imagination, I generated a lot of my own paranoia. It's just that feeling of being an outsider, a feeling that never leaves you. You don't belong. When I got to Iowa City, it was like going to heaven. My God, there were people there who read books!

It's funny now, but Christ I can't tell you what kind of a *hick* I was. I was fortunate, in lots of ways, to be taught to be polite, so that I could fake it. I remember all those country things, like knowing which fork to use and shit like that. Now I feel like I'm comfortable any place in the world, it doesn't bother me, but I'm sure I went out of south Texas with a giant chip on my shoulder about all of that shit. I was more than willing to get physical with people.

Ralph Beer told the story of how the two of you met: how you stood up in a bar and said, "I'm the strongest guy in this bar." And Ralph stood up and said, "No, you're not."

What I actually said – fucking Ralph! – writers lie so much! They love to gossip, and they'd rather lie than tell the truth; I don't blame them, because I'm that way myself. At one time, though, I could say that I'd never been beaten in arm-wrestling except by two pro football players, which was okay as long as I didn't mention that one was a halfback; and that I'd only been held once, and that was by a psychotic. I don't know exactly how Ralph and I twisted arms, but it was some sort of male-bonding ritual.

Still, that kind of thing is common between country people. I've noticed it a lot over the years, particularly among writers. There has to be some sort of physical thing that takes place between men who are uncomfortable being writers. Nobody in my family ever went to college; my father never finished high school. Coming out of that background, I found it difficult to adjust to trying to be an intellectual; a lot of people feel that way now, where there used to be only a few – so that when we run into one another we've got to do something to verify our roots. Goddamn Ralph and I, we twisted arms until we nearly died and we finally gave up. I don't do that anymore, and I hadn't done it for five or six years when Ralph and I did that – shit, I hurt all the way down to the back of my left heel.

Let me ask you something that's related to that male-bonding idea. Your work possesses a strong moral strain, one linked to the definition of machismo *given in your essay from* Rolling Stone, *entitled "The Heavy":* "machismo *means we will be gentlemen no matter how twisted by drink and drugs and life we find ourselves, and, as Ezra Pound so gracefully said, there is some shit we will not eat; no more, no less" –*

I think it was e. e. cummings, actually –

Okay. This definition seems akin to the notion promoted in The Last Good Kiss, *of "living without flinching." In a violent world, the best one can do is develop a moral code that reacts to that violence – an ethics of violence? You re-marked in a previous interview that, as a writer of detective fiction, you sought a "set of moral precepts that seemed flexible." How would you define those precepts?*

I have an old friend who accuses me of still being a Baptist, which I find interesting, and he may be hallucinating. It's always seemed to me that conventional morality is something that we simply make up, and it strikes me that a lot of conventional morality is an attempt by the powers-that-be, whether they be corporate, political, or what, to control the populace, to keep them nice and sweet so they'll stay at their machines. You can't get a guy to stand on an assembly line unless you convince him that it's necessary, that it's not just a way to make money but that it's a moral necessity to stand there on that assembly line. I think the conspiracy of power is much broader than anyone has ever suspected.

So I'm always uncomfortable with that conventional morality; it doesn't serve the purpose that it should. I do think there are certain things that you have to do, in order just to live in the world. I think you have to be polite. I think you can't lie – lying is like the basest of sins, if you want to put it like that. I think you owe something back to the world, whether it be time or money or generosity of spirit. I think you have to be tolerant of other people; that's one of the things that I like about most writers, is that they're very seldom bigots: we may hate yuppies, but we don't hate yuppies individually! It's like trying to talk to your kids and convince them that it's okay to say "Fuck," but if you say it at school you're going to get into trouble. Or it's like trying to explain to some old woman at a Pen and Quill Society why language isn't dirty. I guess a lot of my reaction to morality has to do with my reaction to religion; I can't stomach any kind of organized religion, it offends me, in a moral way. It's that lip service: we can go to heaven if we don't say "fuck." That doesn't quite cut it.

Do you find any kind of spiritual quality in your ethic?

I'm a child of the sixties, so I've fiddled around with meditation and chanting. I don't have any trouble with the spiritual side of life; it's when somebody decides how that spirituality is organized and what it means that I become suspicious. I don't disbelieve in spiritual things at all; it's just when it's put into a religious context that it gives me trouble. I don't know that it's a good idea for society as a whole to give up conventional morality, and it's hard to teach people how to behave without that set of conventions.

Morality is not the driving force of my life, but it's something I think about a great deal and something I guess I try to work around. The novel is, in some ways, moral instruction; it can't help but be. But I don't set out deliberately to pose those kinds of moral questions. Maybe the best answer to all that is this: a lot of people confuse Abraham Trahearne with Dick Hugo, rather than with Jim Dickey, whom I might have modeled Trahearne after. But I think what Trahearne is, is the selfish, mean side of myself more than anything else, that willingness to put everything aside for your own personal ambition – ambition, not in the sense of being a success or making money, but just getting to the typewriter and getting the work out. That's not just what I do, that's also who I am; so consequently I have made mistakes in judgment, out of selfishness and out of that kind of ambition, out of my desire to write a great book. And I'm not so sure anymore that that's a good trade-off. When I was younger, I was willing to say, "I don't care. This work is what's important." I'm less sure of that now. I don't have any regrets about my life; I'm sorry I don't see more of my children, but when I do see them it's a good time: I'm still friends with my older children whom I adopted and raised, I'm good friends with my boys, with my younger kids. I just am no longer so certain – besides, if you don't become more uncertain as you get older, you turn into a pompous ass!

Do you sense any special spiritual kinship with the Native American way? The Native American presence in your fiction certainly is not a major *presence. In* Dancing Bear, *you give the contemporary Indian condition your fullest treatment, working the "Benniwah" legend and the modern problems of Indian life into the fabric of the novel. Do you feel any sort of responsibility to deal with this presence in your West?*

I guess not. I'm not sure where all of that Benniwah stuff came from originally. One of the reasons I made up this tribe was that I didn't feel qualified to speak for a real tribe, and I thought it would be presumptuous and wrong to try to do so. That's why I made up that tribe and the goofy story connected with it. It turns out that there's a county in Idaho, south of Coeur d'Alene, with a very similar name: Benewah. I like to fiddle around with names; I think all writers like to fiddle around with names. Names have some kind of magical importance.

Let me ask you specifically about your novels. Your first novel, One to Count Cadence, *is a peculiar sort of war novel – if it is* a war novel – in that it spends a relatively short span of time in Vietnam. What sorts of decisions did you have to make in constructing that novel, moving as you do from the Philippines to Vietnam? Do you see* One to Count Cadence *as part of a tradition at all, as part of the American war novel tradition? As part of the growing body of Vietnam literature?*

I started that novel in 1960. When I wrote the short story that grew into the novel – the first short story I ever sat down and wrote for a class – that was in 1962 or 1963 – I had this affinity for the military. I'm not exactly sure why.

When I was a little kid I always wanted to go to military school; my parents, of course, couldn't afford anything like that and so I didn't go. Then I went to college for the first time on a Navy scholarship and planned to be a Marine pilot until I discovered I couldn't see well enough – I probably wouldn't fit into a jet, anyway. Later, when my life went bad after I got out of the Army, one of the things I always thought I would do would be to join up again. So there was just something alluring about the military. I didn't do it well, to say the least: I made private first class three times, and I didn't take well to authority at all, but I was fascinated with the Army.

The first story I wrote was called "Labor Pains." When I went to the Philippines in 1959, there were already advisers in Vietnam. In fact, I flew over with a guy who was on his way to Vietnam. Vietnam was also on my mind a lot because that's what we – this is probably a violation of the National Security Act – but that's what we were working on in the Philippines when I was in the Army Security Agency, we copied Vietnamese military communication nets. So I was familiar with all that, and my first story was about a soldier who'd just come back from a combat experience in Vietnam; some of that story was taken from a story in *Life* magazine about the guy who won the first Medal of Honor in Vietnam.

I was a long time in starting *One to Count Cadence*. It was like a gift book, in some ways. I didn't know where it was going or what it was doing. I think, too, that in lots of ways it was a young man's novel in that I took a pretty big bite, and I had no idea what kind of bite I was taking. It took me a year to start the novel, and three and a half years to write it. What I discovered at the end was that I was putting two of the parts of myself back together – it was a cathartic experience when I finished that book, I fell out of my chair I was so happy.

It took me a long time, too, to go back and look at that novel. I couldn't read it for years. The sentences seemed wrong. It seemed pretentious. It was strange. It was out of print for seventeen goddamn years and when I got that Vintage edition, I have to admit that I came out from the post office and sat in my pick-up truck and cried because it was so nice to see that son of a bitch back. And I reread it. It's got a lot of problems, but I'm not in any kind of way ashamed of it or condescending to it.

Actually, aside from that one story that became the novel, and that nobody liked and nobody ever saw again, I essentially got into the University of Iowa on one story. I don't know if it's in *Whores* or not – "The Ideal Son for the Jenkins Family."

No, it's not.

It's about a father who hits his son in the head accidentally with a sledgehammer. That's a wonderful story. This is a digression, but I guess that's how I knew I was going to be a writer. I'd been working on this story for a creative writing class, and I could never get the story to work: I couldn't get the right voice, I couldn't find the right perspective. Finally, it occurred to me to use the father as the major character. I ended up taking a scene out of my own life, in fact. My father had a great respect for machinery, and I recalled a time when we were trying to pump salt water from the tank battery back into an abandoned well. We couldn't get the nuts off – they'd been on there for fucking years – and we were hitting the pump with this big sledgehammer-wrench. It was raining, it was hot, and these fucking ants were climbing all over us. Finally, Shorty just said, "Fuck it," and put that sledgehammer right through the head of that pump.

They tell you, in a writing class, to take an experience that you really don't understand and to write about it. This was the first time I'd ever seen my father really angry, so I was trying to work with that. When I got back into his point of view, when I got to that point in that story, when he picked up that sledgehammer, instead of hitting the pump he hit the kid in the head. Jesus Christ, what a rush! It still makes the hair on the back of my head stand up. That was the moment in which I knew I was going to be a writer. I didn't worry about it after that.

Cadence changed my life – I didn't write another book for six and a half years. It took it all out of me. A good friend of mine said to me one night when we were drunk, "I don't know how you're ever going to write another book. You've already done everything you could in that book. There's nothing else to write." And I sort of laughed it off, but he wasn't all that wrong. That was a big, ambitious book, and I may never approach that again. I just don't have that kind of arrogance and confidence that I think you need to write that kind of novel. I am not Nabokov. I think having self-doubt may make you into a better person, but it doesn't necessarily make you into a better writer. You need that real arrogance: I know the truth, and this is it. I simply don't have that anymore.

Nor do I have that rage that used to fuel me. I used to be the angriest person that anybody could be; I don't know how I got this far without either killing myself or killing somebody else. It was an absolutely stomach-churning rage, and I wrote out of that rage all the time. One of the things I worry about in being calm is whether or not I'll be able to write again. It seems to be working, though it seems to be working differently. I'm much more concerned about being funny than I am about being serious. I think of my stuff as funny; it makes me laugh, and that's all that counts.

There's a certain comic element to the portrait you draw of the West – of the New West *– in your fiction. Your West is one that is clearly modern and altered. It's a West beleaguered by cocaine and alcohol, by tourists and development, by dou- blewide prefab homes and failed hippie communes and waste dumps.*

You've got to do something with all these goddamn people. I guess I've given up about tourists and about housing developments; these people have to live somewhere, and if they can afford to live here we can use the money. The real problem in the West is not necessarily tourists and housing de- velopments, as much as it is logging companies. The Plum Creek Timber Corporation [based in Seattle] just admitted the other day that when they were cutting up in the Swan Mountains here they weren't trying for sus- tained yield forest, they were just cutting trees. Stone Container, the craft mill, is another example. They make liner board, and I've heard it said with some authority by several lawyers here in town that, given the water pollu- tion laws of Montana, they could shut the Stone Container mill down at any time because they're constantly polluting the Clark Fork.

Environmentalists, though, have to have some give in them. These log- gers, these mill workers need their jobs. You have to find some other kind of way for them to make a living; you can't just shut the plant down. At the same time, people who work in the woods have to stop identifying them- selves with the corporate power structure, because the corporate power structure is going to cut them down just like trees. These people don't understand they are a nonrenewable resource, too. They've got to under- stand that if these fuckers cut down all the trees, there's not going to be any work anyway. I believe that if you let the paper companies loose, they'd cut down every goddamn tree. I understand the necessity for the corporations, but there's a corporate greed and a lack of vision that I think is fucking criminal – it's not just mean and stupid, it should be against the law. Until corporate chiefs are put in jail, they're not going to pay any attention to you; you can't fight them – you have to put the bastards in jail. Until they understand the uniqueness of these ecosystems, these biospheres – until they understand that these systems all fit together, these guys are going to keep fucking it up.

I suspect that we're just going to flat-ass lose, unless there's a war of some kind. Which is where I realized that I didn't exactly fit into the radical movement in the 1960s – when it came to me that nothing was going to change unless you killed somebody – it was that simple – that unless there was a real civil war, nothing was going to change. (This was after *Cadence*.) And I realized that I didn't *believe* it enough to kill anybody, that it just wasn't there anymore. However fucking mad I might be at the world and at myself, I didn't want to kill anybody. Not that I'm a pacifist – I wouldn't hesitate to shoot somebody who was breaking into my house, for instance, or who was fucking with my children or my lady. But to kill people for political reasons seems to be creating an entirely different set of problems.

It seems like you were working some of these questions out in Dancing Bear.

Well, all kinds of frightening shit is happening. I still don't know why BFI has never gotten on my ass – BFI is the garbage company after which EQCS in *Dancing Bear* is modeled. BFI owns something like 42 percent of all the garbage companies in America and is clearly connected with the Mob. They had a dump in New Jersey that caught fire, from spontaneous combustion; and they've been indicted twelve thousand times, and they just plead guilty, pay the fine, and go on. Talk about a clear disregard for public safety.

Obviously, nobody gives a shit. All I can do is write books, and donate money. I'm not going back on the front lines. That bumper sticker that says, "Think Globally, Act Locally" – I think that makes pretty good sense. You have to be able to see the whole picture, and to understand that it's important not to cut down every tree in the rain forest. People should be able to realize that without having to be hit over the head. I guess I have more politics than I think I do, but I really try to stay away from polemics in my novels.

Do you think you offer a "surreal version" of Montana, as one writer commented in a review in Time?

Surreal?! I think part of the trouble is that nobody on either coast really knows much about what goes on out here, so that it *seems* surreal to them. You run into odd sorts of things: a copy editor who doesn't know what a daylight basement is or who's never heard of an El Camino or who's never heard of schnapps. I have a notion that New York and Washington and Los Angeles are really provincial places, and that the true sophisticated cosmopolitan American lives somewhere in between. I find it difficult to think of people as civilized who don't know how to change a tire. I don't *like* to change tires, but at least I can.

Did you know that the Bitterroot Valley is the home of more retired CIA agents than any other place in the country except Arlington, Virginia? The CIA recruited, for years, out of the smoke-jumpers' school here. At least half a dozen guys who worked for Air America, who were line boys and pilots, were recruited right out of the smoke-jumpers helicopter pilot school here – and three guys who were bodyguards for the generals in the Golden Triangle. Some real lunatics. There are about three hundred Hmong families still here, too. Now *that* is the surreal New West!

Do you think, then, that you have a strong sense of place in your work – with Montana being that place?

Yes, I think so. Montana affects me. I don't get out to fish much anymore because my feet can't stand the goddamn cold water. Nor do I hunt much anymore; I'll take a deer if it's standing by the side of the road, but that's about it. I don't take any pleasure from hunting anymore. I *do* like to get out and do some serious driving. The weekend before last I drove up to Big Fork for dinner, which is at the other end of Flathead Lake; that's about 250 miles. Last weekend I drove to Sandpoint, Idaho, because I'd never been there; that was about 500 miles. Next weekend I'm driving down to Jackson Hole.

You get out in the mountains and you feel like you can breathe again. I just don't know what it is about this place, but it's really like coming home. As you can see from driving around, Missoula is not the most attractive town in the world. But the people – the people are a precious commodity here. They're the strangest, nicest people I've ever met in my life.

Think about the scene in *The Wrong Case* where Milo talks with the girl who's manning the Chamber of Commerce booth: that may seem surreal to somebody in New York, but that actually happened. Still, Montana, like all the rest of the world, is slowly becoming California.

Despite the often unflattering portrait you draw of the West, very few characters are compelled to leave that West. The crisis of staying or leaving, of escape – which is a prominent concern of so much contemporary Western fiction – seems of no real significance in your work, except in the story "Cairn." Do you think this is so?

I don't know. "Cairn" for me is a going-home story. That place in "Cairn" is my mother's mother's homeplace outside of Blanco, Texas, and it's a place that is probably more significant in my childhood memories than any of the places where we lived. This is the place where we went deer hunting. It's at the end of the road, and as late as 1953 – I had a driver's license, so it must have been 1953 – they still lived in a half-barn, half-house with a dirt floor. They didn't get electricity or a telephone until my great-uncle Henry built a new house there. That place really sticks in my memory. Of course, when Henry died the family got into a gigantic fight about it. Fifteen or twenty years ago, that 640 acres of Hill Country wasn't worth anything, but now this place is worth probably three million dollars. Henry died without a will; the deed hadn't been changed since Henry's grandfather died. Henry was one of those strange old Hill Country bachelors who never got married until he was fifty-six, and when that wife died he married again. I think what finally happened is that the second wife was going to take half the place, and all the other grandkids would split the other half. They've been in court for years; my mother and her favorite aunt haven't spoken in six years – another one of those strange, unfortunate family fights.

But it's a beautiful place. I think the Hill Country is the reason that I like Montana; when I go back down there and drive out into the Hill Country, I'm reminded again of how much I like to be able to see elevation and evergreen trees and clear creeks. South Texas is like a *swamp*.

I don't know about escaping the West. One of my detectives, Milo Milodragovitch, tries to go to Mexico but he doesn't get there. Maybe in another novel he'll get to Mexico. (There's still another Milo novel kicking around back there, where he doesn't get his money. I'm looking forward to that novel, as much as you can look forward to a fucking detective novel.)

I think people come to Missoula, and they never leave. We call it "the Missoula disease." So when you think about escape, where are you going to go? Helena? The valley of the valium? Actually, the West is where you *go* to escape. We're always running up here. Nobody *ever* goes home.

Could you talk a bit about the evolution of your detective-heroes, Milo Milodragovitch and C.W. Sughrue? How did these two characters individually develop? Why did you feel the need to create two *such characters, two different detectives?*

And how do they continue to develop? For example, in the portion of your uncompleted novel, The Mexican Tree Duck *[then excerpted in* Whores, *and*

now published as a completed novel], we see Sughrue as a man profoundly lacking
"moral certitude" (a quality he claims to possess a bit more of in The Last Good
Kiss*). He is no longer a private investigator, his life has declined into chaos.*
Where is he headed?

And what brought you back to Milo, in Dancing Bear, *after an eight-year*
absence?

When I did the first 160 pages of *The Last Good Kiss,* I did it at Reed College
when I was teaching there. I was a bit uncomfortable at Reed; they had never
hired a fiction writer, and I don't think they had ever seen a redneck. They
were nice to me and wanted me to stay for the two years of my contract, but I
really didn't want to be there, so I got to work right quick. I sent the 160 pages
to my agent in New York saying, "Christ, let's try to get a new book contract.
I've been tied up in book contracts all my life." And he did, but he said,
"Listen, this book is unbelievably cinematic, but can you change this guy's
name?" (United Artists had bought *The Wrong Case* in 1975, so they had
already held the rights to the Milodragovitch name for a certain length of
time.) So I said, "Sure, what the hell?" And I went back into my Texas novel,
where C.W. Sughrue is a major character – he's my voice in that Texas novel –
and transferred him into *The Last Good Kiss.* I thought it would be a relatively
easy transferal, because he already had enough of the background: he'd been a
newspaper reporter and had been in and out of the Army. But I was wrong,
for it really changed the novel; it became a different book entirely. I made the
change for mercenary reasons, which is one of the worst reasons for doing it,
but Sughrue became an important character; and he's the narrator, in all
kinds of ways, in the Texas novel.

But Milo is a good guy. I don't know if this bears on it or not, but when my
marriage broke up my wife took my kids and moved back to Boston. I didn't
miss her exactly, but I certainly missed those kids; it was like tearing a piece
of me off and throwing it away. So I was kind of loping around town,
drinking, moping, and one of the things I said in a drunken moment of truth
was: "Jesus, I can't be all bad. I invented Milo, didn't I?" That sort of
maudlin line stayed in my head. I really like Milo. For me, he's the decentest
of human beings. He's a better person than I am. So I can't give up Milo, but
I'm never sure what voice to use. I tried *Dancing Bear* first with Sughrue's
voice. Their voices may sound similar to the reader, but they're really different voices for me.

You seem comfortable with both.

Schizophrenia! I've spent a lot of time in those voices: I've only written four novels, but I have 100 pages or more of another four or five novels, and I have 800 pages of the Texas novel. So the voices are comfortable. But they do change for me. When I went back to the Milo voice in the early drafts of *Dancing Bear,* it was really pleasant, it was really a pleasure to step behind that old fart's face and into that voice: sentimental and maudlin and half-drunk. I admit to a great deal of fondness for Milo. This is insane – I sit here and talk about characters I've created as if they were real people – but I think that is part of why people respond to them, because they are real to me.

I'm writing in Sughrue's voice again, now. Sughrue is meaner; he'll do things that Milo won't do, like shoot a guy in the foot twice. I could never shoot a guy in the foot like that, but *Sughrue* could! His voice is a little bit odd. I've been back in that voice for about a month now, and *The Mexican Tree Duck* isn't going exactly like the excerpt that's in *Whores.* About the only thing I've saved is the incident with the jukebox; I couldn't give that up.

Both Milo and Sughrue have been described as antiheroes. Do you see them as such?

No, I don't. They're not anything that Clint Eastwood wants to do! I think of the antihero as that wonderful whining voice out of *Notes from Underground* [by Dostoevsky], which I love. Christ, I have no trouble with antiheroes, but I don't think of these guys as whiners.

These men are always set against particularly strong women – or at least strong in their relentless pursuit of whatever it is they want. One type of woman seems to be the very mean woman, the woman with a knifelike edge. Yet at the same time, you've also created (though with lesser frequency and emphasis) the woman who is the artist: Edna Trahearne in The Last Good Kiss, *or the nameless central character in "The Things She Cannot Write About, The Reasons Why," a woman whose creative spirit is bound up with the physical/sexual element of her nature. Still another type – perhaps the prevalent type – seems to be the imperious mothering figure, persistent and necessarily vicious in her claims upon her children. These women can be mothers-in-fact, or they can be women who seek to mother the men whom they supposedly love as husbands or lovers (Catherine Trahearne kills Betty Sue Flowers for the right to "mother" her husband, Abraham Trahearne). Do you feel comfortable with the women you've created?*

"Women, women. What do they want?!" Obviously, I've had a great deal of trouble with my mother over the years, so I'm sure that has informed not just my fiction but also my life. My mother was strong because she was so desperate. She grew up in bare-bones poverty, and that kind of poverty affects people no matter where you are. She was really shy, and really angry, and really wanted to be in charge of shit. My father, meanwhile, was an easygoing guy, so they didn't have a lot of trouble; they fit together fairly well. But I was less easygoing, so when I started adolescence the two of us went to war and we stayed at war for a long time. We're pals now, but it's been a long haul; and I'm sure that has affected me. All the women who have loved me over time have said something about me and my mother – I don't know how true it is. I both like women and am afraid of them. I don't think that's particularly unusual for American men. I understand now what makes women feel like they have to be insidious; that's the only way they have to gain power.

I kind of like the women I've created. People ask me over and over again about Betty Sue Flowers, about how I could kill Betty Sue Flowers off; and I never really have a good answer to that question. I don't control my books – I'm responsible for the language and for rewriting them until they sound right – but I'm not really in charge of them; they're in charge of me. So I had no idea where *The Last Good Kiss* was headed, that it was headed toward the death of Betty Sue Flowers. It just happened. I think it fits in the book, and I don't mind letting my books do that to me. I was asked, from the time that book came out, about the death of Betty Sue Flowers. Finally, one time at a party at a literary conference in North Dakota, somebody asked me that and I blurted out, "I couldn't bear to be in love with one of my characters for the rest of my life, so I killed her!" That's a glib answer, but I am truly fascinated by that woman. Nor is she anybody I know – I pretty much don't write from living character to fictional character. There's just something tough and good and kind about Betty Sue Flowers; she's an artist, and I have a natural affinity for people involved in trying to make art, whatever it may be. But I also like Catherine Trahearne.

This all started in *The Wrong Case* when Helen Duffy's mother showed up. Once again, I don't know where she came from. It seemed like the right thing to have happen at the time. Like everybody, I've known women who create their own histories and they seem to do a better job of it than men do. Because of the way they're treated in the world, it's necessary for women to believe this more than it is perhaps for men, so that they're much more convincing. I think women have a righteous beef with the world. I'm not sure that they should take it out on me, though; I didn't create the problem: there's forty thousand years of hunting and gathering that precedes me!

But just looking at the beginning of what I'm working on now, I don't know that I'm going to change the kind of women I write about. I've been accused, and justifiably so, of occasionally putting men in women's bodies and that seems to be what I do. All my women characters can do anything they want to; they might be driven by some kind of odd psychological quirk, but they're not depressed by social factors. They aren't women who've been shoved aside; they're women who do things.

It's funny, too, that you talk of Catherine Trahearne killing Betty Sue Flowers. This is something I've not admitted before, but I have no *idea* who killed Betty Sue Flowers. That scene doesn't exist in my mind. I never wrote it and it doesn't exist.

As a writer of screenplays, how much violence would you do to your novels in order to give a screenplay what you call a "straight line?"

I don't think books have anything to do with movies. What I am interested in is a good movie, and I don't feel that writerly obligation to defend my book. That's not necessary. Being a novelist and being a screenwriter are two different deals, and I've been at it long enough now so that I think I understand something about the difference. Think about all the bad books that made good movies. *The Graduate*, for instance. It's not a *natural* transition, from book to movie. And I'll probably have a nervous breakdown when I go to the theater and see what they've done to my books.

I really like movies, and I've always been convinced that Abbott and Costello had as much to do with my literary upbringing as Hemingway and Faulkner. We lived in the country and we didn't get to town much; movies were magic and wonderful. So I love movies, and I'd really like to make a movie. There are some parts of the business that I'm not crazy about, but you see the work that's been put into some movies and it's fucking magic. When they say it's magic time, they're not kidding. When it works, it works.

WORKS

Dancing Bear. New York: Random House, 1983. Novel.
The Last Good Kiss. New York: Random House, 1978. Novel.
The Mexican Tree Duck. New York: Mysterious Press, 1993. Novel.

The Muddy Fork & Other Things. Livingston, Mont.: Clark City Press, 1993. Short fiction and nonfiction.

One to Count Cadence. New York: Random House, 1969. Novel.

Whores. Missoula, Mont.: Dennis McMillan Publications, 1988. Short fiction and essays.

The Wrong Case. New York: Random House, 1975. Novel.

Ivan Doig

Though he now lives in Seattle, Washington, and has often written of the Pacific Northwest in his fiction, Ivan Doig is probably best known for his novels of Montana – what might be called his McCaskill Trilogy. Doig himself is a Montana native, born in White Sulphur Springs – a town on the Rocky Mountain Front – in 1939. Doig's eloquent recollection of that growing-up experience, *This House of Sky*, was nominated for the 1978 National Book Award, and his work has received many awards over time.

In 1989, Doig received the Western Literature Association's Distinguished Achievement Award, and it was at the meeting of that association in Coeur d'Alene, Idaho, that this interview took place (and that he read from what was then a forthcoming novel, *Ride with Me, Mariah Montana*, to which he often refers in this interview). Doig suggested we meet in his hotel suite, bright and early, for a 6:00 A.M. conversation over a room-service breakfast. Light had still a long way to come when we began our interview, accented by tea and strawberries. Despite the early hour, however, Doig had no difficulty finding his natural eloquence.

GREGORY MORRIS: *You've criticized contemporary fiction for its minimalist, experimental qualities, but in some ways your own work is very experimental, in the way you work with different narrative forms – diaries, letters.*

IVAN DOIG: What I've tried to take aim at is self-referential fiction where the writer writes about being a writer being written about, that kind of thing. Pyrotechnics that don't go off into life but only whiz around there on the page – that just doesn't seem to me what grown-up writers ought to be doing. Meanwhile you read Nadine Gordimer, and my God, look at what she's writing about in comparison – the moral travails of living in an apartheid society. And her work is at least as sophisticated as any literary gamesman's. I maybe shouldn't single out anyone, but did Donald Barthelme ever write anything which is going to make as much difference to humankind as any one of Nadine Gordimer's books? Goddamn it, life *is* real, life *is* earnest. Sure, we need literary experimentation, but it has to be a lot more daring than academic wordgames. A book like [Russell Hoban's] *Riddley Walker* that takes the language apart and yet manages to tell a hell of a story, that's the real deal. Or Beckett, seeing how far down language can be pared, or Faulkner showing us how wild and wonderful syntax can get – experimentation like that takes real guts, and it ends up being worth it because it shows us new sides of the human story. But the stuff that's just tricks on paper, hermetically sealed – minimalism is the latest version of it – there was an awful lot of that in American writing in the past twenty or thirty years and so we came through an important historical period in this country, I think, without enough fiction writers who looked closely and honestly at that period. And that doesn't chime very well with us out here in the West. What's going on in life – *that's* what there is to write about and experiment with.

So you think Western fiction enjoys a more expansive vision?

It seems to me to. More of a community vision, I think, at least. Which probably comes out of Western life, that you do have to cooperate to overcome weather problems, the facts of distance and sparse population. In a place like Montana, your community may be spread across the width of the entire state – Montana is actually a medium-sized city exploded across a countryside about the size of Spain – but there's a feel of community nonetheless. You'll find in Montana, and in a lot of the rest of the West too, that if you talk to somebody for a couple of minutes on a street corner in Missoula or Superior, he'll say: "By God, yeah – is he your cousin? Yeah, yeah, I went to school with his wife!" And that person you'll have in common is likely to be somebody over in Ekalaka or Billings, four or five hundred miles from where you're having that conversation. Out here, everybody is about one or two removes from knowing somebody in common, so we're aware, I think, that there's more to life and the threads of it we ought to be writing about, than just whatever neurosis it is that somebody wakes up with on a given morning.

Part of "your West" seems to have been Missoula – you acknowledge "the Missoula Gang" in Winter Brothers. *What is the history of that group, and when did it "own the West"?*

"This one is for the Missoula Gang, when we owned the West," you're talking about. That dedication was in commemoration of a conference Bill Kittredge thought up, at the University of Montana in 1979. Kittredge called together there in Missoula a tribal gathering of Western writers and historians, with the conference idea and title "Who Owns the West?" I met A. B. Guthrie and Norman Maclean for the first time, and I watched Guthrie and Maclean meet for the first time. Dorothy Johnson was alive yet, Dick Hugo was still alive, Jim Welch and Madeline DeFrees gave readings – it turned out to be a great gathering of writers. So, out of that, I ran that epigraph for what I thought was a literary coming-of-age. And as with so much else in writing about the American West, Kittredge was the linchpin.

Was it sort of a homecoming for you, too, coming back to Montana?

No, I'd been back to Montana a lot.

You didn't feel severed from Montana?

Not at that point. I *did* feel severed in the early 1970s – after my grandmother's death, the last of my family in what had seemed to me a hard history of the Doigs and Ringers, there were a few years in there when Carol and I deliberately did not go to Montana. All the deaths back there, the economic hardship which I'd originally been pushed out by – those things kept me away until a little healing could happen. Really not until the summer of 1977, when I went back to do the final couple of months of research on *This House of Sky*, when I went around to all the places mentioned in the book where I'd lived, did I return to Montana on good terms with the place. My high school class's twentieth reunion happened to coincide with that visit and I was also writing a travel piece for the *New York Times* on Highway 89, the road between Yellowstone Park and Glacier National Park, and Carol and I also hiked the Bob Marshall Wilderness for five glorious days on a backpack trip. So, with all of that, the summer of 1977 was my homecoming to Montana, a piece of time that said to me, My God, look at all that's here, how much it means to you.

The professional camaraderie started the next year, the autumn that *House of Sky* came out. Missoula had an excellent, highly literary bookstore at that time called The Fine Print, and I did one of the very first signings for *House of Sky* there. I didn't really know anyone in town, but one guy came up and said, "I'm Jim Crumley," and another guy came up and said, "All I want to say is, goddamn, you wrote the book I wanted to write" – that was Kittredge. And it went through the afternoon like that, and on into the night at a party the bookseller, Julie Golding, gave – friendships counting up until they became the couple dozen in the "Missoula gang" dedication.

Allow me here one slightly off-the-wall question: Given the rather condescending view taken of the sheepherder and his sheep by the cowboy, do you feel any real consciousness of that attitude in writing about the McCaskills? Do you feel yourself, intentionally or not, a defender of sheep and sheepherder?

Well, I don't have any thumping philosophical justification for this, but just as a gut reaction – you bet, I'm writing against the cowboy myth. The West was settled by a hell of a lot of people, different kinds of people – miners, homesteaders, schoolteachers, merchants, sheep ranchers, Chinese laundrymen – and the guy out herding cows was pretty minimal among them in most cases. So I find it bizarre that the cowboy is the emblematic Western figure that so much potboiling fiction has made him.

The cowboy myth is persistent, but I think it's also an outdated romantic distortion. For example, the major media event of Montana's centennial year was the cattle drive, even though historians point out that the significant cattle trade into Montana in the 1880s was by railroad boxcar from the Midwest, instead of up the trail from Texas. It turns out that the organizers of the centennial trail drive got the idea from the *television* version of [Larry

McMurtry's] *Lonesome Dove,* so there was this circle from media event to media event. But that emphasis on Montana's supposed cowboy past ignores the bigger historical story – that as the historian Bill Lang has pointed out, the homestead boom in Montana was the largest agricultural migration in North American history. And to come into everyday history with this kind of example, there were any number of ranchers in Montana during the Depression, and for that matter other periods of their lives, too, who ranched sheep in order to be able to afford to look like cowboys.

So, yeah, it is intentional with me, to the point where Jick in *Ride with Me, Mariah Montana,* is still a sheepman. The sheep culture seems to me a rich topic which hasn't had that much written about it, even though I think it's a more complex agricultural way of life, and at least as colorful as cattle-raising.

Turning to the Two Medicine novels, I'm curious about the conception of those works. Judging from the notes to English Creek, *you originally conceived of this project as a trilogy; but the order in which the novels have been written – and are being written – was that also an original intention, particularly the working backward from the first to the second novel? If so, why this order of composition?*

Yes, I did think of this as a trilogy from the very start. *English Creek* I wrote first out of a professional reason: it was a two-year book to write rather than a three-year book, as the other two have been. In essence, I was getting into print and making a living a year earlier. I didn't see any great problem in spreading the chronology out both directions from *English Creek.* In that book I was interested in establishing the voice, the family, the general situation, and then thinking both ahead and back, leaving some avenues for the other two plots to go down. For instance, in *English Creek,* Beth is badgered by Jick, "Why did your mother make that wagon trip up there to the Two Medicine?" – and I didn't really *know* what that wagon trip was about when I wrote that. But I wanted some kind of family secret, and worked it out in the writing of *Rascal Fair.*

So that you and Jick and reader put the pieces together – together – discovering how they came to be.

That's right. And you heard an example of that discovery process last night [in a reading from *Ride with Me, Mariah Montana*]. I've never gone near the grizzly bear issue before, haven't wanted to. I have friends on all sides of that issue, and it takes people over. Talk about a potent symbolic environmental issue. So I really didn't want to write about grizzlies – so many other people already were writing about them. But while I was working on the book I thought, Jesus, that's what my characters Riley and Mariah, as newspaper people, are going to be out looking at. And so I pulled out some research I'd gathered while I was writing *English Creek*, talking to a rancher who, without Jick's qualms, had to trap and kill grizzlies probably a couple of dozen times. So the details of how to trap a grizzly come from him. The shooting is my invention – I asked him about what it takes to kill a grizzly, and he just said, "Aw, you shoot 'em like a dog." He didn't mean it contemptuously – he said it more flatly. By the same token, I got in touch with a wildlife biologist in charge of nurturing grizzly bear habitat along the Rocky Mountain Front, and learned all I could from him about what he calls "the relocation process," and Jick and I call "bear moving," when grizzly ecology and human residency collide too badly.

You mention your concern with establishing a voice in English Creek. *Why the selection of voices, and were those voices intended? Why the return to Jick in the third novel? Some reasons are obvious and necessary – the demands of chronology, of having a narrator alive to narrate action within his time – but did you know who would narrate each novel of the trilogy when you conceived of the trilogy? Or has that choice been made with the evolution of the works themselves, a sort of organic development of voice?*

They were intended voices, absolutely. You have to choose your symmetries. You have to match it up; either you're going to have three different things in a trilogy, or you're going to have bookends, so to speak. I decided that Jick would provide the bookends of his life. Part of the reason is that Jick's is a congenial voice for me, a voice I find fascinating to write in. Naturally it crossed my mind that the voice in this final book could be Mariah's or Riley's, to provide a younger generational symmetry through the three books. But I wanted to cut against the grain, not have that absolutely tidy generational scheme – I believed it'd be more interesting to have Jick talking at age sixty-five in contrast to his voice of a fifteen-year-old in *English Creek*.

There's a lot of humor in his voice, too, I think.

Montana is often a highly humorous place, I'm happy to say. It has a sense of dressing up the language, and telling yarns. A lot of what I gather, the lingo, the jokes, come from everyday Montana. There's a fine folklorist at Notre Dame named Barbara Allen – a great name for a folklorist, right? – whom I met at a big conference in Billings this past summer. In her paper Dr. Allen mentioned that folklorists do the same thing that I do: they go into small-town cafés and eavesdrop. There's a table where guys all come in for coffee the first thing in the morning – she calls that "the big table," and I've always called it the geezer table – but, just there at breakfast with those guys ribbing each other, you hear all kinds of stuff to put in a book.

I'd like to talk a little about your conception of the West. In This House of Sky, *you describe "the landscapes of a Western mind," and I note that you specify a Western mind. How would you characterize your Western mind at this point in your career?*

In Winter Brothers *you talk of the "many Wests," of the "intermingled Wests" – is the West still that way, is there the same multiplicity? Or has the West grown more homogeneous? And your "personal West" – are there any more Wests that you want? What of the "westernness in your family"* (Winter Brothers) *– is it still a part of that family? Is "that portion of restlessness," inherited from your father, still there? You seem to have settled now in the Northwest, a self-described "suburban druid," having exchanged Montana for Washington and Seattle, and you seem comfortable in that exchange.*

I should say, first, that the phrase, "landscapes of a Western mind," is not mine except by wholehearted adoption – my editor on *This House of Sky*, Carol Hill, thought it up. The title was one of the last things we did; in fact, I went back and wrote it into the final manuscript after Carol and I came up with it. So we agreed on that title, and then I got a call from Carol after a sales conference, and she said, "Okay, the book's going to be called *This House of Sky: Landscapes of a Western Mind!* How do you like it?" And I said, Yeah, that's really pretty terrific!

As for my notions of the West, I don't have vast concepts, or as one of my characters jokes in *Ride with Me, Mariah Montana*, maybe even any half-vast ones. I try to look at what I see as the situation – at *how* people are doing, at *what* people are doing – and go from there. The Rocky Mountain region has just become the poorest in the country in terms of personal income and is probably still sinking. Driving Montana for these books the past decade, it's utterly evident and stark that a lot of that country is empty-ing out. My wife Carol and I went through a county seat in north central

Montana this summer, one of Montana's fifty-six counties; the town is Winnett, and its total population is 200 – not 2,000, but 200. The county itself is bigger than the Los Angeles basin; the population of that county is 650. Weeds were growing in the street of Winnett; I had Carol take slides for me to write from, and it shows up in *Ride with Me, Mariah Montana.* There are other Winnetts out there. At the same time, the West I live in now, the Puget Sound country, is undergoing Los Angelization. Within the next decade or fifteen years metropolitan Seattle probably is going to be built to the base of the Cascade Mountains, and quite possibly to the border, in this case the Canadian border; we're going to have something fairly similar to the Los Angeles-San Diego corridor, a northern mirror image, if we don't come to our senses before letting that happen.

These are major tides of event. We don't see them nearly as quickly as we see what's going on in Eastern Europe right now, where you just utterly say, Jesus, here is history happening even as we watch. But apparently here is history happening to us in somewhat slower motion. The shift to the coasts, which of course is part of my own life, continues and continues. I have a friend in Billings who has four grown children; two years ago they were all in Montana, and now they all four live here on the Pacific coast. So I don't feel I particularly have to work from a concept on this; the tectonic shifts occurring within the West right now show up perfectly plainly in people's lives.

I still have "other Wests," yes, which may show up as soon as my next book.

But it sounds as though you're comfortable where you are now?

So far so good. Seattle has been a highly congenial place, not only to live but particularly for my work, a good quiet, wetly fertile place to write. For me, a Puget Sound suburb has been a way to keep my professional life orderly, systematic. I have these six books to show for the calm of suburbia.

I'd like to talk a bit about your technique, about the "blending" of fact and fiction, of history and imagination. You are not, strictly speaking, a historical novelist, though you certainly chronicle the Western past and the stuff of history in your fiction. You write what you call a "blend" – inhabiting an actual geographical place with a fictional populace. What led you to such a technique? What part, for instance, did your Ph.D. in U.S. frontier history play in your development as a

73

novelist, and in the techniques you would adopt? Why did you feel it necessary to "stretch geography" (as you put it in your Acknowledgments to English Creek*) by creating the Two Medicine Country?*

I figured that was a commonsense way of doing it. I want my characters to exist within historical laws of gravity. That's how people *do* exist, after all. Irony and angst are not the only things – or even the main things – that operate on people. Declarations of war operate on them, as World War II did on Alec McCaskill (in *English Creek*) and Jick too – you're an eighteen-year-old cowboy in Montana in 1939, and by God, you might be in Tunisia or the Aleutians a couple years later, with somebody shooting at you. *That's* the big stuff of life, not wan little ironies and personal angsts. The market forces in agriculture, the weather – those are big things to the people I write about, the cosmos they live in. Now, within that cosmos in my books happen a lot of personal complications for my characters – but unlike much of modern "canonical" fiction, those personal complications don't constitute the whole of my characters and plotlines. I just think there's bigger game than that.

And, too, I quite frankly just find the flow of history interesting. I suppose that's why after journalism I went back to graduate school in history; I find fact, as Jick would say in *Ride with Me, Mariah Montana*, "highly interesting." There are troves, motherlodes of telling detail on people's lives, out there in history to sculpt books from.

Do you see your work evolving in any particular way, in style or in genre –

I want each book to be different. Maybe this is Scotch pragmatism or pedantry, but why should I have to write the same book all the time, when there are so many terrific different stories to be told? I've had very generous reviews, but whenever somebody is not so generous, usually what's at the heart of their objection is that I didn't write the previous book again, that this one is, well, gee, *different* from the last one. But that's not what I'm up to – turning out the same book over and over. I admire writers like the Australian novelist Thomas Keneally, whose each book is done on its own terms.

It's how different each book is, its particular form, that pulls me along, keeps me interested. For me the whetstone of each book is to work against its major problem, solving its form. To do the diary of a diary, for example, and make it become *Winter Brothers*; to have *The Sea Runners* click along short scene by short scene to emulate the sixty days its characters spend jittering down the Northwest Coast; to have *English Creek* loop out in month-long pieces of life, as a Montana summer of rural life does – the rhythms of the seasons setting the rhythms of life; then to explode that, in *Dancing at the Rascal Fair,* into thirty years of Montana life, bracketing the great hopes at the time of statehood with the killing winter of 1919. And in *Ride with Me, Mariah Montana* I'm trying to gauge both past and present as they flow through my characters' lives. So, the problem of form each time concentrates the mind wonderfully. I've always got that challenge of form to work against. That whetstone, if you see what I mean, that I can sit there for two or three years and sharpen the book against.

Do you see yourself as a political writer, in any sense?

I think writing is automatically political. I do sometimes read a little Orwell and think, damn it, we're not nearly *overtly* political enough in fiction in this country. On the other hand, it's difficult – outside of daily or weekly journalism – to be meaningfully political. By the time you can do a book and get it into print, the circumstances you're writing about have changed in that two or three years. The major glacier of politics maybe won't have changed, but you can't help but be out of phase on the current events. James Watt was appointed Secretary of the Interior [by Ronald Reagan in 1980] and I knew immediately, probably every writer and every environmentalist out here in the West knew immediately, the consequences that had for the land. I semiseriously sat down and thought, now there's a Watt book here that ought to be done, but how *can* it be done? By the time you get the book into print, Watt will have done his worst. And he did.

So I suppose I'm trying to deal with politics historically, in my fiction. It's difficult, in a society as present-fixated as America is, to get people to realize that the consequences of what happened in the past go on and on. But I think writers have got to try. So my McCaskills don't let Hoover off the hook in *English Creek,* or Reagan and the Watt mentality off the hook in *Ride with Me, Mariah Montana.* As politicians they had effects on the land, and on the economic and cultural and, for that matter, familial structures trying to exist on that land, and I think it's the province of the writer to speak out on those effects. I try to be political in my books mostly as my characters are political, but they and I both think political leaders have done a lot of upsetting things, not only in the West but in this society.

Do you feel that your style has evolved? We talked about Jick's voice before, but it strikes me that the writing style in the earlier books is somehow different. There's an incredible vivacity to the language, there are striking uses of the language in Sea Runners *and* Winter Brothers *that, while not absent from the trilogy, are not as frequent.*

That's mostly a matter of voice. The Two Medicine trilogy is a deliberate, almost decade's worth of decision to write in colloquial first person, to use Montana narrators who are not me or even of my own generation. Why? Because of the folk poetry in those colloquial languages, those distinctive generations. Unless I make my fictional characters writers or college professors, they can't really speak as I did in *This House of Sky, Winter Brothers,* and *The Sea Runners.* The narrative device here in the trilogy forecloses that kind of rich, densely poetic language I deliberately tried to put into every line of my first three books. I don't know how else to do even a little of that language in this trilogy except as you heard me read it here last night; one of my characters, Riley, is a newspaper columnist, and lo and behold, I could put in a bit of fancy language about the tribal battle between humans and grizzlies as he'd write it in the paper. But I can't put that elevated language into a character such as Jick as he goes around doing the ranch chores and make that rhetoric believable, can I? So, sheerly in terms of the tools in the books, absolutely, there's been a decade-long shift in the sound of the language on my pages. A lot of writers spin the language brilliantly, but I didn't see all that many trying to use the folk poetry of spoken language from working people in the West. That poetry of the vernacular that I've tried to get into these two books told in Jick's voice and one in his grandfather Angus's still seems worth having put ten years in on.

The voice of Jick has become so clearly defined, rings so clear to the reader's ear –

Although, *Ride with Me, Mariah Montana* probably does conclude Jick. After these three sizable Two Medicine novels I now want to do a shorter, more reflective book. I may go back toward a more *House of Sky*-ish voice in it. We'll see.

Fiction or nonfiction?

More likely nonfiction. It's still evolving, perking in my head, but the best description I've had to tell people so far is that it'll maybe be something like a novella-length essay disguised as a memoir.

But the West is still a concern of yours?

Yes, but it's not my only concern. That's one of the reasons why I spoke about "the eloquence of the edge of the world" last night – writers out there doing brilliant work, in Australia and South Africa and elsewhere. In fact, I don't begin to read everything written about the West. I read what my friends write and various other things, but I'm interested in *writing*, not specifically in Western writing. I'm trying to see what the other literary rivers of the world look like.

Do you see yourself writing outside of the boundaries of the United States?

Could happen. I don't think a writer should foreclose anything. I have in mind a novel which wouldn't necessarily have to be set in the American West.

But the West seems such a significant place.

Significant, sure. But in almost every speech I make, I tuck in the line that I'm utterly convinced that a writer of real caliber can ground himself in specific land and lingo and yet be writing about that larger country: life. Part of what Western writers have had to cope with – it's not just us, it's writers in any given geography – is being looked at as merely regionalists. I don't think any of us that I know of out here are deliberately writing as regionalists. We are deliberately *writing*. Period. We're writing in the region of the literature of life. It happens that we are from the West, we have chosen the West, and one way or another know something about the West, and that's what we bring to our writing. Fortunately it's not asked as much anymore, but out in my state of Washington it used to be that I'd be invited someplace to a conference and the first question from a professor would be, Is there a Pacific Northwest literature? And I'd shrug and say, If there isn't, what the hell am I doing here? Yeah, there's a Northwest literature – there's a bunch of us writing here! Now what it adds up to, and what its confluences and boundaries are, that's your job to say out there in academia. We're just writing, trying to be citizens of literature.

A lot of your work deals with the past, with the familial past, and a lot of your characters learn from the past –

They *try* to learn, you bet –

Right, they try to learn from the past. Can they get too concerned with the past, become stuck within that past? And do you, as a writer, worry about that problem, about turning that concern with the past into nostalgia?

No, my characters and I, by the kinds of lives we've led, are inoculated against inordinate nostalgia. The remembering of my characters, and that I did myself in *This House of Sky*, isn't some pleasant haze of how wonderful everything was in olden times. Instead, we're simply aware of the past along the lines of Loren Eiseley's view of life, as that long skein of existence of which we happen to be a part. You find in *Ride with Me, Mariah Montana* that Jick is pretty radically spooked by memories, the stories our own lives tell us. He discovers he has to work damn hard to balance the past and the future, which I think is a healthy enough definition of the present.

So that as a writer you are not just the "king's remembrancer," as you call it?

The "king's remembrancer" and other representations of the past are the form, the encoded brilliance of language. Life as we lead it has to take on its story component, so the past is where that happens, in my work. The past is the treasury of event.

I was struck by that connection between yourself and Swan in Winter Brothers, *and by that marvelous, artful spanning of time. How did you first come to recognize that link between these two men in time and place?*

I worked that out in the course of the book, which I think is the kind of exploring that books are supposed to do. My original draw to Swan was to Swan the writer – what he had written into his thousands of diary pages across thousands of days. I only ever had two English courses in my college career, but I must have heard in one of them that form should fit content, and so I thought that since Swan wrote a diary, my doing a journal of his diary might be an interesting form. Then within that arc – my books often have an arc in time – I worked on the specifics of linking the two of us. Words tend to bring ideas to me, rather than vice versa. The notion of a community of time came out of my fingers in *Winter Brothers* rather than my head.

And in Sea Runners, *that voyage you make of your own down that coast, that was a deliberate effort to experience what those men might have experienced?*

To see the country and, as it turned out, to deliberately experience the seasickness. Yes, in all my writing I try to turn my eyes toward land that earlier eyes had seen.

Do you, like your characters, have "arithmetic" in your eyes?

I'm a sum juggler in my work habits, definitely, writing so many words a day, so many days a week, so many weeks a year, to produce so many books. That kind of arithmetical endurance is a particular habit or skill or talent of mine.

Do you see the land, though, with that sort of arithmetical sense of the map-maker?

Maps do interest me a lot, sure – great metaphor material. A way to write about patterns. *Dancing at the Rascal Fair* is dedicated to Vernon Carstensen, a leading historian of the American land system, and I've liked his notion of "patterns on the land." When I was in graduate school, hearing him talk about the rectangular survey, a lot of what I'd grown up as a kid knowing but didn't know I knew, all of a sudden made sense – what a school section was all about, for instance. I'd heard that phrase all my life from my dad in his ranchwork, without realizing its significance – that the school section, that square mile of land, provided money to help support the local school, which in turn means that the whole Jeffersonian mesh of the rectangular survey across the West produced those one-room schools, ground-level democratic education. And the way rural roads run, making right-angle turns to follow section lines – again, patterns on the land, patterns of society created by how we've mapped ourselves onto the land.

You may be thinking in your question, too, about actual maps I've used in my writing? *The Sea Runners* would be the best example of that. My last day of research at the State Historical Library in Juneau [Alaska] for that book, I asked the librarian, Phyllis DeMuth, if she could think of anything more I ought to see, and she thought and said, "Maybe you want to see the Tebenkov maps." And there they were, from the Bering Strait to Fort Ross, California, beautiful nineteenth-century copperplate calligraphy, just exquisite – I put on white surgical gloves to handle them. You don't have to be a rocket scientist to know that you want to put something that intriguing into the book, and so a set of Tebenkov maps went right into the plot of *The Sea Runners*.

One last thing about maps, and the directions they lead me to think, is that cultural geography seems to have a lot to offer a writer. The cultural geographers are on to something when they talk about signatures on the land. Right now we're sitting in a signature on the land, and on society: this upscale resort hotel which can be seen from anywhere in the Coeur d'Alene Lake area and halfway to Spokane on the freeway, this declares that Coeur d'Alene is now a big-league resort town, as the smelter stack looming over Great Falls, Montana, used to say this is where the Black Eagle smelter is, this is copper country owned in Boston and New York. Reading the land seems to me the best way to write about it.

WORKS

Dancing at the Rascal Fair. New York: Atheneum, 1987. Novel.

English Creek. New York: Atheneum, 1984. Novel.

Heart Earth. New York: Atheneum, 1993. Autobiographical nonfiction.

This House of Sky: Landscapes of a Western Mind. New York: Harcourt, Brace, Jovanovich, 1978. Autobiographical nonfiction.

Inside This House of Sky. Text by Ivan Doig. Photographs by Duncan Kelso. New York: Atheneum, 1984. Nonfiction and photographs.

With Carol M. Doig. *News: A Consumer's Guide.* New York: Prentice-Hall, 1972. Nonfiction.

Ride with Me, Mariah Montana. New York: Atheneum, 1990. Novel.

The Sea Runners. New York: Atheneum, 1982. Novel.

Winter Brothers: A Season at the Edge of America. New York: Harcourt, Brace, Jovanovich, 1982. Fiction and nonfiction.

Gretel Ehrlich

Born in California in 1946, Gretel Ehrlich waited thirty years to come to Wyoming, and even then she came there not with the intention of putting down roots but to shoot a documentary film on sheepherders. During the making of that film, Ehrlich suffered the death of her lover, and in the healing process that followed she found herself gradually making a home in the Big Horn Basin. It is there that she now lives and ranches. And it is of that landscape that Ehrlich most often writes, both in her fiction and her essays (her essay collection, *The Solace of Open Spaces*, received an award from the American Academy of Arts and Letters in 1986). Besides continuing to work as a fiction writer and an essayist, Ehrlich has also adapted her novel, *Heart Mountain*, for the screen.

This interview took place in 1990 on her ranch, in an old brick house flanked by alfalfa pastures, on a June morning made white by a late spring snowfall. Our conversation was punctuated by the barkings and fartings of Ehrlich's two dogs, Rusty and Frenchy; and by the occasional comments of Ehrlich's husband Press Stephens, a transplanted Easterner who shares the day-to-day operations of the ranch with Ehrlich. (The interview was wedged in between trips outdoors to move irrigation gates and to bring in cattle. Ehrlich and Stephens feature naturally raised beef on their Hudson Falls Ranch and practice holistic, "conservationally sound" grazing management on their range.) Because the snow had turned the road leading to their place to gumbo, I left Ehrlich's ranch in a wagon pulled by two of their pack horses.

GREGORY MORRIS: *Though generally associated with the American West, you are a writer significantly influenced by Eastern – Oriental – art and culture. I'm curious as to what draws you to this perspective.*

GRETEL EHRLICH: It really has been a lifelong interest. I was born in California and I think that had a lot to do with it, in that there is a huge Asian population there. I always had Japanese and Japanese-American friends growing up; there were Buddhist churches and Japanese grocery stores everywhere. So it wasn't anything particularly exotic to me.

Then when I was about fourteen, I entered boarding school, where I was very unhappy and where I read D. T. Suzuki's books on Zen. This was around 1960, and there was very little available to read about Zen; at that point I wasn't aware there was even a practice related to it or that it was practiced by anyone in America. Meanwhile, I was at a boarding school where you had to go to chapel twice a day, every day; it was an Episcopalian girls' school – it was like being in San Quentin. Nothing I heard in those stints in chapel made any sense to me. I appreciated, I guess, the basic morality of any religion (and at that point I hadn't heard of the contemplative orders, the Trappist and the Benedictine, whom I really admired – really, I should have been a Catholic!), but I was pretty discouraged by having to participate in this charade. So when I was in choir, I would put D. T. Suzuki's book inside my hymnal. Eventually, I went to the head-mistress's office and said, as long as I don't believe in God or anything else, that I would refuse to kneel, that I would refuse to say the Lord's Prayer, that I would sit there quietly and sing in the choir, because I liked to sing. And she grudgingly said, Okay.

As more work came out on Zen, and translations of novels started appearing, I read everything I could get my hands on. Then, in the late 1960s, I went to Japan for the first time. What we received was pretty much an outsider's view; we didn't have an interpreter, and I was generally gawking at things. Frankly, though Japan as a society intrigues me, I don't take the society, wholesale, as anything perfect; Japan has a lot of problems, a lot of glaring faults. But there was something about the sensibility that ran through the literature that really affected me – the sense of transcending ego, and of going beyond always trying to solidify identity by material means or by these elaborate reference points. This idea of nonpossession of one's own life and the world around it appealed to me. When I was in high school I read all the existential writers, like most "serious young students" do, and theirs was a sort of a negative detachment from the world; whereas the Eastern writers had a sense of celebration in their work, which certainly the French guys didn't – even though I'm a great admirer of Camus. So I liked that, it was the perfect blend for me, and it was really quite innocent in that I didn't know it was "hip" to be into Zen – I was way too young to think that way. Suddenly, it just made sense, suddenly certain truths revealed themselves.

Later, after I came back from that first trip to Japan, I became a serious student of Zen. I studied with Miazumi Roshi in Los Angeles and Suzuki Roshi in San Francisco, and then with Trungpa Rinpoche, who was a Tibetan lama in Colorado – then I bought a ranch in Wyoming, and I haven't sat since!

So it's not something you still practice seriously?

Not in terms of sitting practice. I spent long periods of time in monasteries, doing retreats; and at a certain point, once Zen is a part of your life it's always a part of your life. Life is your practice. I never wanted to be a monk; I was never very ambitious spiritually, except in a very personal, private way. I did everything I wanted to do with it, and I feel that in my life here, especially in this place, I'm living the teachings as well as I might. I'm not talking about being "a good girl" or anything; I'm just talking about being mindful of my own fucked-up qualities. Zen gives you a sense of humor about yourself.

I would never write a book about the years I spent practicing because I don't think it's very interesting, and it's nobody's business anyway. But I feel that influence is obvious in my work, and other people who have studied and who read my work see it right away.

Since we're talking about this Eastern influence, let's talk a bit about the work in which that influence exerts itself most strongly, your novel Heart Mountain. *I'd like to talk first about the origins of that novel, which seem to lie in your book* Wyoming Stories. *Clearly, those stories evolved into the novel?*

Sure, I wrote the stories first.

With the novel in mind?

Only vaguely. I didn't know whether I was really capable of writing a novel or not, or if it was only enough material for a novella. I was just testing the waters. I wrote the stories pretty cold, off the top of my head, and realized that (a) they weren't very successful short stories, and that (b) I had many more to write: 650 pages later, I finally put my pen down. It was probably not a good idea to have them published, but it was done innocently in that I didn't know where they were leading. My editor, after completing work on *Heart Mountain,* said jokingly, Please, make your next book short. It took us a long time to get through that material; we would both forget what was going on – he had to hire an outside reader to keep track of things.

Actually, I wrote five drafts of the novel, and for the last draft I wrote 250 new pages, which involved totally revamping the character of Kai.

Revamped in what way?

It's hard to explain, but I guess I made him more overtly political, and strengthened him. I just needed more time to get to know him. Having so many characters in a novel is like having a bunch of kids – somebody always gets neglected, though not on purpose.

Was there a specific reason for making Kai a student of history?

Certainly. Historians always think about the past, and here he was *making* history; he was part of a living history which everybody realized, as it was happening, would be a part of American history, good or bad. There was a great sense of that in the camps [World War II Japanese internment camps], and not only among the Japanese-Americans; the feds who were running the camps asked the camp people to keep diaries – why, I don't know. But there was a historical sense about the whole experience that I thought was interesting: that transferal of the past to the present, that idea that the past *is* also the present, that everything is the present. I think that notion hit home with Kai and changed his ideas about what history is and how you write about it.

Is that part of the reason why you use different types of narrative in the novel – diaries, letters – to reflect the historical reality? Were you trying to do anything specific technically through the use of those forms?

85

No, I don't think that way about literature. I didn't have a sort of technical architecture in mind. I just did what I thought was necessary to illuminate the content. And certainly, the diaries and the letters were there because they were the narrative forms used by the internees themselves. They provided a voice for the voiceless people in those camps.

How did the historical material for Heart Mountain *come to you? Was the relocation camp something you knew about before coming to Wyoming?*

I knew about the existence of relocation camps, because growing up in California, I knew kids who had been born in them; I knew about Manzanar [in California], for example. Later, after I moved to Wyoming, I happened to be driving down the highway one day when I saw this little sign that said "Heart Mountain Relocation Camp." I knew right away what it was, and I knew right away I wanted to write a novel about it somehow. I'm very interested in cultural exchanges and cultural straddling and the ways in which immigrant communities assimilate and what happens in the overlays of viewpoints. So part of my interest was political; part of it was finding a situation where I could elaborate upon my own interest in Japanese culture within the Western context. I mean, I was intrigued by the fact that I had this ranch setting, in the middle of which I also had these people who were involved in traditional Japanese activities. And the political situation interested me, it always had; I couldn't understand, as a youngster, why this historical circumstance had occurred, even though my parents were pretty anti-Japanese – you know, Santa Barbara was shelled by the Japanese, and they took it real hard even though, Christ, they never suffered the way a lot of people suffered.

The more I researched the idea – and I researched it for years and years – the more fascinating it all became. I researched not just the people in the camps, but anyone who did anything in the Pacific Theater during the war. I talked to all of my parents' friends and to friends of their friends, and to people at West Point, and to people who'd been on the Bataan Death March. Now I find myself being a sort of World War II buff, at least for the Pacific portion of it!

But the war, because it was a global war, involved so much dislocation for so many people for all kinds of reasons. Right in this county – Park County – there was Heart Mountain Relocation Camp, which had 10,000 people in it and which was the second biggest city in Wyoming. Then, on the other side of the [Bighorn] Basin, was a German prisoner-of-war camp, just a little one. There were people all over the place, all over the world, in these little prison camps. So strange.

One of the ways in which you capture this "overlay of cultures" in the novel seems to be through your technique, and through your adoption of Eastern aesthetics for the telling of your story. Specifically, you mentioned in an interview on National Public Radio that you adapted the "roof blown off" style of painting that Mariko, in the novel, uses in her work, to the writing of Heart Mountain *itself. Could you explain that further?*

I suppose that if there's any particular aesthetic influence upon the novel, from the Oriental tradition, that it is in this artistic approach, what the Japanese call "the roof blown off perspective." It's an approach that literally tried to blow the roof off of a scene, so that simultaneous actions are revealed simultaneously. I liked that sense of synchronicity among people's lives; I think it's silly to think that you're not aware of everybody's lives. That's how my mind works: I have all these people in all these lives and settings, all at the same time, and they're all moving and evolving together. So I wanted to present that sense of synchronicity without doing something that was technically obtrusive, like cutting up dialogue, as in William Gaddis's *JR*. That sort of thing is interesting, but I didn't want to do that. So I alternated chapters, and constantly interwove the stories – it's more an emotional or mental landscape of interwoven stories. Everybody had all the other people in the book in mind somehow in their lives, and they were all carrying each other forward through this four years.

You also make clear and acknowledged use of the Eastern literary tradition, specifically the Crazy Cloud Anthology, *the poems of Tu Mu, the* Kokinshu. *Of particular interest to me is the way you use those sources in* Heart Mountain, *and how they come to color the sensibilities of people like McKay Allison, the novel's protagonist.*

Well, I never have an agenda about anything. As I said, I read widely in Japanese literature, and so those references were simply things that were in my mind. Actually, though, one of the untold influences upon the novel was my love for Murasaki's *The Tale of Genji*. My use of *The Tale of Genji* in *Heart Mountain*, I suppose, was a conscious effort to work a source into the novel. I would start thinking of McKay as Genji, because he was pursuing this woman and never quite getting her.

It's interesting about *Genji*. I was first exposed to it when I was a film editor at WNET in New York in the mid-1960s. WNET bought the Japanese television version of *The Tale of Genji*, and I dubbed it; I was the sound editor. I had no idea what the work was – it sounded like something ancient and boring. Then I saw this beautifully done series, and of course I watched every second of it. And because I was dubbing the English in, I had to use the text, so then I really began reading it. Things that you read deeply, especially when you're young, just stay a part of you; so that character, that person so full of love and passion and a certain sensitivity to nature and the change in seasons, just stuck with me. Everyone asks, Well, who's McKay? And I say, I don't know but I'd sure like to meet him!

He's an attractive character, a strong character, but then so is Mariko.

It was interesting, sorting out the characters, because what I really wanted to avoid was the obvious, awful, clichéd thing of a white man going for the subservient Asian woman. So in a certain way, I made Mariko much stronger than McKay; McKay, in a clichéd sense, has the woman's role in his uncertainty and in his willingness to put his life in her hands, just sort of giving himself up to her all the time. And she's saying, That's far enough, I can't do this. She holds the emotional power.

You said, in that same interview with National Public Radio, that the camp scenes were the most difficult parts of the novel to write, partly because you were imagining an experience and a culture that were foreign to you. You've attracted a certain amount of criticism for trying to capture that experience, that culture, for the presumption of trying to describe that experience through a Western imagination. How do you respond to that criticism?

Well, I was afraid of being accused of doing the same old racist stuff in the story, and hoped that people would see that I didn't do it. Because I wasn't *at* a camp, I had to rely on my so-called informants. Too, I read all the diaries – I read everything that exists: all the material at the Bancroft Library at Berkeley, all the material at the National Archives. I sat with people for hours and hours and hours and they told me everything they could remember. And I just sort of pieced together this material.

It was hard, because I was writing about somebody else's culture, and that's a very delicate matter – which is why I framed it in a single person's diary for the most part, except when Mariko goes outside of the camp and it becomes her story. I felt that I could keep it under control that way.

Still, I got a lot of racial backlash. I think it's absurd to think you can't write about something that you *aren't*.

It's part of the imaginative, fictive process.

And also, the Japanese-American culture was a culture I grew up with. I wouldn't feel comfortable writing about Polish immigrants, for example, but I could write about any of the people I saw while growing up in California: Mexican-Americans, Japanese-Americans, Chinese-Americans. I think that what you take in as a child is far more elaborate and complex than people give children credit for. All I know is that I seem to know more than I know I know about everything that I grew up with; that entire surrounding, from landscape to people to my own and my parents' own social set – I just know it. I have faith in that kind of understanding – backed up by *lots* of research! Still, it wasn't like I just had a political idea and researched it, it wasn't that hard-boiled.

Do you consider yourself a political writer?

Oh, God, no! I avoid politics like the plague.

Even in your nonfiction? You don't think there's a political element to that work?

Well, everything is political in the sense that if you care enough about anything and write about it, then you're being political. The root word of politics has to do with the human condition and how we survive, and certainly I'm concerned with that matter and am political to that extent. Most political issues are so well articulated in the newspapers and elsewhere, that it seems sort of redundant to write about them as politics. But there's a deeper concern, there are deeper conflicts. I mean everyone's concerned with racism in one way or the other; that's been a lifelong concern of mine. I grew up in a pretty white neighborhood where the people of color you saw generally were people's servants. On the other hand, we lived part of the time in Mexico, and as a child I could not figure out what the problem was, why if you were a Mexican in California you didn't go to all of the same places as the people in my parents' milieu did. That was naïve, and obviously I know now the answers to those questions. Still, I notice those things, and have to grapple with those things all the time, but I don't see myself as grappling with them on a strictly political level.

Does being here in this place, and being a rancher in the West impose any sort of political responsibility on you?

Oh, yeah, it's forced us to get involved. My husband, Press Stephens, does most of the actual footwork and most of the homework. But when you own land and when you're trying to preserve land and treat it properly and trying to learn about how to do that, and when you're working with all kinds of people from all kinds of places – you learn pretty quickly what you have to do. We go to meetings all of the time; we testify, we write letters, we call our own meetings, we protest vigorously about things, we call the governor – we do anything, anything it takes.

But that's not something that makes its way into your writing?

Well, I think it would be pretty boring to write about land-use issues. In my new book of essays I'm certainly writing about the new ways in which we're treating our grazing land – I do write about that, but it's in the context of a personal journal, a rancher's journal, what you do and why. What I really am writing about is discipline and compassion in this setting: how you treat animals compassionately, how you form a real relationship with a working horse and a working dog, and how you treat your animals and why, and how you treat the land and how the land and the animals are a mirror of your own sensibility. Everything is a reflection of everything else. Real compassion comes from an extraordinary use of self-discipline in every moment. It's really hard to do. It's hard to go out in a snowstorm and change fence when the cows have to be moved – that's just the tip of the iceberg. Not that I'm patting myself on the back – everybody does these things – I just think that's what it's going to take to save the planet and to save our own skins. As somebody pointed out, this whole involvement with the environment is totally self-serving, because the insects don't give a shit whether the humans survive or not; and in eight million years the sun is going to disappear and it's all going to go anyway, so it's all sort of temporary. That's the interesting catch with personal morality, I guess, and with the whole Eastern sensibility: on the one hand you know that everything is impermanent, and on the other hand you have to be on the spot all the time with yourself, with reality, with your ego. I suppose people could use this idea that the sun is going to vanish as an excuse for just screwing the place up, but that won't do.

So, I guess these things involve me politically and make me political. But when you say politics, I think of dopey guys in business suits haggling over things for the wrong reasons.

One of the things writers in the West seem to be concerned with is the empowerment issue; they see the West as being politically underempowered.

Yeah, it's been a Third World country, but of course it's people's own fault. You can be anything you want to be, and nobody said we had to be treated like a Third World country. It just drives me crazy. Develop cottage industries; demand what you want; stop supplying the rest of the world with your product on their terms – create your own terms, your own standards. Make them come to you. Christ, it's not like we're dying of malnutrition here! Everybody has the opportunity to do anything they want. I just get mad with people here complaining – I think we're a country full of complainers, except for the people who are really undernourished and in a poverty cycle. There's no excuse for anything to go wrong in this country; everybody is empowered in this country, unlike a whole lot of other places in the world. But it's absolutely true: it's a Third World state, it's a boom and bust economy. It's ridiculous. Very few people take a longer view of things and prepare for a future of bad years – they're all so stubborn, refuse to be flexible, refuse to adapt. Everybody goes around killing coyotes – well, they're the most adaptable animal on earth – you could learn everything you needed to know from a coyote. Or the horse: they're the most patient animal in the world, they let us use them, carry us around, and we never see them as having anything to teach us.

That seems an attitude quite foreign to our culture.

Well, we're coming around a little, and these things always seem to take a long time – you can learn these things in about ten minutes if you want to, but people don't avail themselves of this kind of education. The way we manage our place here, for example, using holistic management – anyone can go and take these courses, anyone can find out about this stuff. But people say, Whoa, something new! and they put on their brakes. It's just false pride; the ruination of this country is false pride.

One of the things I've thought about with regard to women in this business of ranching and agriculture, as opposed to men – and I hate to say these sorts of chauvinistic things – but I know that my coming here and learning about ranching, in certain ways, has been easier because I'm not afraid to ask anyone a question, and I've asked some really dumb questions, and still do. I couldn't care less if I look rat-dumb, because the expectation isn't that I'm supposed to know anything anyway, although a lot of women in Wyoming are really capable. I have nothing to lose. But it's a lot harder for Press sometimes – harder for men in general just to call each other up and say, Hey, what *do* you do when this happens? It's just harder within the framework of this culture.

But is it easier for a woman like yourself, coming from outside of the West and into this culture and asking these kinds of questions, than it is for a woman born in this culture?

I guess if you grew up here it wouldn't be harder to ask the questions, but you'd have to be *motivated* to ask them, and maybe you'd be sort of bored with the prospect.

I think of Mary Clearman Blew's work, who writes of "growing up female in Charlie Russell country," and I wonder, what is it like coming into Charlie Russell country, so to speak, from outside? Is that advantageous?

In a certain way, yes. Although the women that I work with around here, I think they ask a lot of questions and try stuff out; but there's a lowered expectation. It's sort of the same idea that if you're poor, you have nothing to lose – these situations can be used to our own benefit. If there is a lowered expectation of women, you can use it to your advantage and actually empower yourself.

One of the things you do with this landscape is see it from a feminine perspective, often describing that landscape, for instance, in terms of the male physiology, giving the landscape an erotic charge. It seems a vision that comes from outside the region.

I don't know about all that inside-outside business. They make such a big deal about it in Wyoming; there's a fuckin' fence around this state. I write the same way about California, and I was born and raised there. I think that that's people's way of being territorial. I feel that I could live anywhere in the world and I would write from the same point of view and in the same way – obviously, the landscape would be drastically different, but I would write about it somehow and it probably would be similar in certain ways. A writer *is* an outsider; you're always observing what's going on around you, whether you're a part of it or not. So I think it has more to do with the function of the writer in society than with what your goddamned birthright is. Just because I grew up in Santa Barbara doesn't mean I can't write about it, and I *am* writing about in my new book, in very much the same way and just as lovingly as I write about Wyoming. I don't live with it every day as I live with this landscape, but that California landscape has inspired me as much, means as much to me as this landscape.

You talked earlier of "culture straddling," and in her introduction to your book of poetry, To Touch the Water, *Lucien Stryk called you "a sophisticate of both coasts." I wondered if you see yourself as culture straddler?*

No, because I only belong to one, rather revolting culture. Although my father had a business in Mexico City, and I did spend a lot of my young life there, on and off. That's my only claim to a culture-straddling fame. Also, California is such a wonderfully confused group of people.

Do you still look for the Marlboro Man when you go to New York?

Yes, I do. In the sense that I am a city person *and* a ranching person, I guess I straddle two cultures, but I don't particularly see that as a difficult leap to make; it's been happening for a long time now.

And is that Marlboro Man one of your "androgynous cowboys" (as you describe him in the essay "About Men," in Solace*)? You suggest in that essay, and in that description, the odd but necessary combination of masculine and feminine that often goes into making the cowboy's nature. In that same essay, you write:*

The geographical vastness and the social isolation here make emotional evolution seem impossible. Those contradictions of the heart between

93

respectability, logic, and convention on the one hand, and impulse, passion, and intuition on the other, played out wordlessly against the paradisical beauty of the West, give cowboys a wide-eyed but drawn look. Their lips pucker up, not with kisses but with immutability. They may want to break out, staying up all night with a lover just to talk, but they don't know how and can't imagine what the consequences will be. Those rare occasions when they do bare themselves result in confusion. "I feel as if I'd sprained my heart," one friend told me a month after such a meeting.

Someone said to me, No one really said that to you! But someone did – it's not my line.

But those "contradictions of the heart" seem to be at the center of your fiction. There's an impulse within this androgynous cowboy that pushes in one direction, and another impulse that pushes in another direction. Do you think this tension is especially significant to your fiction?

I guess so, but it stems from my own past. I hardly talked until I was seventeen, because I was the kind of person who had great difficulty articulating anything, and I still am; I was feeling a lot of different things, intensely, but was sort of paralyzed by speech. Maybe that's why I feel so comfortable here in Wyoming, because I can really sympathize with these people. The difference is that I had the vocabulary to express anything I wanted, and a lot of people here don't; but then, a lot of them do, and they still don't.

Is that peculiar to the cowboy?

No, I think it's just peculiar to certain kinds of people. It's kind of the style here. I think it's partly because of ethnicity, partly because of the geography, partly because of the kind of work people do here; when you're doing ranchwork, you don't see too many people and you don't really have a whole lot of time to discuss things, the work is pretty action-oriented. It has to do with physical work; for instance, I think the same would be true of fishermen, who don't say much, yet there's an enormous amount of communication that goes on. I don't feel that I'm deprived of communication with people here, by any means; I feel a real intimacy with the people I work with.

It's just that we don't always hash out ideas, the way I do with other friends; and if we do, it's just done with a different set of words, fewer of them maybe and phrased in different ways.

But I sure don't want to remythologize the cowboy. People don't understand that there are ranchers and there are cowboys. Cowboys are just people who do day-work or hire on at a place; they're like the menial labor. A rancher, who also does cowboy work, is the person who owns the place or manages the place. This word, "cowboy," is very confusing to everybody. The word has been such a misused word, the concept such a misused concept.

This aversion to mythology and mythologizing seems to work its way through your fiction and your nonfiction. Is this a result of your work as a journalist? Do you see yourself still as a journalist at all?

No, I'm a terrible journalist.

But it's something you did earlier in your career.

Well, I got published in magazines because that was the way to get published. I was also desperately poor. So I wrote portrait pieces that helped me get started and to make some money. I still do: I write for *Time* magazine sometimes and a few little things here and there. Actually, those are the hardest things for me to write, and usually the least successful. I'm much more apt to get a rejection letter for some little 1,500-word journalistic piece than I am for a 10,000-word personal essay. Part of my training in film school was in documentary films; I have a real lively interest in other people's lives. But I don't think my strongest point is writing a journalistic piece about other people. I think of myself more as a contemplative writer.

You strike me as both a contemplative and a revelatory writer.

I see those two things as going hand in hand: contemplation leads to revelation, and vice versa. And too much revelry leads to the quiet life!

You mentioned your work in film, and of course your documentary film, Sheepherders, *is what brought you to Wyoming in the first place. Is that interest in film something you've pretty much exhausted?*

95

No, I'm writing two screenplays, one of which is the screenplay for *Heart Mountain,* in fact. This young producer who bought my novel is really wonderful, and for the first time since my friend David died (while I was making *Sheepherders*), I can imagine actually working in film. Of course, this fellow just does Hollywood films, but I can imagine actually working on a film with him because he has this sensibility that I admire – he's bright and thoughtful, and there aren't too many of those people around in Hollywood. He showed up just a few months ago and opened up a door in my life that I thought had been closed forever. He's already asked me to work on some other projects, which I haven't decided on yet. It's not like I'm going to give up writing books, of course; between books, I just like doing something else, just kind of living for a while so I'll have something to write about later.

I think that's a problem with certain writers, especially university-connected writers who spend all year teaching and then go to all of these silly summer workshops; except for their domestic life, when do they ever see the world? And I think it's reflected in their fiction, in these awful domestic dramas – they're so hermetic and boring. It's like they really have nothing to write about. I'd rather go work on a shrimp boat in Mexico – anything, rather than teach at a university. Of course, most of these people teach in order to survive, but I think it's more invigorating to do something completely outside of your vocation. It seems to me, from the little teaching I've done, that it really zaps your energy, sort of the same *arena* of energy that you use to write from. You have to do something that uses another kind of energy. Maybe I just have a smaller energy field than other people have, am more fragile.

Does your work life also affect your sense of style?

What *is* my style?

You seem more of the storyteller, and less of the antiseptic, self-involved writer of narrative.

Probably, yes, because all of these people around here *are* great storytellers. That's what ranchers and cowboys do; you work long, hard days and then you go to the bar and you tell each other the stories of what happened that day. Then you remember your grandfather's stories, and you tell those. It's a great tradition up here.

Your comments here, and the nature of your own work, suggest a distaste for what has come to be called minimalist fiction.

Well, I don't like to make blanket statements. The work of particular writers doesn't appeal to me, and I guess those writers would be included in that minimalist school, that domestic drama school: where the opening chapter is always in some university professor's kitchen, you know. I certainly liked all the real sources of that fiction – the early twentieth-century French writers – and to me, the most wonderful book that occurs only in someone's mind and which is totally self-concerned is Malcolm Lowry's *Under the Volcano*.

I'm willing to read anything about anything – if it's good. I just don't think a lot of this stuff is very good. I don't think it's a question of subject matter, but what you do with it, because ultimately we're all writing about ourselves; some people just draw larger boundaries around themselves, some people include more. It doesn't mean that they're richer, it's just that their horizon is larger; if you have a small one, it might be a richer vein going vertically.

Do you feel yourself a part of any particular tradition as a writer in the West? Do you feel any sort of kinship with Western writers?

I feel lots of kinships, but I'm not sure they represent a tradition. Like anyone who writes about landscape, I've read Thoreau and Emerson, but I certainly don't think I'm part of their tradition. I don't know, I guess, what tradition there is.

I was thinking of that Western tradition that includes writers like Stegner and Guthrie.

Well, except for Stegner and Guthrie and others, we're all pretty much contemporaries of each other, so we don't think of ourselves as being part of a specific, common tradition. If you do, I think you're making a terrible mistake because you're creating a scene that doesn't exist yet. That's for future generations to decide, whether this was a tradition or not. We're all just doing our work; we just happen to live within eight or nine hours' drive of each other. I ended up living here by mistake; I didn't come to Wyoming to write about it. It's not like I moved to Walden Pond so I could write like Thoreau. A person would be insane to do that. I ended up here by chance, by mistake because I was too emotionally paralyzed to move on, and I just wrote about it. I don't really care if anybody else in the world is writing about anything related to this or not. It's great to have these friends, but they could be writing about Mars, for all I care; and certainly my fiction is very different from everyone else's.

It's been said that there are too many books about ranchers and ranching in Wyoming, that ranchlife is actually a very small part of life in Wyoming, and that other elements of that life need to be written about.

I don't know how small a part of the population ranchlife represents, I don't know if that's really true. In fact, I think there are too many books about *town* people! Still, I don't feel any responsibility to write about anything. Who gives a shit if I ever write a book again; I'm sure nobody does. I just write about what I can write about. I don't know from one book to the next what it's going to be; but like I say, I don't have an agenda, hidden or otherwise. I write about the part of the West that I know, and that's ranching life. The town part of life that I know is mostly the bars – at least, that's the part of any interest, because that's the social center – and I write about bars within that social context.

I get so pissed off at comments like that, partly because I sense a class thing – that I'm a moral and political cheat because I'm not writing about the working class. As far as I'm concerned, we're *all* the working class; a sheepherder sure as hell isn't on top of the world. Maybe I'm being paranoid. There are always these struggles between groups, wherever you are: you've got the town people and the oil field workers and the miners and the ranchers and the cowboys.

I hope that what any of us writes transcends the costume of the day. What I'm writing about is, I hope, the human condition, and not about whether you're a cowboy or a sheepherder. Yet I think that people are so hung up with the stupidity of myth. To me cowboys and ranchers and sheepherders are just working people who work with their hands and work with animals and live outdoors, just like a whole lot of other people doing a whole lot of other jobs.

But many readers see the version of the West described in The Solace of Open Spaces *as being a romanticized version of the West and of the ranching life.*

Well, the vision there was romanticized in a certain way, and there are reasons for that. First of all, I had just arrived, basically, when I wrote that book, so there was a lot I didn't know. Second of all, I lived in the communities that I was writing about, and you just can't write certain things when you're in that situation; you can't write about a whole *lot* of things! Which is why I started writing fiction, because certainly in my novel there was a real complexity of class and characters that wasn't in those first essays. So that was sort of my dilemma: I had to be self-censoring, if I planned to stay here.

Solace is a book about surviving a loss, it's a book written in the throes of grief, so what I was reaching for were the things that were saving my life. And those were all the good things about the place and the people, which are *there;* I wrote about the things that they offered me in response to my emotional situation. I didn't change anything about how they behaved toward me and how I felt about the place; so I think the book has to be seen from that point of view. I wasn't writing the *The Compleat Book of Ranchlife in Wyoming,* which is what everyone seems to want. Readers want what they want, and writers write what they can write, and never the twain shall meet.

I was also naïve in that I didn't think, first of all, that anyone would ever publish the book, and second of all, that anyone would ever read it if it did get published. I *certainly* didn't think I was writing about anything of any particular interest to anybody: I lived in this little, dinky Mormon town with these broken-down sheepherders and an illiterate rancher, and I just didn't think it was very spectacular. I didn't live on this dreamranch where we had ropings every week; I've been on some fancy ranches since then, and I know what they can be like. Well, I wasn't living that life, it was pretty poverty-stricken. In that sense I was naïve, because now I understand, from the response to *Solace,* that there were many other ranching worlds that I was not a part of, and that I was not addressing; and that people had certain expectations of what all this represents, mythologically, to them, expectations which I really wasn't aware of. I was brought up around ranchers and horse people – we raised horses – and it was just no big deal to me. I've ridden with cowboys all my life – they were just low-paid people, that's all I knew about them.

One of the other hats you wear, of course, as a writer is that of a naturalist. Does your work as a rancher inhibit your works as a naturalist at all? Do the values of one vocation conflict with the values of the other?

No, the one *complements* the other. If I have a mission in life, it's to prove to myself and then to the world that you can run a ranch in a way that's environmentally sound, that's compassionate, that protects land from subdivision without preventing people from using it to ride or walk through.

That's been a slow revelation for me, too, because when I got here, what did I know about any of these things? Coming from California, the Big Horn Basin looked about as pristine as you could get, until I looked quite closely. But that's really my mission, to try to educate everybody to be a little more progressive in how they manage the land, and to educate the people who don't know anything about what takes place here, so that they understand that this can be done, and that taking away these lands from ranchers could mean, in the wrong hands, the demise of the land. Ranchers have been unwitting conservationists for all these years ir that they have owned large blocks of land, and for the most part have been unwilling to let them go and subdivide them. It's subdivision, it's these "ranchettes" that screw up habitat for wildlife and that pollute and that desertify these little places for their backyard horses. To me, that's the worst kind of damage you can do; give me a big ugly old city any day.

I didn't know these things could be done, either; I've just happened to meet these wonderful people, these visionaries, along the way who have taught me things. People like Allan Savory, who taught me about holistic grazing. People like Ray Hunt, an old broken-down Nevada cowboy who works with young horses, who taught me more about life than any Zen master. People like this are everywhere, and interestingly enough, their ideas are making their way through the ranching community. Sure, some people take to those ideas more slowly than others, and of course, I always leap on those ideas and get laughed at. But then, a few years later, I'll notice one of my neighbors sneaking down to take one of these clinics, and I know something good is happening. The best you can do is to set an example, to do things that change the land – and a horse's mind – for the better.

WORKS

Arctic Heart: A Poem Cycle. Santa Barbara, Calif.: Capra Press, 1992. Poetry.
Drinking Dry Clouds: Stories from Wyoming. Santa Barbara, Calif.: Capra Press, 1991. Short fiction.
Geode/Rock Body. Santa Barbara, Calif.: Capricorn Press, 1970. Poetry.

Heart Mountain. New York: Viking, 1988. Novel.
Islands, the Universe, Home. New York: Viking, 1991. Essays.
The Solace of Open Spaces. New York: Viking, 1985. Essays.
To Touch the Water. Boise, Id.: Ahsahta Press, 1981. Poetry.
Wyoming Stories. Santa Barbara, Calif.: Capra Press, 1986. Short fiction.

Richard Ford

Richard Ford is a Southerner by birth, born in Jackson, Mississippi, in 1944 and raised in both Mississippi and Arkansas. He was educated at Michigan State University and dates his beginnings as a writer exactly: a moment in January 1968 when he said to himself, "I think I will try to make myself a writer." Ford went on to take writing classes at the University of California-Irvine, studying with Oakley Hall and E. L. Doctorow. In subsequent years, Ford's fiction has received numerous awards, and his story "Great Falls" was made into a film, *Bright Angel,* for which Ford wrote the screenplay.

Since 1983 Ford has made his home, for part of the year, in Montana; when this interview took place (in 1990), Ford was living outside Dutton, Montana, with his wife Katrina (with sincerity and without embarrassment, Ford and his wife call each other "Angel" and "Baby" and "Sweetheart") in a rented blue house surrounded by wheat fields. Ford's two birddogs roamed the house. Ford speaks with the drawl of his Mississippi origins; his face was shadowed by stubble, and he smoked a thick Macanudo cigar as we talked.

The next day would be opening day of pheasant season, and in between visits to the fields, we would fit in a trip to Choteau where Ford would speak, along with Mary Clearman Blew, on writers and writing. There, too, would occur a memorable meeting between Ford and A. B. Guthrie (in whose honor the Choteau gatherings were held) at Guthrie's home: two writers linked, perhaps tenuously, by the West; two writers separated, aesthetically, by an unimaginable distance.

GREGORY MORRIS: *One of the things I'm curious about is the turn your writing recently has taken to the essay, to nonfiction prose – for example, in the several essays about your family.*

RICHARD FORD: Well, I always thought, when I was first writing stories, that I knew more than was getting into the stories. Young writers, though certainly not all of them, start with a narrow scope, even if they have a lot of material, and as they use up what they come equipped with they have to widen their scope. I suppose you do that by learning new things to write about; and by devising ways to get more of what you know into what you write.

I'd never written any essays before 1982, though I'd wanted to. Rust Hills, at that time, asked me if I wanted to write an essay about Faulkner, Hemingway, and Fitzgerald, for the *Esquire* fiftieth anniversary issue. I demurred as much as I could because I didn't think I was a good enough writer – though I think I secretly wanted to do it. But Rust carried on to say several semi-insulting things about how my work had been compared to Hemingway, and to Faulkner, and that since those writers had "clearly" influenced me, I was at least qualified to write about why. He also said, "Look, Philip Roth turned this down. We don't know who else to ask."

When both of us got down to desperation I realized that I probably didn't know anything original about Faulkner or Hemingway or Fitzgerald, but I had read them all and not so long ago. I didn't have time to bone up. So I'd have to write about those writers "in my life," which is how I wrote the essay, and which is how my family came to be partial subjects.

And that's how I've gone about writing essays – in a personal way. Not that I have such an exalted opinion of my responses or of what I know; my responses and what I know are probably like most people's. But I do have the habit of language, and a habit of reflection that goes along with writing, and an admiration for literature which translated into a wish to compose. And it's possible with these as your habits, to make up something that wouldn't otherwise have existed.

Do you see that affection for words as evolving in any way? In that essay on Hemingway, Faulkner, and Fitzgerald, you talk of the evolution of the rhythms and noises of words – do you see a similar development in your own writing?

Sure. If you look at the books, they're certainly various. Anyone's "style" will reflect in some way, or be influenced by his changing life – getting older, having used up certain strategies, having read things you like. There's certainly no formula for it. Although it should be said that most writers' style is not one thing, not one mode of utterance, not one sentence length. From one bit of writing to the next, from one period in one's life to another, these qualities change, and in fact they often more or less coexist in a single period. Carver is said to have a "Carver Style." But really you have to freeze time for that to be even slightly accurate. Later, his sentences lengthened, his grasp of subjects widened. To define a style in that way, in that narrow way, is really to take away from a writer what she or he is trying mostly to do – widen the reader's view; and it's often done by a critic or would-be critic in behalf of making her or his job easier, by delimiting the subject more narrowly than is accurate, but narrow enough to make easy conclusions.

You talk of how life influences style. That concern with your life again emerges in your essays – the essays about your family, about both your mother and your father. I'm curious as to why this has emerged as a subject now.

Well, about my mother and my father there's nothing really profound to say. I thought I had a pretty good relationship with them, and in neither of their cases did I have anything particularly organized intellectually, or even chronologically. I suppose, once again, it seemed worthwhile to commit what I had lived to my habits of language, and see what sense I made, if it was surprising, or informative – this, for the purposes of whoever would read the essay. I suppose I thought that we are innately interested in our parents, and that the point of view of a fellow – me – who's had a good life with his parents, and who wasn't bound up in too many clichés about that life, might be of use to a reader. I've always thought it was only worthwhile, given my peculiar and not very major intelligence, to assign myself to writing only about the most important things I know. That way I'd get the most out of myself. Although I've not always written about obviously momentous things. I've written about Bruce Springsteen's music, and James Michener's novels, and about a lot of things not so high powered, such as parenthood. But I've always tried to think I had found, in doing the writing, something that wasn't known before, and that became important when it was revealed.

That interest in family, certainly, makes its way into your fiction: in Wildlife, *for example, and the business of parent and child and familial understanding.*

I've always been interested in what seem to me the unnecessary impediments to love being expressed or recognized – in families and without. And conventional wisdom is one of those impediments. Something as conventional as Tolstoy's famous bromidic beginning, that happy families are all alike. I suppose I just dispute that sentiment, because I haven't found it to be true. I've found that possibly we don't look closely enough at families, and that possibly we miss noticing that what may seem an unhappy family is just one trying to solve its problems and to be happi-*er*. That's one of the things that *Wildlife* is about: a family trying to stay together in the face of disruptions. And for the reader it's a book that would try to rethread conventional understanding about families in such distress.

At the end of "Optimists," though, there the family has gone asunder, but the family's story still can be told in an orderly way, as a whole. The narrator looks back on his family's bad luck and hard times with a sense of affection, an affection and a sense of integrity that are proved in the telling. At the end the speaker's mother comes back into his life briefly to testify that years ago they all loved each other, and that it's not a tragedy – just a thing that happened. And in doing that she tells him, her son, that what he should do is make the best of things how he can, not to give over to such clichés as "I came from a broken family." Include all the facts.

For me, it's an act of affection and sympathy to write about these people, and to say that their lives were better than convention might describe them, and to prove it just to invite a closer look.

That confidence in the future comes through in your work, both in the stories and in Wildlife, *where Jean Brinson says to her son Joe: "Tomorrow might be a better day . . . Something'll happen to make things seem different." And you said you're an optimist by nature.*

The belief is that it *could* – that the future is not irretrievably bad; that with the requisite small amount of good luck and a continuing interest in the particulars of your life, you can make your life quite bearable, quite livable.

As Frank Bascombe does in The Sportswriter?

Just the act of Frank's deciding: I have all these things in my life which I can't control – my son's death and its effect on my marriage, and God knows what all else – with these things in front of me, I still have all this time left. I'm either not going to use that time and do what Walter does (commit suicide), or I'm going to try to steer myself forward with clearer expectations.

So it's basically an affirmative act that you perform?

I think every time you write a story it's an affirmative act; because, among other things you've said, "Here, quit what you're doing and read this"; or put differently it affirms an interest in life sufficient to be written and read by another. It's a positive act when I make something the best I possibly can, from a medium as lively as language, and give it to another.

Another element that I'm curious about is the spiritual element in your work. You've mentioned, again in your essays, that you did not inherit your mother's Catholicism, for instance.

Well, my mother wasn't Catholic. She was educated in a Catholic girls' school in Fort Smith [Arkansas] – that is to say as far as she went, the tenth grade or so. But she was rather religious, or it might be that she had faith, and found her faith supported by, well, liturgy and ceremony. I think she might've gone on and been Catholic if she hadn't married my father, whose mother was from Ireland and rather crisply opposed to Catholics. My mother never lost her sense of humor – that seems most important – and she never tried to beat religion into me.

In my nuts and bolts way I've always distrusted (long before I knew I distrusted it) the impulse to seek authority for one's acts outside oneself. A godly authority, that. Not that you can always be responsible for what happens to you. But you can try to be. I've always disliked the sense of disempowerment. Maybe it's what makes one a novelist. I've thought of that before – the possibility of authorizing a great deal.

My mother was quite a bit this way, too. I think she was probably a Christian existentialist, and sometimes she got out on the dark end of self-responsibility, and secretly wished she could creep into a cathedral and just relax, tell somebody her troubles. I don't wish that. And, in truth, she didn't do that.

It seems to come around to the idea of individual responsibility, that if you prohibit the chance of external influence upon your characters' actions –

Well, you can't prohibit those things, of course. But, again, you can try to be the person who acts. Sometimes people have said about my books that fate plays a strong role, but I don't really agree, if I know what fate even is. Or maybe it's that most people believe they're in control of their lives absolutely, and the possibility that they're not is a reproach, and to the extent they aren't they think something – fate – is. I just think that things happen to you and you try to make the best of them, try to authorize what of your actions you possibly can. That's all I know about fate. Mary Gordon once wrote that fate is "the villain of the American dream." But I really disagree with that. Maybe it's the villain of the American neurosis.

But you don't rule out the element of luck?

Luck, well, luck is not exactly fate, I guess. Luck's a sort of unreliable antidote to bad events befalling you. We need it for the things we can't authorize better. There's the old putatively Arab proverb saying, "Luck is the residue of design." My version is that the "appearance of design is often the residue of luck."

Yet it seems that in many of the stories in Rock Springs, *the reins are taken out of some folks' hands.*

Well, again, those characters may say so and they may think so, and that may be their way of explaining their circumstance. Like Earl, in "Rock Springs," says: he "can't quite get his acts reconciled with his intentions." That's his way of explaining it, and that's offered, for the reader, as a possible explanation for how humans get into the fixes that they get into. But it's not meant to be the last word in that particular fictive paradigm, because I'm sure that when most people read that they think to themselves, Yeah, yeah, yeah, that's *his* explanation. I think a story offers a lot of explanations for human conduct, and never finally says what the final explanation is, except that it leaves you – and this is one of the reasons why I think the stories in *Rock Springs* are redemptive – it leaves you with a speaker speaking a story who is finally the only person left in the whole fiction, the whole story who *can* be responsible. Fate and family and affection and all kinds of things are not final causes; they are contributive causes to all kinds of human actions, and finally all that we have left are ourselves and our responsibility for our own actions.

108

Does landscape *contribute, in any way, to human action?*

Well, I suppose it does, in one way or another. If it's cold where you live, then you tend to stay in a lot and get cabin fever. If it's hot, then maybe you wear fewer clothes and have more sexual adventures. But I think, more commonly that *we* say it contributes in our attempts to explain our lives to ourselves: why this happened, why we feel this way, why we're having this problem. The drama is in us, not the mountain range to the west of here. I think landscape is inert, and that we attribute to it qualities, strengths that we say affect our lives. If our explanations persuade us and others, then the relationship to landscape which we've advanced becomes true.

So you have no special relationship to landscape, sentimental or emotional or emotive? Different landscapes don't pose different problems?

No, not really, not in an important way. Oh, when I'm in the South, sometimes I miss Montana terribly. And I do feel without sentimentalizing that I'm a Southerner, that the South is my home. But that's just an accident of birth, and I don't attribute to it any special qualities outside the obvious ones. So I guess I shouldn't say I have *no* relationship with landscape. But, again, I think that saying I miss Montana is just expressing a feeling of need of mine in terms of place, likewise saying Mississippi is my home. I could express that need differently, but for some reason, something like instinct, I express it in terms of place, landscape.

This is one of the reasons I so strongly resist the notion of regionalism – in literature, in defining culture. My life has simply shown me that we're more in the same boat wherever we are, and that recognizing that fact might enable us to adapt to our situations more successfully. That's, in my mind, one of literature's concerns regarding its readership. If a reader thinks he or she finds the logic of my stories, or their observation of place to be peculiar to Montana, or the Eastern Front, I just think that the reader has performed a transaction in his mind, a transaction which identifies my words with his appreciation. I, though, am never trying to write stories that are unique to Montana. I feel sure that if I'd come to Nebraska in 1983, I'd be writing the same sort of stories, and they'd be Nebraska stories.

When you study the West in your fiction, you seem to study exclusively the New West, the West at present, rife as it is with the burdens and detritus of its history.

It's a West full of "empty moments" (as a character says in "Sweethearts"), full of unbridgeable gaps between expectation and achievement –

I wouldn't say that the *West* is a place full of "empty moments." I would just say that some people's *lives* suffer these moments. It isn't anything unique to the West, by any means. There are as many empty moments that people have to bridge with language or with affection or with patience or tolerance or forbearance, taking place in Chicago or in Dallas as there are in Montana. There's nothing that I write about, in writing about Montana, that I think is unique about Montana, unless it be that there is a town called Great Falls. But there are towns called Great Falls elsewhere.

With regard to place, then, you remarked elsewhere: "I really think that human beings accommodating themselves to a landscape, to a place, is natively dramatic." Your characters often seem caught up in this act of accommodation, an act that contains special significance for those characters. What is it about this act that is "natively dramatic"?

Well, there's conflict. There's something I want, and I don't have it (familiarity with where I live, say), and I have to get it, and I try and either succeed or don't. Those are basic constituents of a story. Or else those conflicting elements are in the background of another story, and add to that primary story's drama: I'm in a town where I don't name the streets, and where I haven't yet seen a winter, and my parents are breaking up.

In the western United States white people came looking for something they didn't find elsewhere. The climate is rather vividly forbidding sometimes. So, it's historically and factually a good place to show some human enterprise striving to succeed. Though, still, it's my, I suppose, "philosophical" position as an American, that nothing important to human affairs goes on out here that doesn't go on anyplace in America.

Is there a language, an idiom that is native to the West or to Montana, one that you've tried to capture in your fiction?

If there is, I haven't tried to capture it, but I'm not so sure there is – so many people being from elsewhere, and the history of the state for white people being relatively brief. I've just tried to do what any writer does, make up a language, a lingo, a dialect that's suitable for a story, not for the place. And here, I'm just talking about Montana. If we were talking about the South, then I think I'd have a somewhat different answer. But in writing about Montana I've been able to draw from what I know of regional language far from here – idioms, rhythms of speech. They've seemed – from what readers tell me – to fit into Montana-speak, whatever that is.

Do people in Montana say that?

Sometimes they do. But it's because they've made a connection themselves. It may help in making that connection that I use language as much as possible in the service of what I hope will be important stories for a reader. But my language decisions are trying to be as widely referential as possible, and not regional or based on what I think is right for Montana. (Of course I suppose I wouldn't use a phrase if I just simply thought it was wrong, for whatever reason.) I set stories here because I've lived here and continue to live here, and because I like the names of things out here, because living here made me feel free – after living in the South – to do what I wanted to do.

You talk about "exhausting" your interest in a place, too. Is that when you move on, either artistically or physically?

Maybe. So far I haven't exhausted my interest in a place yet. Sometimes I think I've exhausted my interest in the South. But I know it's just that I haven't found a way to think I could write anything interesting about the South. It's sort of the opposite of exhaustion.

It sounds like you've made a very clear distinction between your life in Montana and the Montana or the West that you create in your fiction?

Well, I don't write about myself, if that's what you mean. My characters aren't me, though I'm sure I contrive dramatic situations with which I have some sympathy, if not exactly some experience. I do like the notion that while stories can take you back to your life renewed, one of the reasons they can is that they're made up of lively language instead of life experience. They're special in that way. They have a referred relationship to life, but they are not life itself – except that you use up your life when you read them, and in that way they are part of life. But I very much like to think of stories as being purely matters of language artfully contrived, at least as a first principle. There's a line from R. P. Blackmur, in his essay "The Critic's Job of Work," which goes something like: "poetry is distinctive because of the animating presence of fresh idiom, which expresses the matter at hand and adds to the stock of available reality." Paul West wrote someplace else that language can never accurately report the truth of anything, anyway. So, the distinction between my stories set in the West and the West itself exists the instant I use language to refer to place at all.

It's an interesting stance you take, divorcing yourself from the literary and historical tradition of the place in which and of which you write.

Well, I try to write stories that don't rely on history much – that is, other than the characters' personal histories. It's just a matter of what I like to write about. I think that early on I grew somewhat disillusioned about the study of history, because, among other reasons, I grew up in Mississippi and spent my early school years going over and over the history of the South with my teachers and classmates (now, it sounds incredible) trying to rationalize the South's defeat in the Civil War, trying to make the case that the war wasn't about slavery (which still goes on, by the way), and trying to make other spurious cases using history. Based on that early "learning experience," it's not surprising I'd want to invent histories that approached truth in a more reliable way. I think, too, that I must want to invent something I can take absolute responsibility for.

That distancing from tradition and that invention of history allow you a certain aesthetic freedom.

Well, okay. So I'm free to write what I want. Literary tradition certainly figures into my story writing, but not as far as I'm concerned in an especially inhibiting way. I don't really know much about the literary tradition of the Western United States. I know quite a lot about the literary tradition of England and America, and each of those has devolved on me in such a way as to make writing stories seem appealing. But I don't think of myself as doing more than making this obvious nod to literary tradition and going on about my business.

Place doesn't control me for reasons we've talked about already. I just make the place up out of words and call it what I want to call it. I could call it Mars. I'm sure, in the case of this place, Montana, that I've been affected, and my life has been, by living here. But I don't feel responsible for recording that, or for explaining it in prose, or for reporting on it in any way. I use those effects rather intuitively in writing stories, and when I run out of them I make up the rest. My story, for a reader, may comprise or represent a credible linkage between humans and place, and if so then I accede. Literature can do that for a reader – posit a relationship. But I don't think I'm trying to posit that, and I don't think there is *one* fundamental relationship, and I don't rely on there being one that's uniquely Western any more than I think there's a uniquely Southern one. We may just want to believe there is and find it in stories. In my own mind, I'm usually trying to do something simpler.

So you can go out tomorrow morning and hunt pheasant and walk the landscape, and not feel the need to translate that experience, that emotional relationship between you and the landscape, into language?

Well, more or less that's right. I don't come in from hunting and think to myself: I have to sit down now and describe that sunset in my notebook. If I did do that, it undoubtedly would be less because of the sunset than because of some description that was in my mind that I liked. Later on, the reader does with this what she or he will. Most of the ways I've felt when I've been exposed to nature's grandeur, or to its menace, have seemed to me, as I expressed my feelings to myself, sentimental. And so what I want to do is write something new and not sentimental, something that owes itself more to the imagination than to a responsibility to a place.

But there's no link between language and landscape for you there?

I have to, in a way, be a kind of almost adversarial proponent of the things that I care about in talking to you in order that I just tug away from sentimentality, tug away from what I think are less significant but more conspicuous impulses in the way we read literature. My work may not seem to bear much relationship to Donald Barthelme's, but certainly on that postmodernistic principle we agree. We just diverge rather widely in what schemes we use to create verisimilitude. *The French Lieutenant's Woman* [by John Fowles] is another book worth reading on this point. But you have to keep insisting, insisting, insisting; otherwise you give way to word-pictures, you give away something of the language which is so instrumental and so basic to our experience of literature that once we ignore it, literature gets arrogated into the minds of sentimentalists.

So these guys who look at the mountains and want to write descriptions of the mountains, what I think is: Hell, go to the mountains! Forget about writing pictures of them. If you want to write pictures of them, make it interesting word for word. Forget about the mountains. That's why I don't have a lot of word-pictures in my stories. I don't have the patience to write them.

For that reason, then, you never describe Jerry Brinson fighting those fires in Wildlife?

Maybe that's right. I thought about describing it. I certainly could've gone up to the fires and seen what went on there because a lot was on fire in Montana then. 1988. But, I thought that a description of the fire was not what the story was about, and I was as always trying to stay close to what I felt was my story. I think I was probably more interested in the consequence of the fire more than the fire – that is, in terms of my story's economies. For me, one of fiction's compelling qualities, and one that interests us because it seems like life, is that fiction's about consequences. Consequences of our acts, of events outside our control. Most of our life is spent dealing with those things, trying to better the next set that comes along.

Some of your readers have been "suspicious" of the voices in which your narrators "communicate." Some readers have complained that the language used by those narrators seems beyond their capabilities –

"Seems" is right. First of all, I don't think eloquence is denied anybody. Just as a general, democratic attitude, I think anybody can be eloquent, particularly when she or he is talking about the most important things of their life. The stress, the telling, the importance of telling, the importance of what's told can imbue the teller with language and language possibilities not known before. I also think people have possibilities for eloquence which conventional wisdom doesn't suppose they have. So to imbue them with eloquence is an act of faith in humankind. Likewise, in the presence of great things, great events, language explodes.

Another matter is that I don't wish a reader reading a story of mine to forget for a moment that he's reading a story, that he's having practiced upon him the art of literature, and that the art of literature is an art which includes illusions, and also extends the realm of your credibility as the everyday, everyman reader. Therefore, in behalf of telling you something you couldn't have known but that you read my story, I may make demands on you proportionate to what you're getting. There's a certain self-reflexiveness that I want any reader to experience, and in experiencing that sense of self-reflexiveness, the reader sees himself reading a story, knows he's reading a story, isn't trying to live in the "referred reality." That little intellectual gymnastic will open him up, make him curious.

We do this all the time. We do it every time we read about King Lear. We know there probably never was a King Lear, but for the purposes of letting Shakespeare do what he will to us, we suppose there was: we suppose a man can blind himself, we suppose a man can do all kinds of things. Give speeches on the moor which we can see and hear. Well, there's no difference in supposing that and allowing characters to speak words that, were there such a person, they might not – I still won't concede this – *might* not be able to speak. Every time we open a book and we have a third-person narration and we are exposed to the thoughts of characters – well, we can't really know what people are thinking, but we allow the writer to do that. So, you can tell me that I haven't done what I do successfully, but you cannot tell me that I may not try. What's the difference in a Henry James character who thinks in paragraphs and sentences that are twenty-five lines long, and a character in my story who wants – for the purposes of doing exactly what the Jamesian character wants to do – to extend the limits of the known into the unknown?

Do you think your narrators ever find that solace in language?

Well, Frank does in *The Sportswriter*. Oh, yes, yes, yes! Because, in a first-person narration, what a speaker does in a story like "Optimists" is that he takes consolation in the putting together of his story, in the choice of the words he will use, the choice of the incidents he will tell, the way in which he makes a shape out of it. His practice is very much like my practice. So, yes – maybe it isn't a self-conscious pleasure in the words: maybe it's an associational pleasure, maybe it's a sort of nonintellectual pleasure of suffusing himself in language, maybe it's the referential value that language has as it trips memory. But I think that in all the first-person narrations, for instance, the speaker in the story adopts language because it consoles him.

Since we're talking about language, do you see yourself experimenting at all in your fiction? I think, for example, of A Piece of My Heart, *with its dual narration.*

That was certainly an experiment. That was an experiment to see if a dumb boy could write a good book. That was the ultimate experiment of my life. Beyond that, I'm not entirely sure I know what's meant by "experiment." I suppose you mean so-called technical experiment. But really and truly in linear, narrative terms there's nothing that hasn't been tried, I guess. We thought Barthelme and Borges were experimental, when I was in school. But Borges was writing his stories in the 1930s. Joyce wrote *Ulysses* quite a while ago. So we're not talking about exactly cutting-edge issues, I guess. There's a way in which, for me or any writer, writing any story is an experiment, irrespective of its technical conceits or formal strategies; getting together all the components of a story and making a compelling whole out of it, is challenge enough. Experiment, I suppose, is finding ways in your work to extend yourself; extend what you knew at the beginning into the realms of what you don't know by the complicated act of writing a story. For instance, when I began writing *Wildlife,* I wanted to seize some of the working principles from prior stories of mine and extend them so as to achieve effects, uncover human complications, that those other stories didn't achieve and uncover. *Wildlife* may sound like, say, "Optimists" from time to time. But it's not "Optimists." It's a wholly different construction with much different, wider aspirations. To me, that's experiment of a high order. It's something different from, I guess, "pyrotechnics" and multiple points of view, and magical realism. Though those things are fine, too.

On another tack, there's the need, as one gets on in one's life and work, not to let yourself narrow, not to just play to your supposed strengths, not to accept limits to what you might do as a writer. I've just had accepted by *Granta* a novella called *The Womanizer.* And for me that was a considerable experiment, relative to what I'd *been* doing. It's set in Paris, it's a third-person narration, it's a length I'd never written before. It goes against quite a few principles I'd employed previously. So, it's an experiment also.

Was the compression of Wildlife *part of the experiment?*

I don't know. Really and truly it just came out the way it came out. For a long time, at least in the last fifteen or so years, I've liked moving a story from strong moment to strong moment, with side stories rather stringently proportioned to their effect on the whole, and keeping the story as close to tolerance's limit as I can. So, I guess, no, it wasn't precisely part of the experiment.

We were speaking of narrators earlier. Those narrators are often men working to comprehend their relation to women, to make themselves comprehensible to women. Lisa Lombardi has written that you describe a "landscape west where women serve as foci for hope and communion . . . [and as] oases, offering hope by their mere survival." More recently, Vivian Gornick has declared of you and of certain other male fiction writers: "At the heart of their work lies a keen regret that things are no longer as they once were between men and women, a regret so strong that it amounts to longing. It's this longing, endowed with the appearance of reality, that informs much of their writing. But from where I stand, the hard reality is this: that question about why things are not as they once were has got to be asked honestly, not rhetorically."

How do things look from where you stand? Are you asking the right question, and are you asking it "honestly"? What has transformed the relationship between men and women?

I don't have any relationship to those claims at all. Whether they're right or wrong, it doesn't strike a responsive chord in me. I don't know what Gornick's talking about. I don't even disavow it – I just don't know what she's talking about. She could have said the opposite and I still wouldn't know what she is talking about.

You obviously feel that you're asking the right questions?

I'm asking the best questions I can ask. I'm asking the ones that seem to be as close to the heart of the matter; that seems to me to be affectionate relationships between women and men. And men and men. Or women and women, if I get around to that. I think those affectionate relationships are probably the most important ones we have, outside of being what Frank Bascombe described as "being within one's self." It's those relationships that make our lives livable and bearable. I'm not trying to write role models; I'm just trying to portray people doing things which they can only do, with whatever frailties and limitations human beings suffer. So if Ms. Gornick would have me be better, so would I. But it is silly for her to suppose she knows what questions I *should* ask, based on a rather lopsided reading of one book.

I've written some other books too, and in order to really pin me to the bias, Ms. Gornick would have to take into consideration not one but all of them. That includes *A Piece of My Heart,* which represents, in some ways, a retrograde attitude toward women – at least some people have said so. Also, the whole business of trying to figure out what somebody is doing in the middle of his writing life, and fix his limitations at that point – not to say on one book – just seems to me to be, finally, fruitless. You try to write as much as you can in any book, you try to make the book as round and as admissive of experience as you can. Then you go on and you learn something else, and you try to make the next book as round and as whole and as admissive of new experience as you can. But, stepped back from, what you see is somebody charting out a big picture of what she or he believes the world is about. And one book, as whole and round as it may be, will only cover up that one spot. The next book will cover up another spot which gets revealed because the first one was covered, and so you cover that one. Finally, you'll either get them all covered. Or you won't.

What too many critics try to do is take the same attitudes that they have toward dead writers or finished writers and apply them to ongoing work. Ms. Gornick doesn't say what she should say: This guy's still working – there are other books I'm not talking about. It's like book reviewers who make what seems to me to be final judgments about books without ever saying: Of course, I think literature is good when it's this way and bad when it's that way, and this book falls on the bad side of my line. They don't ever bring into a clear focus what *their* intellectual bias is – and I don't mean bias in a strong sense, I just mean that if you write about one book and not another, you have a certain bias, and the point that you try to make, if it's a large point on the basis of that book, is somewhat biased against the alternative argument that the other book might make. All I can tell you is that it doesn't make me mad.

I thought it interesting, though, the comment Gornick made about the men, and the sensitivities and sympathies shared by those men.

That something's wrong with them? Well, maybe something is wrong with them. Maybe they're not all God could possibly hope for. I just don't know anything about it. I'm not a categorizer. It's not my enterprise to think in the sorts of ideological, combative terms which she chooses. It's fine. If it encourages someone to read my book, I hope it succeeds. If it discourages someone from reading my book, I hope it fails.

You have a tremendous respect for the reader.

That's why you write. I think the primary reason people write is for the reader, though not the only reason.

Many writers will claim the opposite.

Maybe it's a useful thing to tell oneself; maybe it's a lie that allows them to be more honest on the page – thinking they're only telling themselves their story and are only secondarily interested in the reader. But I don't like either the notion of writing as self-congratulation or the notion of writing as self-confession or self-exposure. Many of those impulses go into writing stories, to varying degrees, but ultimately it's all done so somebody can read. By factoring in that other person – the reader – an allowance is made for sympathy, if you have any need for sympathy.

WORKS

The Best American Short Stories 1990. Edited with Shannon Ravenel. Introduction by
    Richard Ford. Boston: Houghton Mifflin, 1990. Short fiction.
A Piece of My Heart. New York: Harper & Row, 1976. Novel.
Rock Springs: Stories. New York: Atlantic Monthly Press, 1987. Short fiction.
The Sportswriter. New York: Random House, 1986. Novel.
The Ultimate Good Luck. Boston: Houghton Mifflin, 1981. Novel.
Wildlife. New York: Atlantic Monthly Press, 1990. Novel.
The Womanizer. In *Granta* 40 (Summer 1992). Novella.

Photograph by Pat Zagelow

Molly Gloss

Molly Gloss is a native Oregonian (born there in 1944) who has taken the Pacific Northwest as the setting for much of her fiction. She is also a writer who came to fiction writing somewhat later in life. Her work includes several science fiction stories (published in such journals as *Calyx, Fantasy & Science Fiction,* and *Isaac Asimov's Magazine of Science Fiction*), as well as a novel for young adults. Her (adult) novel, *The Jump-Off Creek,* was nominated for the 1990 PEN/Faulkner Award for Fiction and received the 1990 Pacific Northwest Booksellers Association Award for Fiction.

Gloss chose to conduct this interview in writing, feeling that (as she told me over the phone) she could get herself to "sound a little more significant" by writing out her responses than she might by answering questions on tape. The interview was completed late in 1990.

GREGORY MORRIS: *You have written many types of fiction, yet you came relatively late to full-time writing. Could you talk about the circumstances that delayed your "emergence," and what finally allowed for that emergence? Were there special pressures in being a woman, writing? In being a mother?*

MOLLY GLOSS: I think I followed a not-uncommon path for women, though it's the inverse of what people usually think. I began to be a writer by first being a mother. I'd always liked to write, but it was something I kind of played at off and on if I happened to have an "idea," and I'd never actually written anything all the way to the end. I didn't take it seriously, I guess. Then I had a son and became a full-time mother. Motherhood puts you in touch, every day, with the big issues of life – heavy-duty things like Love, and Loss, and Conflict, and Tolerance, and Dignity, which are the issues, incidentally, that make great novels! But the daily tasks of mothering are trivial, or anyway they're consuming, and tiring. And all at once writing became important to me, because it was a way I could make a coherent space for myself, in a world filled with redundancy. I began by writing desperate journal entries, and when gradually I was less desperate, I wrote little fictional anecdotes, and then beginnings or middles or ends of imitative novels. It's very, very hard to find large blocks of time for writing when you're caring for a baby or a young child, and so for several more years I still didn't finish anything. But when my son went off to school, with the five hours a day of unclaimed time, I finally wrote the beginning, middle, and end of the *same* novel. It was a perfectly awful book, but I subscribe to the theory that, if good writing can't be *taught*, it can be *learned*, and mostly by the old-fangled method of practicing a lot. That book was the one I practiced on. And afterward I began to write short fiction, and almost right away I was selling what I was writing. Not every piece, but enough to begin to take myself seriously as a writer. It was years afterward, by the way, before I saw this connection between being a mother and becoming a writer. My responsibilities as a mother had kept me from spending as much time writing as I'd wanted to, and for a while that obscured the other truth – that mothering had driven me to write in the first place.

Up until your novel The Jump-Off Creek, *you were probably best known as the author of several science fiction stories. What was it about that genre that drew you to it and continues to attract you to sf?*

I don't read very much science fiction, actually, because so much of it seems to be about hardware and high-tech futures. The sciences that interest me are the people sciences – sociology, anthropology, psychology. It's hard to find, among the thousands of new sf books every year, the handful that are about people. I know I like the metaphoric uses of sf, and its castle-building possibilities. I seem to be drawn to write about people making connections with one another – the points of human contact, even in a world that's technological – and science fiction, because of its freedom of metaphor, lets me explore those connections right out to their edges. In science fiction, I can play around with aspects of things that interest me, a landscape, or a society, or a way of perceiving things, which aren't part of the world here and now – I can see how something would work, whether it might not become possible, might not have value. I love that openness to possibilities.

Much of that science fiction concerns itself with human consciousness, with telep-athy, with the healing potential that can accompany the penetrating conscious-ness. We see this idea at work in your stories "Joining" and "Seaborne"; we also see it in your children's novel, Outside the Gates. *Do you feel this "fictional" motif is grounded in some personal belief, in a sense of the reality of such a phenomenon? Can our consciousness and our selves be "joined"? What is the power of this idea for you?*

I had thought those were just metaphors, for the ways people communicate and connect with one another! But you're probably right, there's a little more to it than that. I never have experienced anything like a "joining" in my own life, and I'm generally a skeptic if someone tells me a ghost story or a telepathy experience. But I'm fascinated by the *possibility* of those things, I always have been. I think children are more open to them than adults. They aren't yet fully organized for dealing with the world, and so they see the invisible as a reality. I said I hadn't had a "joining" experience myself, but actually I can remember some very powerful experiences I had as a child, ghosts for instance, and waking dreams, that I've since explained to myself in rational ways. But I'm sorry for what I've lost, by explaining them away. Some cultures, even technological cultures, seem to keep into adulthood that willingness to believe in the unseen. It isn't superstition I'm talking about, but a kind of spiritualism, or mysticism. I envy that, and I'm sorry we've lost it in our own culture. I think there's truth in those experiences, at some level, and it may be that I'm trying to find it, in my fiction. I would love to have an unequivocal experience – to sit bolt upright in bed at exactly the moment my husband or my child's life is threatened in some city 3,000 miles away! It would be wonderful to have that affirmation of the invisible connections that bind people to one another.

One of the elements of your science fictional world is what you call the "ruralist" sector – farmers, both onshore and (in your story "Seaborne," where aquaculture plays a part) offshore. And what you seem to paint is a picture of some sort of futuristic agrarianism, one full of detail – detail of labor and effort – in which a certain moral quality, a certain ethic attaches itself to that rural life. Do you see some sort of Wendell Berry-like saving grace to this way of life? And is this ruralist element a link, a transition to your most recent work in The Jump-Off Creek, *where you depict the life of the frontier rancher?*

For a while, I didn't notice I was doing that – writing about agrarian peoples in my futuristic stories. But when I look back, I can see it has been a thread running through most of my fiction, that I do tend to write about people living close to the land. But I don't think I'm attaching a moral quality to the rural life. In our society, in fact, it's often the farmer, the hunter, the logger, who is least able to see the value in an unmanaged landscape. We have a long history, as a culture, of doing battle with the wilderness. A mythology of conquest. We've lost a sense of ourselves as part of the world. We try to make everything around us human-scaled, or contrive to make it amenable to humans, and we imagine we're the center of things, that everything else exists to benefit us. We can cut all the trees, kill all the wolves, because it benefits us. We no longer see ourselves as part of the natural world, but apart from it, and entitled to manipulate it to our interest. One of the reasons I'm drawn to science fiction is that it lets me reimagine our encounter with the wilderness – to make the governing myth one of wholeness rather than conquest.

Another link established in these stories seems to be the portrayal of strong, central female characters: Lisel in "Seaborne," Teo in "Interlocking Pieces," Dulce in "Wenonah's Gift." In your story "Interlocking Pieces" you deal specifically with matters of gender, when you suggest the exchange of imaginations and selves between the male donor, Dhavir, and the female recipient, Teo. Do you look for some androgynous self in your fiction, some happy combination of male and female?

In science fiction, right now, it's popular to give the sword to the woman, to put her into the fray with the men. But letting women play hardball with the boys isn't my idea of gender equality. What I find I'm doing, more often, is trying to imagine a world in which so-called women's issues of love and family and home and peace, are valued – by both men and women – above the so-called men's issues of power, competition, sexual predation, war. Even in a story like "Joining" – which was one of my earliest, and has a male protagonist and a violent beginning – the governing motif has to do with bonds of love, and fear of aloneness. And that character, Myles, who's modeled on the hero peacekeepers of Western fiction, is a man who weeps easily and perceives the emotions of other people as a visible aura. And it's his feelings of grief and loneliness, really, that move that story forward. I'm interested in strong women, yes, and also strong men. I just want their strengths to be, for instance, responsibility, and nurturing, and compassion, and the kind of peaceable, authentic courage that invests everyday lives.

The world you describe, finally, is a postapocalyptic world, a world that, in "Wenonah's Gift" and in your novel Outside the Gates, *is primitive, naturalistic, brutal in ways. Sacrifices are demanded; dark, ironic gifts are bestowed. Yet it's also a world informed with an inextinguishable humanity that springs from the human heart. Do you see that fiction as being particularly "moral" in any way?*

I'm not sure I understand what you mean. I do think I'm inclined to write about people who are fundamentally kind. As a reader, I'm not very patient with books that seem too cynical or bitter. There's a whole class of rather cold-blooded "literary" novels that I haven't been able to like. I'm interested in characters who are driven by loneliness to do mean things, but I'm not as interested in characters who are just completely mean-spirited. And actually, I think the only postapocalyptic world I've described is in "Wenonah's Gift." Most people have perceived *Outside the Gates* to be a fantasy, not set in a recognizable historical world at all. And most all of my other stories are just set on the frontiers of "Outspace," or in a near-future that is just an extrapolation from where we are now.

You moved from short fiction into the novel with your children's book Outside the Gates. *What is the history behind this novel, and what led you to the novel form? Did it serve as a comfortable way of "growing" into the writing of a novel? And*

*do you think this novel is intended for a particularly mature juvenile conscious-
ness, considering its style and subject matter?*

Outside the Gates was an "accidental" book. I had a notion to write a story for
my son, who was then ten years old, I think. I intended to write fifteen or
twenty pages of adventure, the kinds of things I knew lived in my son's
fantasies, and I even thought I might illustrate it, and then bind it with
poster paper and yarn and give it to Ben as one of his Christmas gifts. When
I started, I thought Vren, the boy in the story, would be going off to hunt for
his missing parents. But I didn't have an outline, I couldn't see the shape the
piece would take, and so I just had to follow the boy wherever he led me, and
eventually I realized he wasn't hunting his parents, and the reason he was
outside the Gates was much more complicated than I had thought . . . and
then I saw this wasn't going to be a fifteen-page story, but something much
longer, and I gave up trying to get it finished for Christmas! That was
fortunate in one way, because it never was a book for a ten-year-old, and by
the time I finished it and saw it into print, Ben was twelve or thirteen, which
was a more apt age for reading it.

Yes, it did actually serve very well as a way of "growing" into the novel
form, just because it was a short novel with not many characters, and so I
had an easier time than I might have, keeping kite strings from tangling. But
I wasn't thinking about that at the time. I was just following Vren! I did
worry, when I saw the direction he was taking me, that the book might not
be easy for children to read. Not that the language was too difficult, but that
it was a dark novel in some ways – the boy's parents had let him be cast out,
for one thing – and maybe not as plot-driven as I imagined children's books
should be. But a certain kind of reader is drawn to it. I think I would have
liked it, myself, when I was thirteen. It speaks to the isolation of adolescence. And adults seem to be moved by the book – teachers and librarians
seem to love it. I do think it's not the kind of book that kids tell their friends
about, that becomes widely popular by word of mouth.

I'd like to ask you now about the beginnings of The Jump-Off Creek, *about
what led you to the writing of that novel. First of all, did you find it difficult to go
from writing about the future to writing about the past; to go from dealing with
hypothesis and prediction to dealing with history? Both processes, of course,
involve imagination and vision, but slightly different sorts of imagination and
vision. What was the transformation like for you?*

Well, the big leap was the opposite of what you've described, actually, because I had started out, in my baby-coping days, writing Westerns, and only
later turned to science fiction. *The Jump-Off Creek* was a return, for me, to
old familiar forms. In fact, the book I wrote the year my son started school,
the book I "practiced" on, was a Western. I had grown up reading Westerns,
traditional genre Western fiction, and by the time that got tiresome, by the
time I had started to value good writing about adventure, I had stumbled on
the real Western literature, which wasn't shelved with "Westerns" at all in
the public library, books like Clark's *The Ox-Bow Incident,* Davis's *Honey in
the Horn,* Guthrie's *The Way West,* Wister's *The Virginian,* and those books
sustained my interest in the genre. People always say you should stick to
writing about what you know, but when I started to write, I took that to
mean I could write Westerns, because I'd read so many of them! After that
first Western novel, I wrote one more Western piece, a short story, but then I
looked around and realized I didn't have any place to send it. The market for
short Western fiction was completely gone. Even the Western movie was
moribund, and Louis L'Amour owned the book market. So I started to
write science fiction. There were a lot of magazines publishing sf stories, so
it was in many ways just a practical marketing choice. I'd been reading
science fiction for a few years by then, and I knew there was a place in it, for
the kind of thing I liked to write. Science fiction is a very open field of
literature. A lot of it is about hardware and physics and reptilian aliens, yes,
but there's a healthy sidestream that is thoughtful, that concerns itself with
human issues and feelings. And it allowed me to reimagine Western landscapes and themes – something I wasn't consciously aware of, at first. But I
must have realized it on some level, because I know I didn't find the "jump"
very hard to make.

*Obviously, you were prompted to write the novel for a reason, having a story to
tell. I'd like to know about some of the stories you heard from those "westering
women" in your own family. You seem to possess a familial tradition of colorful,
strong, imaginative women, and you apparently grew up listening to their
stories.*

The dust-jacket writer may be to blame for giving you that idea! The family
stories I heard were just little anecdotes, there wasn't enough in them to
really influence *The Jump-Off Creek.* The story that was most often told in
our family was that my great-grandmother Lena had come across the West

in a covered wagon when she was a girl. Her parents were German immigrants. The husband she would marry, Marx, was German too, and as a boy he had come around the Horn to San Francisco and by steamer up the coast to Vancouver, Washington. I also knew another great-grandmother had been widowed when her husband fell from a horse. And one of my great-grandmothers had named her last-born son "Z." I knew in a general sort of way that they were all rural women, and that they'd come West during the homesteading days. It was my work on *The Jump-Off Creek* that got up my interest in those things, instead of the other way around. I'd been reading dozens of journals and letters and memoirs of pioneering women, and I wondered if there might not be a diary or some letters of my great-grandmothers if I scratched around a little. There weren't. But I dug in family trunks and sorted through obituary clippings and photos and mementos, and I learned a few more things about each woman.

Emmaline, Emma, was twenty-three and had two little babies when her husband was killed falling off a horse. She married a man about twenty years older, a Civil War veteran, and had four more children, and then that husband just, as they say, up and left. Emma moved to Walla Walla, Washington, and never remarried. She supported her six children by taking in other people's laundry. She was so shamed by that husband who had left her, it was still a whispered family secret when I was growing up. I was in my twenties, probably, before I heard it said out loud, even though Emma by then had been dead for years.

Nancy's husband was a doctor and a preacher who brought his young wife to west Texas from someplace in Missouri. She had seven children. One of them was reported to be the first white child born in Irion County, Texas. Her husband died fairly young, he was forty-three I think, and she moved to Dimmett, Texas, and didn't marry again. I don't know how she supported her seven children. In later years she didn't have a permanent home, she spent a month at a time at the houses of each of her children.

Magdalene, Lena, was the German girl who came with her family in a covered wagon. Her husband worked as a nurseryman, he planted the trees that still stand along the roads in old Fort Vancouver. Lena was prone to miscarriages, and she only had three children who lived. Molly was the great-grandmother I was named for, in part because she died the year I was born. Her husband had been a Georgia well-driller and cotton weigher, and he brought her out to west Texas to take up farming. She had twelve children. The last born were twins, and she named them Y and Z. Baby Y died seventeen days after the birth, but my Great-Uncle Z is still living in Texas; I get a letter from him every once in a while.

I used to think I must be rare to have these four westering women rooting my family tree, each one of them with a good story there between the lines of what was known. But since *The Jump-Off Creek* has come out, people have been bringing me their histories, and I've realized probably my great-grandmothers are just fairly representative of the kinds of women who settled the West. Every one of them has a good story that is waiting to be heard. I wish my great-grandmothers had left me a greater record of their lives. If they had, I might be able to answer yes, *The Jump-Off Creek* was inspired by their stories. But it wasn't.

Were there other stories, then, compelling enough to make you change the course of your own career as a writer, to move into a completely different historical and imaginative framework? Stories uncovered in your historical research?

It might have been *My Ántonia* that led me to write *The Jump-Off Creek*. I don't know how, but I'd missed Willa Cather when I'd been reading the classic Western literature, and I was in my thirties before I tumbled on *My Ántonia*. And I then read *O Pioneers* and *Death Comes for the Archbishop*, and *Song of the Lark*, all of Cather's "Western" books, and went hunting for more. I thought there must be other women writers I'd missed, who had written that kind of lyrical prose about ordinary people on a western landscape. Well, of course, nobody else had. There's only one Cather! But in the hunt, I did find writers I'd missed, women who'd written at about the same time as Willa Cather, but closer to the mainstream of "Westerns." Mary Hallock Foote, Mary Austin, Sarah Orne Jewett. I had quit reading Westerns a long time ago, but when I found this forgotten bunch I went on a tear, looking for them in the library stacks, and at used-book stores and friends-of-the-library books sales and garage sales. I learned to look for a woman author on a frayed old binding, and some giveaway word in the title – "horse" or "Montana" or "mountain" or "prairie," something like that. I found and read, I don't know, fifteen or twenty of them. They were fairly conventional Westerns with a strong male hero, but they always had a strong woman in there somewhere too, some lovely, fragile-looking thing who, it turns out, is brave as any man, and doesn't need rescuing, and usually by the end has given up civilization to happily make a home with her man in the wilds. They were old-fashioned, in a way that Cather's work wasn't, and they were romantic, after the style of *The Virginian*, and clichéd, as so much of the genre always has been. But once I was started reading them, I realized I had missed reading Westerns. I found, I still had a yen to write in the Western form. And almost before I knew what I was doing, I had started *The Jump-Off Creek*. For a long time I didn't think it was going well, because the woman in it struck me wrong. I had made her independent and strong, and I had her doing a man's work, and I didn't have a sense of what sort of nineteenth-century woman would choose that kind of life, so probably what I was doing was writing Lydia as a man, and just putting skirts on him.

Well, eventually I started to read pioneering women's diaries, letters, memoirs, because there wasn't much straightforward material about women's daily lives in the ranching West, and I needed to know what women really did in those days – for instance, did they actually help with heavy work like branding cattle, and if they did, were they wearing their long skirts while doing it? And once I got started reading the diaries, well, they just swept me away. They changed everything. I realized I wasn't interested in writing about a lovely, fragile-looking thing who was brave as a man. And I didn't have to write about a man in a skirt. There were these real women who had done everything men had done and more, and they interested me more. At the beginning, I had thought I could just give myself a standard Homesteader Plot and pummel it a little to fit a woman. But when eventually I started to write Lydia's journal, and she told me who she was, what kind of a woman she was, the Homesteader Plot wouldn't fit. I did other research, at the Oregon Historical Society, and the Multnomah County Library, and Portland State University Library, and in Pendleton and La Grande, but it was the indigenous literature, the diaries and memoirs, I turned to most often. And the more diaries I read, the further I got from a genre Western.

I know you've been a bit surprised by the reception of your novel, by the awards it has won (including its nomination for the PEN/*Faulkner Award), and by the broad readership it has found. Why were you surprised, and what about the novel strikes so many emotional chords among its readers, do you think?*

For the two years I was at work on *The Jump-Off Creek*, I considered that the book might have to be a sort of gift to Lydia Sanderson. That I might be writing it, as Lydia had written her diary, just to please and instruct myself! I had an agent whose area of expertise and interest was science fiction. The only editors who knew my name were asking me for science fiction stories, or another children's fantasy novel. People's interest in the Western form, as far as I could see, was dead. I was so pessimistic that I had already decided, if my agent didn't want to handle a Western novel – which I thought was a definite possibility – I wouldn't break my heart over this book. I'd give it one or two tries on my own and then put it away and try to forget about it. Even when my agent wrote and said she liked the book, I still thought she might not find a willing publisher. And when Houghton Mifflin took it, I thought it might just sink like a stone down a well. And when Susan Shreve called to tell me it had been nominated for the PEN/Faulkner, in the minute or so before she'd got to the point – while she was telling me what PEN was, and what the award was about – I was wondering, why is this woman calling me? And guessing, first, that she wanted a donation for PEN. Or second, that she wanted to ask me for Ursula Le Guin's unlisted phone number! Which is not to sound humble. I knew *The Jump-Off Creek* wasn't shoot-'em-up pulp fiction, I knew it was a serious book, but I really still thought it would be perceived as a little book about a woman homesteader. Not Louis L'Amour, not a Western, but not serious Western literature, either.

Obviously, one of the things The Jump-Off Creek *features is a strong, independent woman, Lydia Sanderson – widowed, and lucky to be so, forced as she was into a bad marriage; settling, alone, on an Oregon farmstead in the last decade of the nineteenth century; finding herself bound by social convention, even in the wilderness, and by an inescapable loneliness; and finally moving toward some sort of emotional involvement with a man, equally alone now. Was it necessary to kill off Blue Odell before Lydia could accept Tim Whiteaker as a man, and not just as another hard-pressed rancher? What kind of working-out of the male-female problem was at work in this novel? The reader notices how Lydia, even though a rancher, gathers with the women and wives at social gatherings in the region. How does she reconcile this sort of gender ambiguity?*

I'm very familiar with the old Western plot necessity of killing off the faithful sidekick before the hero and heroine can get together. So it's interesting, and a little disturbing, that you see Lydia "accepting Tim as a man," after Blue's death. I certainly wanted to show them moving toward a deeper friendship – which I think was happening before Blue died – because I like Tim, and his loneliness just makes me ache for him, and makes Lydia ache for him. And I wanted to suggest, just slightly, Tim moving toward a more feminine ethic of sharing and generosity. I'm not sure if you inferred they would eventually become lovers. What I've found, is that about half the people who write to me or talk to me at book signings, say they "hope Tim and Lydia get together" eventually. One person said, "I know they get together, because I know what 'making hay' means, and at the end they're making hay!" But about half want to thank me for letting Lydia keep her independence at the end. I'm happy with any of those resolutions. Blue's death was necessary, but not for getting out of the way of a romance between Lydia and Tim. I think it was just inevitable, given the slow aggravation of the conflict between Tim and the wolfers, the fated working out of the male story.

As for Lydia associating herself with the women and wives rather than the ranchers, I don't think it would have occurred to Lydia to do otherwise. Women ranchers and homesteaders were much more common than is supposed – probably one in seven homestead claims was filed by a woman, and their rates of proving up were better than the men's. And women did much other men's work in the West, delivering the mails, hauling freight, and so forth. But in the diary evidence, you don't see many occasions of women including themselves in men's society because they're doing men's work. Lydia, though she's taken up ranching, isn't a man in skirts, and she naturally feels more at ease in the company of other nonranching women than of ranching men. I imagine that "gender ambiguity" might be something she wouldn't have recognized or considered.

One of the areas in which Lydia differs from the men in the novel, I think, is in her sexuality, which seems contained or perhaps absent. Both Tim and Blue are allowed their commerce with whores, but Lydia lacks any sort of sexual activity (at least any that is directly stated or described). Yet there's clearly a sexual undercurrent to the novel. Do you see Lydia's celibacy as appropriate, acceptable, fair?

I had been reading Western novels since I was eleven or twelve, but the journals and memoirs I read for *The Jump-Off Creek* reported things I hadn't seen very often, if at all, in novels – plain hard working, and sickness, and tedious childcare, and grief, and loneliness, and poverty, and a necessary kind of "sudden" friendship. In their diaries, women liked to make lists of books they'd read, or music they'd learned to play, embroidery finished, recipes, prescriptions for dosing illness. They liked to write poems to their husbands or children, and long, sentimental prayers. They often wrote down their resolve to be braver, or stronger. They wrote about lost love, or a child gone wrong, or an elderly parent failing. What they didn't write about were bodily functions, sex, childbirth, birth control, menstruation. You can find occasional oblique references to these things, euphemisms for pregnancy for instance, but no where did I find a woman openly writing about her sexual experience. I meant to be true to that ethic, in keeping those references out of Lydia's journal. As for her celibacy, it's certainly appropriate, I think, given the moral climate of the times, and given that she had had what I imagine was a sexually unsatisfying marriage. The sexual tension is on the men's side. Lydia finds her celibacy both acceptable and fair.

Do you see, then, this novel as a "feminist novel of the West" and yourself as a "feminist novelist of the West"? Did you write the novel with any political intent, any political program in mind?

I wanted to write a Western novel with a woman holding up the center. Women's experience of the frontier hasn't been explored very much in fiction, and I wanted to do it because it hadn't been done very often. Once I was well started, I saw there were some things I was learning or discovering, and then the book became a working out of some of the different ways men and women confronted the frontier. But I never felt I had a political intent. I want to keep on doing that kind of exploring, if I can, because it interests me. But I don't really think good fiction springs from political programs.

You do some interesting things stylistically in this novel, also. For example, you include, sporadically, excerpts from Lydia's journal, supplementing the third-person narrative with these direct, intimate insights from Lydia's consciousness. The journal, of course, was a common narrative form used by these westering women, but why the combining of forms? And were the journal entries all that sporadic? What sort of structural and thematic purposes did these entries serve? Were you ever tempted to let Lydia tell all of her story herself?

I had written more than half the novel before I decided to incorporate Lydia's diary entries into it. I'd been struggling with her, you know, she'd been a cardboard figure, that man-in-skirts. Well, I always take summers off from writing, to catch up reading, and clear the decks for the fall, and that summer, after getting about half done with the book and not thinking it was going very well, I spent three months pretty much just reading pioneering women's journals and memoirs. When I started writing again in September, I wrote a diary for Lydia as a way to start defining her personality for myself. And from the first entry she wrote, on the day she was leaving La Grande to go up to the property she'd bought on the Jump-Off, she told me who she was, in the absolute clearest way. And her personality just seemed to grow organically out of the voice in the diary, and the circumstances I'd placed her in. I had to go back and write the whole book over from the beginning, actually, because now that I had a real nineteenth-century woman in hand, I found other things had to be shifted around, adjusting to her. I had got together the elements of a traditional Western – a marauding grizzly, a cattle roundup, some bad guys rustling cattle. But when I set Lydia down in the middle of it, she skewed everything away from a genre Western storyline. It was her diary that always would see things unsentimentally, and she helped me see them that way too. But I just flat didn't want this to be entirely Lydia's story, nor told entirely in her voice. It's illuminating to see people from more than one viewpoint, and that's some of what I was after. Also I wanted to be writing a parallel men's story, Tim and Blue's story, which impinges on Lydia's story only at a few places. The men's story and the woman's define each other, I think, in ways that wouldn't have been possible if I'd stuck only to one.

You've also written fiction that is more realistic and straightforward. For example, "The Doe" and "Little Hills" and even "Personal Silence" (which is more futuristic) are set in and deal with the contemporary Northwest. Is the Pacific Northwest a generic setting for all of your fiction? Is there something about the Northwest that prompts you not only to live there but to write about it as well?

Do you see yourself as a writer who moves comfortably among styles and genres? Do you envision yourself writing again of the historical West? Do you find the West, in all of its chronological states – past, present, future – equally as interesting and provocative?

I think everything I write reflects the landscape I'm embedded in, the Pacific Northwest, and the Far West. The elements that define all my work as "Western" – sparsely populated landscapes, people living agrarian lifestyles, weather and landforms taking roles almost equal to the characters – I think these things give a kind of emotional shading and context for the other things that interest me, things to do with connecting and communicating.

The book I'm in the midst of right now probably will be called science fiction, but it's as much about landscape, and the human response to it, as *The Jump-Off Creek* was. I realize, it may be hard to get people who loved *The Jump-Off Creek* to read a book that might be labeled science fiction. I hope not. I haven't been able to imagine a different form for saying these particular things. And after that book is finished, I think I want to explore the way attitudes and policies toward "wilderness" were being worked out in the first few years of the twentieth century, when the Forest Service was just getting established. It happens that Lydia's land on the Jump-Off is right in the middle of what would become, by 1908, the Umatilla National Forest [in Oregon], so it may be the book I have in mind is a companion to *The Jump-Off Creek*. I'd just like to keep on trying to write well about whatever interests me, without feeling confined to one genre or style. I like the idea of challenging a genre, pushing its edges out, and out, so that it becomes larger, more encompassing. Sometime, I'd like to write a detective novel, and a swashbuckler adventure.

WORKS

The Jump-Off Creek. Boston: Houghton Mifflin, 1989. Novel.
Outside the Gates. New York: Atheneum, 1986. Children's novel.

Ron Hansen

A writer fascinated by both the historical and the contemporary West, Ron Hansen has spent most of his life in that West. Born in Omaha in 1947, Hansen attended Creighton University in Nebraska, and then went on to the University of Iowa Writers Workshop and to Stanford for graduate study in creative writing. He has held fellowships and teaching positions at the University of Michigan, Cornell, and the University of Arizona, and currently teaches at the University of California–Santa Cruz. Hansen also is the author of a children's book, and in the past has found his novelistic work borrowed (without acknowledgment or financial compensation) by television.

Though I first met Hansen in Ithaca, New York, and talked with him there about his work, he opted to put his responses down on paper rather than on tape. As he wrote, facetiously and with characteristic modesty, in a 1989 letter accompanying the interview: "I'm appallingly stupid when talking about my work, but a little smarter when compelled to write about it."

GREGORY MORRIS: *How much of your Nebraska life was urban, and how much country?*

RON HANSEN: I was born and raised in Omaha, a pretty good-sized city, but for most of my growing up we lived at 3188 Larimore, just about a hundred yards from meadowlands, the Chicago & Western railroad tracks, mulberry bushes, tall sunflowers, wild apple trees, and fields of hard yellow feed corn. We'd even see people on horseback pass by now and then. About twice a year we were told not to play on the tracks, and about twice a year we didn't. We skulked through the cornrows, kicked up pheasants, played with matches, hunkered down in the high weeds and looked at dirty pictures – you couldn't get much more country and still have streetlights and hotrods. We'd hear a tractor in April and run out to see some nameless man plowing, but then the cornfields were ours again until he suddenly appeared with his harvester in the fall. I haven't seen a farmer work so little since. We also have relatives who farm in Antelope County, Nebraska; Harrison County, Iowa; and Yuma County, Colorado; so I get some rural talk and feelings just passing the mashed potatoes; but I'll still feel like a city slicker if you ask me to be particular about alfalfa and sorghum.

Do you see yourself as a particular kind of Nebraskan, considering the various regions of the state and their individual identities?

Yes; I'm an Omaha kind of Nebraskan. Omaha means something in Nebraska that it doesn't mean elsewhere in America. In part, Omaha is Mecca, it's the honeymoon, the Christmas shopping trip, it's where high school girls say they're by God going to go just as soon as they graduate; but on the other hand, it's a huge and hostile place full of up-to-no-gooders and crazy ideas. Nebraskans can be real skeptical about us Omahans, and I'd probably be kidding myself if I said Omahans weren't real skeptical about me.

Do you feel that you've emerged from any sort of Nebraska tradition as a writer?

I have read and admired Wright Morris, Mari Sandoz, Willa Cather, and the less well-known Nebraska writers, but have only felt a part of their tradition insofar as we are or were all looking at much the same weather and geography. Even the families are sometimes the same. Writers haven't been taught in Nebraska in the way that William Faulkner is in Mississippi, or

Stephen King is in Maine. Perhaps that will change and the kinships will grow.

You speak (in a letter) of the "stifling provincialism" of Nebraska, and that you felt a need to escape from that sort of environment. Do you see this as the reality of that landscape, of that place?

Aren't you talking about an age-old phenomenon? Willa Cather went to New York and Wright Morris went to California. Scott Fitzgerald left Minnesota, Ernest Hemingway left Illinois, James Joyce left Ireland, Gertrude Stein left Oakland, California, because "there was no there there." William Kennedy has stayed in Albany, and there are a host of other exceptions but nearly every writer I know was raised in one place and now resides elsewhere. Whereas my twin brother, Rob, still lives in Nebraska and loves it. So do my mother and one of my sisters and nearly all the people I grew up with. Probably they're simply more heroic than I am. Weather there is truly horrifying. Hidebound attitudes tend to be entrenched in some places and intellectual pursuits are frequently treated with suspicion. "Weirdos" usually turn out to be artists. Education is being short-changed out of plain old stinginess. And so on. I hate it when I whine. Wonderful art and poetry and theater is being produced in Nebraska, but without a great deal of encouragement, and only against incredible odds. But that's really an American problem. Even a universal one. Omaha has been very good to me and Nebraska is still my home in a way, but I get pretty nasty about it when I'm there for too long.

Do you still feel nostalgic in any way, and might that nostalgia be expressed in a story like "Nebraska"?

Sure.

How does that portrait of the state play against the image captured in a story like "Wickedness"?

"Nebraska" was a fictional fugue on the theme of small-town America and was written specifically for a commemorative issue of *Prairie Schooner.* You could probably read it as part love song, part elegy, and one more part complaint, but all I was trying for was a word-picture that seemed in accordance with my own experience and memories. Sentiment and nostalgia seem acceptable under those circumstances, but I say some hard things in that story, too, just to give it the sting of truth.

"Wickedness," which is about the great blizzard of 1888, is a kind of choral piece that has darker things happening in it; and yet the portrait of Nebraska is ultimately more positive because there was so little room for pettiness then and because heroism is so pervasive in the lives of the pioneers. Elemental and primitive forces were at work in that story, so I tried to write it with the tone and rhythms and passionate dispassion of the book of Genesis. "Nebraska" probably comes later in my Old West testament: Ecclesiastes, say, or The Song of Songs.

You write, too, of the New West, particularly in your story "True Romance." Do you see a radical transformation in the West today? Do you see a change, for example, in the nature of the outlaw and of his or her crimes?

Were you to have asked me that ten years ago, I would have answered differently, but now I think everything is pretty much the same as it always was. Look into history and you'll find a West you still recognize. And outlaws don't seem a great deal different. Laziness, jealousy, greed, pride, selfishness – they are now and always were at the heart of most crimes. "True Romance" could have been placed a hundred years back but for the incidentals and the ironic, twentieth-century device of Riva's deadpan, soap-operatic, and highly unreliable narration. I began that story with the intent of treating my contemporaries in Nebraska farming, but through a great many drafts the story kept changing, from psychological thriller to zany comedy and other outposts in between. So now it's possibly too many things: a parody of romance magazines inside a plot of wrenched hearts and fierce rage, with an overlay of farce and an undercurrent or residue of horror.

What was the source of your interest in the outlaw histories, in the tradition of the Western desperadoes? Can you trace that to your childhood, to your reading there? Or is it more recent than that?

To a certain extent it just came with the territory. My mom and dad gave Rob and me cowboy boots when we were three or four and we would not ever ever take them off. We were later given fancy six-shooters and were hot stuff in the neighborhood. We played on a sheer dirt cliff called Devil's Slide that had a cave in it where it was said that Jesse James hid out on his getaway from the Northfield, Minnesota, raid. We had an old prevaricating grandfather who grew up in the late nineteenth century and he claimed he'd seen the James gang watering their horses on his stepfather's Iowa farm. Writing about outlaws was always a possibility given my interests, but I needed permission to try it and got it from the fabulators and postmodernists of the sixties and seventies who were giving our American myths and legends honest and serious attention. Were it not for John Seelye's *The Kid*, or Michael Ondaatje's *The Collected Works of Billy the Kid*, or E. L. Doctorow's *Welcome to Hard Times* and *Ragtime*, I probably would have been hesitant about squeezing into the tainted pigeonhole of the Old West.

I'm curious, too, about the origins of both Desperadoes *and* The Assassination of Jesse James by the Coward Robert Ford. *Were they in fact published in the order of their composition?*

You bet. I completed *Desperadoes* just after my thirtieth birthday, and *Jesse James* just before my thirty-fifth.

Were they conceived together, or did one grow out of the other?

Oakley Hall had just completed a historical novel called *The Adelita* and an excerpt appeared in *Playboy*. And I thought it would be both lucrative and nifty to write a historically based short story much like it. Looking for a subject, I soon decided that the James gang was just too intimidating, and I couldn't get a handle on some of the other Old West legends I read about. And then I happened on a nonfiction paperback called *The Dalton Gang*, by Harold Preece. While it was not a good book, it did lay out the chronology of the Dalton brothers' criminal journey, ending with Emmett Dalton as a scriptwriter and real estate salesman in Los Angeles. In the 1930s, Emmett returned with his wife to his home town of Coffeyville [Kansas], the scene of the Dalton gang's infamous 1892 raid on the two banks, and he was greeted as a hero. That intrigued me. I began plotting my short story and soon it was so swollen with thrilling event that I foresaw an unmanageable piece of sixty pages. I had just completed a still-unpublished contemporary novel, so a Western seemed a nice change of pace. Hence, on October first, 1976, I opened up a big blank book and wrote in pencil at the top, "Desperadoes – a novel by Ron Hansen." From then on I was committed.

Equally accidental was the book on Jesse James and Robert Ford. The James-Younger gang was a great influence on the Daltons, so I kept coming across tiny details about Frank and Jesse in the Dalton archives. Even when I scanned the nineteenth-century newspapers for a notion of what was happening in the summer of 1892, I stumbled upon the announcement that Robert Ford had been killed in his tent saloon in Creede, Colorado, by a man who thought he was avenging the killing of Jesse James. It was a bit like researching Michelangelo and inadvertently becoming expert on the fourth Pope Sixtus. Shortly after *Desperadoes* was published, I was contacted by William Kittredge saying he was editing a special Western issue of *TriQuarterly* and could I send him something. I sent a postcard saying I'd do a piece on Robert Ford and the assassination of Jesse James. About thirty pages later I knew I'd need a hundred more to get the story right. And so the book was launched.

From the very beginning, I wanted the novels to be paired: *Desperadoes* would be a day book, humorous, attractive, full of adventures, hijinks, nostalgia, and Saturday matinee shootouts; and *The Assassination of Jesse James by the Coward Robert Ford* (then titled *Nighthawks*) would be the night book, the dark side of all that, exhaustively researched, highly moral in tone, serious, even stern, and intricately constructed along the lines of Shakespeare's *Julius Caesar*. The first book was easy to write, the second quite hard, but for me the difficult pairing was essential in order to explore fully my perspectives of the Old West.

As a writer of historical fiction (or perhaps of fictive history), do you see anything specific that characterizes "a late twentieth-century view of the late nineteenth century" (in George Garrett's words)?

We find greater integrity, nobility, and humor in the late nineteenth-century than we do in our late twentieth. Criminals are usually pathetic creeps, but at least in the past their crimes *pretended* to be inspired by high-minded notions of Western chivalry or class vengeance or just continuing the Civil War. Everything now seems to be oriented toward getting a hundred bucks for yet another hit. Elderly people and women are killed for their pocket change these days. In the Old West that just didn't happen. And historical writers are charmed to know that Frank James recited Shakespeare while robbing his trains or that Emmett Dalton was likely to quote accurately from *Ivanhoe* when answering a reporter's questions. We're kidding ourselves if we think outlaws were a great deal different from the punks and hoods in the streets right now, but they did give us a kind of wild humanity that the fried and jazzed-up criminal can't.

Where might you place yourself in that world of historical writers who treat the historical West – writers like Larry McMurtry, Pete Dexter, Michael Ondaatje?

I'm a great fan of their books; I'd be pleased to be seen in their company. We're each doing something slightly different with the historical stock – I'm probably closer to Michael Ondaatje – but that's good for history and American literature.

You seem particularly concerned with blurring the line between representation and distortion of historical fact. You're very careful to acknowledge your sources, to verify the authenticity of your novels' history, and to include in Desperadoes, *at least, maps of the territory and of the town of Coffeyville, Kansas. What kind of responsibility do you see yourself as having to historical truth, as a novelist of these times and of these figures?*

I acknowledge my sources so the troubled or enterprising can check me out and know to what extent I have invented these people. In spite of that there were reviewers who thought I'd made up Emmett Dalton and that it was a reach for me to have put him in Hollywood. And there are gun and horse fanciers who have taken me to task for some pretty basic things that I have ample evidence for. Whereas everything imagined seems to go un-challenged, possibly because I work harder at making it seem real. I have visited the graves of the Jameses and the Daltons; I have prayed for the repose of their souls; I know them as human beings – how could I not then take some responsibility for what is said of them because of me? A movie producer once said she thought that in the film she was making about Jesse James, Robert Ford should have a sexual relationship with Mrs. Jesse James. Well, that would have never happened in that household, particularly with the Zee James I knew, and I said so rather insistently. *Sic transit* big bucks. My instincts are a teacher's as well as a writer's, so I strive for accuracy and clarity and I try to help the reader out.

These two novels are, of course, more than histories. They are portraits of families, of brothers; they imagine the strange ways women and men fall in love (and the odd way that women fall in love with these kinds of men), and the strange pseudonymous lives they are sometimes forced to lead in pursuit of careers that veer outside of the law. One of the most dramatic contrasts revealed in these two novels seems the surprising domesticity of these men and their families set against the violence of their vocations. Do you see this as part of your intent?

Yep; but you could also say they're portraits of families and love relationships precisely *because* they're histories. But for all their addiction to thrills and violence, those guys were your lazy, shiftless, and too-easily bored, common, Midwestern, white trash. Were they around now you'd hear the TV on all day, the house screens would have been punched out, half-painted cars would be up on blocks in the yard, and he or his wife would get drunk and talk about getting out of this dump. Every now and then their buddies would stop by for hot dogs and beer and then suddenly the house would be quiet for five or six days. And then the ne'er-do-well would ride up on a motorcycle and he'd whistle some sweet-tempered tune while he took the bike apart on the porch. In *The Moviegoer,* Walker Percy writes about Perry Mason and of having less interest in his courtroom theatrics than in the ordinary dailiness in the life of Della Street. Those are my sentiments too.

I'm also taken with the way these novels, particularly Desperadoes, *are novels of transition, of the movement from one century to the next. They seem to chronicle the death of an age, an era. And you weave the historical into the fictional to emphasize that change – for example, your use of President Garfield's assassination by Charles Guiteau is especially striking, and, of course, offers a nice parallel to Robert Ford's killing – assassination – of Jesse James.*

I hadn't really known about that until a year or so after I started writing. And then I saw how Charles Guiteau's success in getting attention throughout the trial and during the weeks before his execution must have had a profound effect on a callow, twenty-year-old boy.

More than anything, to my mind, Desperadoes *and* Assassination *seem novels about acting, about modeling: the West as American Theater.*

Exactly.

Your desperadoes are actors, both during and after their careers in crime. Their stories turn into stage productions, films, theatrical events.

I would hate to limit the books to one generalized reading, but both are, to a certain extent, about being famous enough to get ink in the newspapers. The James-Younger gang members were pure in their way because the stories only came after they'd done what they wanted to do. Jesse James began paying attention to his press clippings in the 1870s, and effectively manipulated the editorial pages of the Kansas City papers. And that is how Bob Ford first learned about him and later became obsessed by him and still later pictured how his life would be improved after he had "captured" Jesse James. John Lennon was killed by Mark Chapman and President Reagan was shot by John Hinckley while I was writing *The Assassination of Jesse James by the Coward Robert Ford*, and I borrowed some aspects of Chapman's and Hinckley's psychological profiles in my composite of Robert Ford. His problem was that his deceptions and his overweening desire for cheap fame were all too apparent to the press, and they turned on him within weeks after the killing, and within years were yearning for the great old days when Jesse sold out each edition. The Dalton gang got into outlawry through the back door of police chicanery, but once the press began writing about them they clearly began tailoring their crimes for the stories, invoking memories of the James gang on more than one occasion. The plot to rob two Coffeyville banks at the same time appears to have been hatched less for the money than the infamy of it. Emmett Dalton's prosperity in this century indirectly depended upon having his famous name in the papers, and his recuperation in the eyes of the Kansans he tried to kill came at least partly because the linkage of the Dalton name with theirs had given them stature and notoriety. *Cogito ergo sum* has given way, in the twentieth century, to the media have done me, therefore I am.

Do you see yourself ever returning to this form at all, this tradition of historical fiction? Has it played itself out in your imaginative life, or are there stories that remain to be told for you?

I don't know much else about the Old West that needs saying right now. Crazy Horse ought to be written about, but probably not by me. Buffalo Bill Cody held some fascination for me once, but he seems a hackneyed story now.

Would such fiction necessarily be confined to the American West? Do you ever feel the urge to write of other places, other men and women, within similar historical contexts?

No to the first; yes to the second. Isak Dinesen said she put her stories in the past because she didn't own the present. Likewise about me. The book I'm writing now – and insist upon being mysterious about – is set earlier in this century just for that reason [*Mariette in Ecstasy*]. Wings are added to my imagination whenever I go back in time. Up to this point I haven't been particularly comfortable writing about foreign places – I have to stop to look up the names of trees whenever the *senorita* walks along the *playa* and pretty soon the pages seem tearsheets from some language text. Possibly I'll one day know enough about another country to attempt it, but the story and theme would have to be more important to me than the locale.

The stories in Nebraska *often describe what might be called the life of the New West. Such stories as "True Romance," "Sleepless," and "Red-Letter Days" all imagine life in the contemporary West, and that life is not always that pleasant; in fact, in those first two stories life is menacing, dark, treacherous. And in the latter story, the mood is nostalgic, recollective, shaded by the past. Is this part of your own regional ambiguity?*

I don't try to write unpleasantly about the New West; it's just that the unpleasantness that *is* there seems to me to need expression. Cities are rotting in their centers while the suburbs spread like an oil spill. Ghost towns are on the rise throughout the Midwest and Great Plains. We still have that "pave paradise, put up a parking lot" mentality that Joni Mitchell sang about. I sound like a guy on the stump for some Nature Conservancy votes, but I'm not campaigning for anything in those stories but heedfulness, perspective, sympathy, and self-examination.

Considering the oddities in many of your stories in this collection – the bizarre twists in "Playland" and "Sleepless" and "His Dog" and "The Boogeyman" – is Ron Hansen showing a particularly dark side of his imagination, perhaps as antidote to the historic nostalgia of Desperadoes? *Where does this darkness come from?*

We all begin with hopes and possibilities, but only when we meet interruptions and obstacles do we have plots. Unhappiness is right there in the recipe for any dramatic conflict. And what are those stories about? "Playland" is an updated version of Genesis and the Garden of Eden myth. "Sleepless" is a ghost story about racism and psychic healing. "His Dog" is about brutality, jealousy, emotional detachment, and unrequited love. "The Boogeyman" is about contemporary soldiering in a fabulist landscape. I wasn't intentionally trying for antidotes; the subjects have determined the darkness of the approach. We don't remember dreams unless there were great oddities in them or they were the nightmares we woke up from at three in the morning. Weird things in my stories are what keep my own fascination up. The peculiarities surprise even me and are partly why I continue writing those queer little things.

What compelled you to write a children's book – The Shadowmaker *– using a character that reminds me so much of the late John Gardner?*

My sister Alice persuaded Rob and me to try composing a children's book when we were six. She knew within paragraphs that we were merely plagiarizing the good stuff from our favorite books. From that point on, however, I yearned to put together one of my own, and when I read John Gardner's *Dragon, Dragon,* I knew exactly what kind of kids' book it ought to be. You're perceptive to have seen him in my portrait of the shadowmaker. That was my homage to a great writer, teacher, and friend.

Is this something that will happen again?

I have two others that I tool around with when I have what the Irish call a touch of the poet in me. With my novels I'm pretty disciplined in my work habits, but with kids' books I really do wait for inspiration.

Do you find yourself writing beyond that child-audience in such a book? Is it even necessary to look beyond that readership?

Children's books are hard to sell because there are so many censors out there trying to protect the wee ones, and even great editors are too often reading from the perspective of adults. Some famous famous children's book writers are great bores to the kids who have to read or listen to their stories. Wildness and whimsy are what children want. *Little Red Riding Hood* is wonderful not because of the horror or the high-toned message, but because the wolf dresses up in the grandmother's clothes and the wily little girl foils his nefarious plot. I try to think about that with kids' books, and then hope that child in my grown-up readers will respond just as the younger ones do.

I was struck by the aesthetic choices you made as editor of the anthology of love stories, You Don't Know What Love Is. *You stated your preference for "stories of emotional persistence"; you declared that it is "spirit, shrewdness, percipience, and a cause or pursuit that matter" that mark a fiction as important, enduring, worth reading. Yet you include in that anthology writers of markedly different styles, traditions, concerns. Is contemporary American fiction so expansive, so capable of embracing such variety and such significance? And do you see yourself as belonging to a particularly conservative aesthetic tradition, the moral tradition (as John Gardner called it)?*

Anthologies are hard to judge because you just never know which stories were excluded because the publication rights were too expensive, that particular theme had already been done slightly better, certain kinds of writers were already represented, and so on. I liked every story in *You Don't Know What Love Is;* I just wish my budget had been bigger and that the collection could have been longer. I do indeed believe that contemporary American fiction is incredibly various and expansive. Stories by Andre Dubus, Amy Hempel, Joyce Carol Oates, Stephanie Vaughn, John L'Heureux, or Jim Shepard have almost nothing in common beyond their individual excellence. I hope that enterprising spirit continues. I don't embrace the wide world as Walt Whitman did, but I do find it hard to hate serious literature. I agreed with a good half of what John Gardner said in his *On Moral Fiction,* but he was just plain wrong about some of the good books he slammed against the wall. And he knew it. Having said that, I'll also say that I don't think I'm especially conservative in my aesthetics, but the Omaha altar boy in me couldn't help but hope to be part of something as highfalutin as a moral tradition in literature, even if none of us can truly know which American writers will be invited to that party.

WORKS

The Assassination of Jesse James by the Coward Robert Ford. New York: Alfred A. Knopf, 1983. Novel.

Desperadoes. New York: Alfred A. Knopf, 1979. Novel.

Mariette in Ecstasy. New York: HarperCollins, 1991.

Nebraska. New York: Atlantic Monthly Press, 1989. Short fiction.

The Shadowmaker. New York: Harper & Row, 1987. Children's novel.

You Don't Know What Love Is: Contemporary American Stories. Edited by Ron Hansen. Princeton, N.J.: Ontario Review Press, 1987. Short fiction.

John Keeble

Though he has lived in eastern Washington for nearly twenty years, John Keeble came to the United States from Winnipeg, Manitoba, where he was born in 1944. Like many other writers in this collection, Keeble attended the University of Iowa Writers Workshop, graduating with an M.F.A. in 1969. Keeble taught in Iowa for a time, and borrowed that Iowa landscape for his second novel, *Mine* (written in collaboration with his good friend, Ransom Jeffery). Since 1973, however, Keeble has taught in the English Department at Eastern Washington University in Cheney, and lives with his family in a rural, hand-hewn home in Medical Lake. More recently, Keeble's interests have taken him to Alaska in pursuit of answers to the 1989 Exxon *Valdez* oil spill; Keeble's analysis found expression in his book *Out of the Channel: The Exxon Valdez Oil Spill in Prince William Sound.* The matter of corporate influence upon the physical and human landscape is a persistent concern of Keeble's fiction, as well.

As with two other interviews in this collection, this conversation with Keeble took place at the 1989 meeting of the Western Literature Association in Coeur d'Alene, Idaho. Keeble spoke there in patient, considered voice about his work, his life; between sentences, or even in mid-sentence, Keeble would pause as if to allow his thought to come full measure before permitting it expression. Remnants of his Canadian origins accented Keeble's speech.

GREGORY MORRIS: *You're a native of Canada and came to the United States when young. In one of your essays you write about the matter of boundaries, of national boundaries, and of nationality being at odds with character. How much of that immigrant experience, which is a major part of your fiction, has been a part of your own experience, has become a part of your own personality?*

JOHN KEEBLE: I came to the United States at a fairly young age, so I wouldn't say that I had an immigrant experience, in the sense that somebody like an Hungarian refugee would have. It was nothing like that. What I did have, from the time when we first began thinking about coming to the United States until our eventual move to this country, was a sense of suspension, a sense of a national suspension, and I think that has worked its way into my fiction.

But the idea that's expressed in *Yellowfish*, that the Canadian West Coast and the U.S. West Coast have more in common than Vancouver does with Montreal is not an original idea. Joel Garreau, in his *Nine Nations of America*, was working on basically the same idea, that the true boundaries of the North American regions are different from the national boundaries and even, of course, from the state boundaries. We're in the "empty quarter," according to Garreau: Montana, Wyoming, eastern Oregon and northern Nevada, and eastern Washington and eastern British Columbia.

Empty in what sense?

It's essentially an area of resource, and there's not much political clout emanating from this area, although eastern Washington now has Tom Foley.

So you do see this portion of the West as politically – not impotent – but underempowered?

Politically, it's underempowered, and it tends to be managed by outside interests, whether they be governmental interests, federal interests, or corporate interests. Moreover, it's managed by these interests to an extent, relative to the input from the people, that is greater than in other areas of the country. I've been going back and forth to Alaska, and so I've really got that state on my mind. Alaska's an even more extreme case. Alaska is really functioning as a resource colony for the United States and other parts of the world. The extent to which life here is governed or run by the federal government or by corporate interests outside is almost nothing compared to what it is in Alaska.

You wrote in one of your letters that you've changed your view on the Exxon oil spill. What did you mean by that?

Well, my views have changed or developed in some very substantial ways that I probably don't fully understand yet. That's why I'm writing the book on the spill, *Out of the Channel.* I think what I was referring to specifically in the letter, was that at first it was oil – oil was everywhere, and that was the preoccupation of anyone who had anything to do with that situation. But then, very rapidly, it became money; the primary concern was money. Money behaved like oil.

How so?

In Prince William Sound, so far as the relationship of the geography of the place or the landforms to the oil is concerned, the most compelling thing you find is the extreme irregularity of the shorelines. So you could go to a beach and find the beach bisected: half of it would be oiled and half would be either not oiled at all or only very lightly oiled. And that was caused by peculiarities of the landform and of tide and of wind and current.

Then the money behaved the same way. The money would find people, and other people wouldn't get found by this money, or they would refuse to have anything to do with it, or they would drag their feet. Maybe they were uncertain whether or not they really wanted to go to work for Exxon or one of its subcontractors, or maybe they objected to it on principle, or maybe they just had bad luck. The money was a mirror of the oil.

That whole incident seems to play on, or play out, your sense of corporate evil that's at work in your fiction, particularly in Broken Ground.

That's one of the things that I'm trying to come to a better understanding of. I think there is a handful of things I have been working to understand that the oil spill will help me bring to some kind of completion. And that's one of them. I'm trying to think this out. It seems to me that Exxon's response is systemic, that they must respond in certain ways, and that they're really powerless to respond in certain other ways; a number of options are not open to them. One of the options that doesn't seem open is to tell the truth, and I'm not sure whose fault that is. If I can figure out the answer to that question, then I suppose my sense of what corporate evil is will have become a little more defined.

One of the most compelling things about the oil spill is the contrast between the response of Exxon people and response of the people who live there, who are frequently very independent-minded. I mean they live on the bottom edge of our time. These are people – especially the fishing people – who are accustomed to making decisions fairly rapidly, and to acting upon those decisions. They have to do that in order to survive. They live lives of action. Every time I've been up there someone has died – fishing or on a tugboat or something. So this is a little different breed of person from your typical American, who is likely to walk *around* the block to avoid trouble.

I haven't encountered anyone there who isn't outraged by the effect of the oil spill upon their place, and these people took action. They enlisted into all kinds of volunteer groups to try to do something about it. That response is just miles apart from the sort of response that a company the size of Exxon made; there's an incredible lag. I think there's something there about the relationship between a large corporation that must behave systemically, and individual people who prefer to be responsible. As you say, this is something I've been concerned with in my fiction all along; this Alaska project is a factual articulation of a previous myth.

You've talked about the "self-mythification" of the Northwest, and I was curious about what you meant by that. What sorts of myths do you see operating within this particular region?

I'm not quite sure what that was. I think that was kind of a caution, wasn't it? I feel very deeply about the place that I live in; I'm really interested in the history of the place, and I like its frontier spirit, insofar as it still exists.

Are you talking about the Northwest, or about Medical Lake, Washington, where you live?

The Northwest. I appreciate the natural beauty of the place. I live in the country myself, but at the same time I think that where self-mythification is concerned, the writers who live here need to be very careful not to become self-indulgent about their pleasure of place. I've served on several literary committees out here – and I think that's what got me to thinking about this, because you read stories about fishing and bird poems until you just can't stand it anymore! They are often little more than merely pretty.

But at the same time, as you say, you're very interested in the history of the place, and you make significant use of that history (and of its artifacts) in your work. Yet you don't descend into that self-mythification.

I hope not. My view is that history has to be kept in a picture along with contemporary reality. So you have to think about *power* and where the economic power is and where the political power is; as long as you keep doing that, I think you'll be more or less okay, because that will keep you honest. What worries me is the number of writers – and I suppose the number of people, too – who sort of descend into an insular idyll.

The lifestyle you've chosen, though, is a country, rural existence, a sort of hand-hewn existence. Is that itself a sort of retreat?

Sure, and that may be one of the things that's in the back of my mind, too, as a form of self-correction.

But in terms of your own way of life – as I understand it, you built your own house, and you've written about the "meditative act" of work. Can you sink too deeply into that work-spirit? For example, Hank Lafleur, in Broken Ground, *seems to come close to being addicted to work or being seduced by work.*

Well, I think that's part of the point, that yes, he comes very, very close to being too enmeshed in his work – and there are reasons for that which have to do with his domestic crisis, so the work is restorative, emotionally. But the danger is just what you were saying: People sink into it so deeply that they fail to see what's going on around the edges or who they're working for.

And in the kind of work that Lafleur does, the operation of machines upon the land and the landforms, you seem to oppose two ideas: the idea that rock is carnal, and the idea that politics is geological. You have those two forces at play in the novel, with Lafleur, as he operates that machine, tearing up that earth and deriving a sort of carnal, erotic satisfaction from operating that machine, and unearthing a whole host of ghosts. At the same time, he's also committing a political act, in a sense.

I think that's really interesting, and this is coming to play again in the whole Alaska business because the people who understood the most about the oil . . . from the very beginning the people who knew best what was going to happen were the fishermen. They, too, are marauders, in a way; they use machinery in order to catch huge quantities of fish. I was just talking to someone yesterday who told me a record was broken for the number of fish caught in one day by a single seining boat – it was 225,000 salmon. That's a lot of fish! But you've got a sonar device and radar and all that high-tech stuff, and big seining nets, the whole deal. At the same time, though, a person like that knows more about the natural world than just about anybody else because they're in day-to-day contact with it. So there's a contradiction there. I don't know what the resolution of that contradiction will be.

Speaking of the land again, which always seems at the center of your fiction, you consistently invest that land with a very real spiritual quality. That spiritual quality has its origins in an Eastern, Zen-like perspective. It also seems to come, to a lesser degree, from the Native American tradition; but there isn't a strong Native American presence in your fiction, except in terms of the past and of the aboriginal culture.

Well, there's a writer named Elizabeth Cook-Lynn, a Sioux who also teaches at Eastern Washington University; she's brought me to understand that white people have a bad habit of dealing with Indians as if they were all the same. She says the tribes are different. When you say "coyote tale," for example, which tribe are you talking about? I used to think that the coyote tales were commonly held stories. Liz Cook made me aware that one has to be very careful, and I backed off. I think I made more use of Native American material earlier in my work than I have lately, and I've become more interested in white mythology. I'm really interested in Native American culture, but one simply has to be very careful and scrupulous about it. You need to have knowledge. If you don't have it, then you'd better just wait until you get it.

On this question of spiritualism, I'm looking for a proof of God. If I could find it, then I would know.

Is it something to be found, though, in a white mythology? Given what has happened recently to the landscape – in Prince William Sound, in the West – is such a spiritual essence possible within a white belief structure?

That's a good question. So much white activity is antispiritual. The division between secular activity and sacred activity is very clear in our society, and it's also very clear which one is dominant.

Let me shift direction a bit here, and ask you about your first two novels, Crab Canon *and* Mine. *Both of those works seem part of that 1960s and 1970s style of parody and of self-reflexive fiction. Clearly, there was a radical shift in your fiction after those first two novels, a shift that demands more of the reader and of the reader's patience – the storytelling is slower and steadier. Whereas in those early works, you do a lot of technical experimentation: the shifting of narrative perspective in* Crab Canon *and the collaborative effort in* Mine. *These early works demand something different of the reader than what is demanded in* Yellowfish *and* Broken Ground.

I hadn't thought of the *pace* of the early works. I always had thought that *Crab Canon* was almost impossibly difficult. I was twenty-four when I finished writing that book – I don't know if that means anything or not – but I was fairly young. There *is* a lot of parody in it. But I think that *Crab Canon* probably contains the seeds of everything that I've written since then; some things have become more carefully worked out – for instance, we were talking about the Native American material, and certainly there's a big contrast between the way that's handled in *Crab Canon* and the way it's handled in *Yellowfish* or *Broken Ground.* There's a definite development there for the better.

Point of view? I don't know. It's certainly true that there was experimentation with point of view going on in *Crab Canon.* I started writing it in third person, then changed it. In a way, it's like a very early twentieth-century European novel – maybe because I was reading the European writers very seriously during the time I wrote that. It's also an antiwar novel, which is the purpose of the seemingly senseless violence in it, and maybe it's a work of deconstruction, too, though I had never heard that term then. The various points of view in conflict, so that there are questions of veracity. One of my ideas was to make a work of art that ripped itself apart before the reader's eyes, which is what I felt our society was doing.

Mine was written in six months.

Did you each – you and Ransom Jeffery, who wrote the novel with you – did you each adopt a voice of one of the two narrators, Rag or St. James?

Yes, and we drafted it by mail. Actually, it started out as kind of a joke because we each had sort of an empty space and we decided to fill it with this project. The technique was to try to put the other narrator in an inextricable position, so it actually was written as kind of a serial novel. Then we joined together with our families for a couple of months and put the book together. As for the voices, I wrote the St. James portions; a lot of people guess the opposite.

I wish we had been older when we did it, because I think it was a fascinating idea. Of course, both *Crab Canon* and *Mine* were coming out of the sixties, but in a certain way *Mine* was a step forward. The rather postured fragmentation of view in *Crab Canon* evolved into a work of collaboration by two truly different beings – Ransom and myself. So, to me, *Mine* was an act of healing through story and friendship.

Part of that novel seems to come out of your own experience at the University of Iowa. Did you have any particular influences there, at Iowa, upon your work?

A man named William Murray essentially told me that it was okay for me to write, which was what I needed to hear. I didn't realize until later how important it was for somebody to tell me that, because I was very unsure about my work. I can vividly remember writing *Crab Canon*. I can remember perfectly the order in which the chapters were written, and I still think of the book *that* way as opposed to the way it came out. The novel was restructured by an editor, who instead should have made me bear down on it in some areas and clean it up in other areas. I wish he had. Anyway, I can still see the narrators of the chapters coming out of this hall of mirrors, which is the book. There's a long history section in it, broken into two chapters, the McGrath chapters. That was one of the last things I wrote, that and the two short chapters which are still at the end. And if I think about those two little chapters and the big historical chapters as the *end* of that project, then it becomes very clear to me how I got to *Yellowfish*.

There was a significant interval of years in between those two books.

I wrote a play in there –

Salt?

Yes. And we published *Mine* in 1974. I also did some short stories. One, "The Transmission," came out in 1976 [*American Review 25*], and as I drafted it, I worked out the third-person narration I would use in the later novels, but the story came out as a first-person narration after all. *Yellowfish* didn't come out until 1980.

Is Salt *a Western play?*

It's set in Missouri. It's a play about real estate. You'd probably see the same kind of change going on there that you see in my fiction; it was very political. You see, *Crab Canon* was political, but it kind of attacked positions while I think *Yellowfish* tries to locate a position. One of the big problems for writers, especially writers nowadays, is how to not avoid position, and at the same time not compromise the complexity of experience they're trying to represent. And I feel I've solved that, for my own work anyway.

You see, that's why I think Yellowfish *and* Broken Ground *are much more substantial. Maybe it's because you take the time to work out the narrative detail, but they're more traditional kinds of fiction; the characters are thinking, and the reader is thinking out the complexities. They're demanding in a different kind of way.*

Well, maybe it's a matter of maturity. One eventually realizes that to come on to something straightforwardly does not necessarily mean that it's not going to be complicated. That's maturation.

You mention in your essay "Making Things Up in the West," [Willow Springs, Fall 1982] Wallace Stegner's notion that the Western hero has died as a possibility. Yet your own heroes seem to "walk down" (as Stegner puts it) their crises, their moral dilemmas. Do you think people like Wesley Erks, in Yellowfish, *and Hank Lafleur, in* Broken Ground, *fit the notion of the hero? Perhaps they're a new kind of hero, or Western hero, if you want to be that specific.*

There are differences in each man's situation. Erks, legally, is in a much more complex situation. And Lafleur is older. Erks is also a little more bigger than life than Lafleur is. In each case, though, I think it's an act of faith on the writer's part to go ahead and create such characters. Partly, it's for the sake of the reader, who must be weary of all these characters at dead ends, their lives leading nowhere. John Hawkes and Beckett are great writers, but I'm of a different generation and I too am bored with all that, I'm tired. I'm interested in characters who actually are going to try to *do* something, even though it may be futile. I guess I'm trading in the description of the existential dilemma for existential action.

You've talked before about the capable male presence in your work, how it's elemental. But what seems to be absent in your work is a successful and satisfactory relationship between men and women. Erks and Ruby know some satisfaction in their relationship, but there's also a real strong undercurrent of tension, a real strong hint of the possibility of ruin.

Well, they're powerful people, they're dynamic people, both of them. Ruby has a lot of power, and I think the two of them are likely to stay together against the world. Actually, I was following my own subconscious route as I wrote, but at certain points I would think, Ha! What's going to happen if you write a book with a hero that's a little larger than life, and a book that's promarriage and a book that has a child in it that actually is not the offspring of presently divorced parents?

And even the relationship that Lafleur, in Broken Ground, *has with the woman at the construction site – with Iris – she too has power, though she's sort of been seduced by the corporation. But there's a very real and very satisfactory erotic element in that relationship.*

That was scary, for me, that character. She was one of the scariest characters I've ever written, for reasons that I still don't fully understand.

She's a very ambiguous character – she's a very attractive character, but in the end she conspires to get rid of Sabat and to become part of that corporate conspiracy of power.

She's putting herself forward.

But in a morally ambiguous way, as opposed to somebody like Ruby, who is strong and capable and powerful but in a more moral way.

Well, what she did was, she knew what was happening and she didn't tell Lafleur. She understood before he did what was going on, and she didn't tell him. She let him float toward trouble so that he wouldn't impede her advantage. That's the evil element in her action.

One thing I want to get to is the "weird telemetry" that operates in your novels, that idea of measuring distance between self and place, and between self and time. For example, your use of the Colnett journals in Broken Ground *and of the drawings in those journals –*

Those are amazing drawings. I had to find a way to get those drawings into the novel, I was so struck by them.

They're fascinating exercises in perspective.

Well, my use of that telemetry has to do with relationship and exploration, with the relationship between your position and what you're looking at. I suppose that ultimately it moves toward the dissolution of the surveyor's triangulation; I think that's where it's headed. To dissolve that, I think, and to merge with the substance, would be the objective. I'm not sure if either Erks or Lafleur have got that yet.

Well, it doesn't seem so for Erks. But I was thinking it was a matter of consciousness, of being consciously in relation to things.

For Lafleur, certainly, it's almost occupational – it *is* occupational. It has to do with the writer, also, and with the writer's relation to the material. The writer is either in the material or outside the material, or both, kind of like the map and Colnett's ship.

Do you see yourself as an anti-institutional writer?

Sure. I'm sort of an insurrectionist, I think, doing as much as I can do, without hurting my children.

That sense of familial responsibility and of familial community comes through strongly in your work. Hank Lafleur, for example, holds out the possibility that he will return, that that fractured family will cohere again, will heal even after the loss.

What happened to them – their daughter's drowning – is something that came from the outside. Even though he blames himself – he's wrong, of course, to blame himself, and he knows that – the fact that it is something that happened from the outside is what will cause them to come back together again. It's really not between them, it's exterior, although it had an incredible interior impact.

The dramatic choice of that kind of event, of that child's drowning, which I had previously linked to Hector Zeta and the death of their child –

That story's true, by the way, but it's not Hector Zeta who's involved, it's someone else. Everything in that little story, "Zeta's House," is true, except that the characters are fiction, including Hector Zeta.

So all the material in Broken Ground *from* The Manifesto of Spirits *is fictional, is material you created?*

Yes. I probably shouldn't have told you. I probably should have kept it secret!

Broken Ground *and* Yellowfish *seem attempts to move beyond (or behind) postmodernism, and postmodern technique –*

Yellowfish and *Broken Ground* are reactions against "postmodernism," or even against "modernism." *Crab Canon* asserts my connection to this course of reaction. I'm not alone. There are quite a few writers – Toni Morrison, for example – writing in a different way about a very different life. Writers who are interested in engaging fiction with the world in a direct way, and in investing fiction with a sense of political reality and also a sense of mythical reality. So I think there's the generational business in operation here. I have two ways of looking at it: one is from the standpoint of me, the writer. It's been a struggle to work through and to continue to work through some of

162

these concerns. At the same time, insofar as I may be a literary phenome-non, what I'm doing is a parallel to things that other writers are doing in their work.

I think there is this reaction, and I see it largely in the West, where I think myth is such a large part of existence. And so is politics.

Yes, and the West has a really shallow literary tradition. I mean the roots of it, the written language, don't go very far back. At least in the white tradi-tion. And it's exciting, all these very good writers.

And perhaps undervalued writers?

Yeah, but that's okay. Then we can sneak up on 'em. I mean the East Coast still doesn't really understand what, say, James Welch is doing or what Ivan Doig is doing, or even what Wallace Stegner and Ursula Le Guin have done. How could they? They'd have to give some time to it.

So the West, the region, generates its own literary culture, with its magazines and its communities of writers?

Yes, but the other part of that is what we were talking about previously – I think it's important that Western writers not become entrenched in their Westernness, because the world doesn't operate that way anymore. I mean, the Alaskan fishery is controlled by the Japanese; you can't write poems about salmon without knowing that.

You were once identified as an "adventure writer," and I suppose the elements of the genre are there in your fiction: the elements of mystery and threat and voyage and that sort of thing. But to define your last two novels as "adventure novels" –

Well, I would never have imagined that I was an adventure writer until the paperback book cover of *Yellowfish* said that it was a "thriller" or something like that. Then *Writer* magazine contacted me and wanted me to write an article on writing the "adventure novel." Which I did, but it's really just an indicator of commerce so they know where to stock the book in the book-stores.

But I liked [Robert Louis] Stevenson when I was a kid. He's a great writer, a much better stylist than he's given credit for, and he writes these great tales. I loved Dickens too; I started reading Dickens when I was in high school. I wouldn't classify Dickens as an adventure writer, but he has a very strong sense of story.

And of character. I really think that's what it comes down to in your later two novels, that the characters are so substantial.

Well, I like something that has a sense of strong motion. Again, that sort of fits into that antipostmodern position. For a while, I was raised to think, when I was taking literature courses in college in the late 1960s, that if you wrote a novel that had a really strong plot, it was by definition no good. Later, I corrected my thinking because I remembered that I loved Stevenson and Dickens.

What you describe as your concerns as a writer seems to fit into John Gardner's definition of moral fiction, with its emphasis upon strong plot, strong narrative, strong character. Do you see yourself as part of that school?

I read that book [*On Moral Fiction*] and I agree with what he said, for the most part, but I don't agree with his handling of examples; most everybody gets trashed in the book. But if you write a book with action, then that in itself says something about your position in relation to all these things we've been talking about. If you write action, then obviously the characters are going to have to act, and that's different from sitting in a trashcan through the entire play. We now understand that the world is limited, we understand that there are no ultimate answers available to us. We don't even have very many workable illusions left anymore. But at the same time, does that mean you can conduct your life without making a decision and then acting upon that decision and taking the consequences of that action? That's the way I see it. So then I started writing novels that had a coherent and thought-out line of action, and the line of action was created by characters.

So there you have it – maybe that's antipostmodernism. I think it's simultaneously forward-looking and reactionary. Which is sort of where I am politically, also.

I think Beckett is a great writer. I love Beckett, and yet I can hardly stand to read him anymore. It's like he went out as far as he could go, he explored the nether regions of emptiness – and that's great, but how long can you do that? How long does it take you to realize that, yeah, we're doomed – now what? There has to be time for laughter and thrill and tears during our brief sojourn on earth.

WORKS

Broken Ground. New York: Harper & Row, 1987. Novel.

Crab Canon. New York: Grossman, 1971. Novel.

With Ransom Jeffery. *Mine.* New York: Grossman, 1974. Novel.

Out of the Channel: The Exxon Valdez Oil Spill in Prince William Sound. New York: HarperCollins, 1991. Nonfiction.

Yellowfish. New York: Harper & Row, 1980. Novel.

William Kittredge

William Kittredge was born in 1932 in southeastern Oregon, and grew up there on his family's large desert cattle ranch. Kittredge managed the operation until 1967, when the farm was sold. Following a stint at the University of Iowa Writers Workshop in 1968–69, Kittredge took a position at the University of Montana, in Missoula, where he continues to teach and to direct the creative writing program. Kittredge has exerted a special influence upon contemporary Western writing, as a fiction writer, as an essayist, and as an editor. One of his most significant efforts has been the putting together, with Annick Smith, of the volume of Montana writers titled *The Last Best Place: A Montana Anthology* (Smith and Kittredge were also two of the three coproducers of the film version of Norman Maclean's *A River Runs Through It*).

Kittredge was one of a trio of writers interviewed at the 1989 Western Literature Association conference held in Coeur d'Alene, Idaho. The towering resort hotel which housed the conference served as an appropriately ironic backdrop for Kittredge's comments on the West, on what it has become and is becoming. Kittredge is a hefty, impressively headed man. His laugh, which rises often in accompaniment to his words, takes a deep seat. As he talks, he smokes.

GREGORY MORRIS: *I'm interested in how you seem to have become a spokesman for Western fiction* –

WILLIAM KITTREDGE: You mean shooting my mouth off every chance I get?

No, no! I mean, you seem to have established a voice for the literature of the New West – for example, in your essay "Doors to Our House."

Well, in about 1978, I felt I really was not going much of anyplace – writing a story here and there and drinking a lot and chasing around – and I started going to some symposiums. At Sun Valley [Idaho], in 1976, they had a thing on Western film – a brilliant symposium. I don't know where they got the money, but they had every old actor and every old director still alive; they showed about three hundred movies, and they had every academic who had ever published in the field. The symposium lasted for four days and it was astonishing. I suddenly discovered a whole field and received a liberal education in it in four days. I started thinking about a lot of issues that I'd never thought about before, and began to get some *political* ideas. And at that point I discovered I had some things to say about these matters. It started there.

Then Terry McDonald, who started *Rocky Mountain Magazine* in 1979, asked me to write an essay for him. I said, I don't know how to write an essay. And he said, Well, it's not very hard, and he told me how on the telephone. He made it easy. After three or four more of these essays I began to think, Let's see if we can't get a certain kind of arc into this and maybe make a book out of it. Then in about – I don't know when I put that book (*Owning It All*) together, 1985 or 1986, whenever it was – I sat down and spent two or three months rescrambling some of that stuff (a lot of that book is not the way it originally appeared) and making a book manuscript out of it. I didn't expect much from the book, but it's had a life and a nice response.

The whole phenomenon of Western fiction – and of Montana fiction, in particular – seems to have drawn a strong response. Why do you think that is?

A lot of energy has accumulated in Western writing of late. People are paying attention to it; I know that in Montana, at least, a lot of attention is paid to writers and to their ideas. That attention is due both to historical accident and to the work of a lot of people.

A man named H. G. Merriam started the writing program long ago at Missoula. He also started a magazine called *Frontier and Midland;* it was a wonderful literary magazine, from right after the First World War on. Then in 1946, Leslie Fiedler came to Missoula, and Montanans hated him in ways and loved him in ways; but he was a great teacher and you see his influence all over Montana – you go to Circle and you'll find people who want to tell you about the course they took from Fiedler thirty-five years ago and how it's changed their life. So Montana's covered with these people who take ideas and books seriously, and a lot of it has to do with Fiedler. Then Dick Hugo came when Fiedler left in 1964, and Hugo had Jim Welch and Rick DeMarinis in the first class he taught. So all these things began to build. There've been a lot of lucky accidents.

It is interesting how Montana has developed as a sort of community of writers, all over Montana.

Yeah, all over the place. Tom McGuane told me that he was really looking for a good town to live in where the fishing was terrific. He said it came down to Bend, Oregon, or Livingston, Montana. He finally picked Livingston, of course. And he had a great talent for attracting his friends, so suddenly everyone was moving to Livingston. And in Bozeman, you've got David Quammen, and in Kalispell you've got David Long. There's just a lot of good writing coming out of the area. Somebody asked me the other day about writers with growing reputations and I said, I don't know, maybe Patricia Henley – she's a wonderful writer, another Bozeman person, and she's just getting better and better and better and better. And there's Mary Blew – I think this book of essays she's doing [*All But the Waltz*] is just going to be a knockout.

Surely, the anthology you did with Annick Smith, The Last Best Place, *had a lot to do with this "renaissance." How did that collection come about?*

We were at a conference in Montana, and all the people who later did *The Last Best Place* were there. None of us knew each other at the time. Afterward, Annick Smith and I were driving home from the conference and we thought, We really ought to do a book of Montana writers, which we envisioned as a slim, modest volume and which ended up being a massive thing: *The Last Best Place!*

Massive, but powerful. The memoir by Richard Hugo, for instance – "The Milltown Union Bar: You Could Love Here" – that's such an emotionally overwhelming essay.

Isn't that great stuff? Hugo had an enormous influence, a great humanizing influence, a kind of antimythological influence in Montana. He kept telling people, Your life is interesting, you can make art out of your life. Kids from Plentywood could not imagine that Plentywood was worthy of art, and Hugo said sure it was – he would tell them that over and over again. It's true: people who've lived in isolation and who've looked into themselves a little bit, once they get some faith in the stories they have to tell and get to know those stories are valuable (which takes a little doing), then suddenly they really bloom. For example, Ralph Beer's a guy who'd dropped out – he had a degree from Bozeman [Montana State University] finally, a degree in English or something – and he was back getting a teacher training certificate in Missoula; he took a class from Bill Bevis and wrote a personal essay in a Montana writers class. Bill showed me the essay and I said, Get that guy over here, we've got to coopt him right away! And we did. He is a wonderful writer.

Did you have some sense, before you (unlike Beer's protagonist) left the ranch, that writing was something you wanted to do?

Oh, yeah. I was one of those guys who went to college because they didn't want to go into the Army, during the Korean War, and ended up in my junior year in college, at Oregon State, taking an English class and realizing that, Jesus Christ, this stuff is pretty good. I was one of those kids who discovers books – like somebody turned the light on. I took a class from Malamud when he was teaching there – he'd just published *The Natural* – Christ, they had him teaching five sections of composition and he had all these jocks in class, friends of mine. I remember he always made them go outside and run around the building during class; he said, If you guys don't do anything else, you might as well get in shape. I kind of hated him, and I'm sure he hated me – I was an arrogant twenty-one-year-old – but I got that idea of being a writer in my head.

When I got out of school, I really tried to write. I went into the Air Force, and worked at it for a year or so; I wrote a novel, which was a terrifically silly novel, and finally abandoned the whole idea as hopeless and pointless. Then at the age of thirty-two or thirty-three – I worked it out once, but I don't remember now exactly when it was – I decided that if I was ever going to do this, I'd better get at it. Just do it every day, whether it works or it doesn't work. The first thing that ever worked came when, after about eight or nine months, I went back and found that old novel that I'd written when I was twenty-one or twenty-two and made a short story out of it. It was the first thing I ever got published. I sent it off to *Northwest Review* – I was sending stuff out all over the place; I figured I'd never see any of these people, so who cared what they thought, they were so foreign to my life. And *Northwest Review* sent it back and said they'd like to publish the story, if I'd work with them to make some changes. I really debated with myself – I didn't want anybody messing with my sacred pages, you know – and finally I said, Well, okay, we'll try it. Thank God I did, because they changed everything but not enough; it was still pretty terrible! Then I was lucky enough to write "The Waterfowl Tree," which they probably sent back ten times for changes; I was perfectly illiterate, you know, may still be – but Ralph Salisbury and Jon Haslip were terrific for me; they kept sending this stuff back and working it through and sending it back and working it through. I know now what an imposition that was on them; I didn't know that at the time, but having been in these positions myself I know how ill-inclined you are to actually pick a story out and work with somebody. I owe those people a lot.

That image, in "The Waterfowl Tree," of those ducks hanging from the tree – that's an image derived from your experience, isn't it? I think you write about that image in one of your essays.

That's true. I started with that notion. I wrote another story called "The Waterfowl Tree," which was no good at all, I knew it and I didn't even send that one out. Then I tried to write this story. My father had had a stroke, and he came back to the Warner Valley, in Oregon, while I was still there, to go hunting with a guy; he had a limp and a cane, and this other guy wanted to go hunting. They had a Jeep Wagoneer – it was one of those thirty below days when there are no clouds in the sky, an actual bluebird day – and the only place there were any birds was across the valley in this swamp. My dad couldn't go out there, but his friend and I waded through tules higher than our heads with flags, and got out there next to this open water and there must have been fifty thousand birds out there. I mean, it was astonishing. We had the wit not to shoot, to just sit there – it would have been like shooting off your shotgun in a cathedral. We looked at this for about forty-five minutes, and then turned around and walked out – that was all we could handle – and we got in the car and said, Aw, I don't think we'll shoot anything, and drove away. Almost immediately I knew there was a story someplace in there. I don't think I managed it necessarily too well, but it was the first story that worked really, and that was lucky again. But I was writing a lot of stories; I was writing, I think, a story every two weeks at that point and mailing them out, and out of every fifty only one was any good.

Then, when the book – *We Are Not in This Together* – was published, Ray Carver went through them all again and marked them up.

He really edited the stories?

Oh, yeah, he made plenty of changes. Sometimes the changes are small, but there'll be lines changed here and there. I took all his changes too, pretty much.

I noticed that some of the stories that appeared first in The Van Gogh Field *and later were included in* We Are Not in This Together *had been changed.*

You bet. Some of them were changes that I saw and some of them were Ray's ideas, and I still have a couple of stories that were originally going to be in that manuscript that weren't in there that will be in the next one, that have changes that he marked in them. His revisions were tremendously useful and educational; I'd say, Okay, I can see what he's talking about, I can see that that doesn't work.

The changes were more stylistic in nature?

Yeah, little changes here and there. I don't think they were anything very major, nothing to do with intent. Once in a while there'd be a line – or a line of dialogue – that bothered him, things like that. I've never been a particularly wonderful writer of dialogue – I think I'm better at it than I used to be, but I never *listened* to people, it was too much in my head. Writing like Ray did was just hard work for me; he had a great ear for the way people talked, and I just never had it. He would listen to people – I remember going to parties with him and coming out and he'd be half-loaded, and then he would say, Did you hear . . . ? And he'd recite to you some five minutes of conversation he'd snooped on over his shoulder between this couple, which he had verbatim. I couldn't remember that stuff for three seconds, and he'd remember every bit of it.

You surely have a marvelous eye for detail, though. Still, what really strikes me, as a reader, is the emotional power of your stories. Thinking of "The Waterfowl Tree," and the story "Hermitage" –

That was a very early story. It was probably the third story I had printed – in the *South Dakota Review,* in about 1967.

Is the theme of that story an early theme of yours, that idea of the son returning? Is it a theme you haven't gone back to?

That father-son stuff? I think so. It's not something that tempts me much anymore. This book I'm writing right now [*Hole in the Sky*] is full of child-hood material and really is a chronological, autobiographical book, but it ends up being an ecology book; it's a story about taking care of ourselves and taking care of the world and how to conduct ourselves in what I conceive to be proper ways. I really believe that if you've spent all the time to learn how to write, to learn how to get this instrument that you've got, that you ought to use it for purposes like that. For instance, I've never written a novel – well, I've written a couple, but they're never any good – but I've never written a novel that connects with the world in ways that seem important to me. And these nonfiction books seem easier for me to do, I'm just more comfortable with the form.

I think it's probably *not* just me – I think that it's happening all over the culture. There's some reason why fiction isn't quite connecting; it has to do with technique, I think, and with the position the writer is in in regard to the material. I'm teaching a personal essay course this quarter, and I have forty people in there, and they're terrific, they're wonderful. They're coming over from other programs like Environmental Studies, which is a good program at the University of Montana, with a lot of really smart students – and those people want to learn how to say things about what they care about. And they all would have wanted to write fiction ten or fifteen years ago, so something is changing.

I think this whole idea of a self-reflexive narrator is just another fashion-able, short-lived way of telling stories. In the 1960s, when John Keeble and I were both in the [Writers] Workshop at Iowa, we both had Bob Coover as our teacher, and everybody there was concerned with the idea of reinventing narrative. It doesn't seem to have been a fruitful direction and nobody's much doing that stuff now, but I think the reinvention really probably came out of New Journalism, going back to voice and back to storytelling. It's the same impulse John Keeble had – you read *Crab Canon,* and you see that that's a technical novel, full of Robbe-Grillet – he was writing that when he was in Iowa City, and it's very different from what he does now. I remembered the stuff that used to be on the worksheets from *Crab Canon* in Iowa City – and then I read *Yellowfish,* and I couldn't believe it was the same guy.

As Keeble said, it's a part of maturation too. I know you've spoken of the maturation of the West, of its necessity – and perhaps this trend toward nonfiction and this desire to tell one's story are part of that maturation process.

I think one thing about writers in the West – and probably the same thing they felt in the South in the 1930s – is that you really do have a chance to have some say about your culture, about your part of the world, and that you can influence it to some degree. Power, political power is important – it gives artists of any kind great heart to think that you're not just working in a vacuum or that you're not just entertaining people or distracting them.

It seems that writers in the West have taken more of an offensive, than a defensive, stance.

Yeah, the feeling that you are actually going to cause some things to change.

John Keeble has spoken of the apparent absence of power here in the West, political power particularly, and how it's almost as if the writers have taken it upon themselves to exert that power.

I think that's really true, because there is no other voice. In Missoula, there are continually things that outrage you in the newspaper every day, and every day I have to step on that letter to the editor I want to write that would get me into huge warfare with somebody. At Ed Abbey's death – it occurred to me and I'm sure it occurred to some other people – suddenly a lot of very political people began to look for somebody to take the role of Ed Abbey at the head in the West, to say the things that Abbey was saying and to take that kind of a political stance. Personally, I'm real leery of it, because I want to be able to be taken as a more reasoned voice than that, although I admired Abbey enormously and he was a friend. But still you feel chicken-shit every goddamned step of the way, you think you're just telling yourself something so you won't have to take the flak! So, who knows? Maybe in five years, I or somebody will do it.

But you drew some response with your essay "In Our Backyard." I thought the interesting thing there was that the complaint wasn't so much with the argument of the essay as with the incident of the tree-cutting that you describe.

Oh, they hated that one. People wrote me letters saying things like, What's he supposed to do, his only core drill is stuck in the tree. Well, leave the son of a bitch there! The description may, in ways, have been a cheap shot, but nevertheless it really happened. Ultimately, I thought, It's a political thing to say, and this time I'm going to say it. I don't mind it.

Something you haven't done, to a great extent, is work with the old myths, though you have done a radio play based on the Lewis and Clark explorations.

I don't think that's ever going to come to anything. I've rewritten it about four times, and it doesn't ever seem to satisfy the producer. But what do you mean by "old myths"?

Well, the myths of the Old West, and your point about the New West and the Real *West, and the need to recognize what that Real West is. Do we want to, do we* need *to create new myths?*

New stories, yes. Essentially, as I've said in *Owning It All*, the old mythology is a mythology of conquest and takeover and law-bringing, it's inherently a racist, sexist imperialist mythology of takeover. Among the few people who know the real West and its real history, this idea is old, redundant: Okay, we've got it now, we've known that one. But out there in the world, it's not redundant; the old mythology is still in place.

It gets back to that question about who's going to take Ed Abbey's place in a sense, because somebody needs to say in Montana that you shouldn't do these things, somebody in Idaho needs to say you shouldn't do these things. Somebody needs to go up in the Tongass Forest and say, You really mustn't cut this cedar forest and ship all those logs to Japan so they can be pickled and be used fifty years in the future. That's a bad idea. I remember going to Powell, Wyoming, and talking about irrigation agriculture and some of the ill effects and a woman saying, Well, this is our life, we can't change our life. And I said, Maybe you have to change your life in some way, because over in Nebraska they're pumping the Ogalalla Aquifer dry, and that's *got* to be a bad idea. You just can't keep doing stuff like that.

So that old mythology is everywhere, but in another sense: Use it up, use it up! You end up with people in the West being powerless, being pawns, being a colony: the loggers in Darby, Montana, are out on strike against the environmentalists, saying We've got to make a living, when you know what's really going on is that the loggers in Darby are ploys for these giant multi-national companies who are in fact making all the money, and the loggers in Darby are just running front for them. On the one hand, you hate to go down to Darby and start telling these people they're fools and the way they're conducting lives is immoral.

It's my hope – and I think it's everybody's hope – with the writers in the West being political, that an accumulation of things – one statement after another statement after another statement after another statement – that things will begin to change. And they *are* changing. In the twenty years since I came to Missoula, things have changed enormously. I keep telling the story of reading a newspaper account about clear-cutting in *The Missoulian,* and the writer used the word "ecology," and I did not know what it meant in 1969. Now, I doubt if you could find somebody on the streets of Coeur d'Alene who doesn't know what ecology means. Things have changed enormously; our consciousness has really changed. Still, you want to change the *conduct.* I mean, I think the way the U.S. Forest Service conducts itself is inexcusable.

Aware as you are, though, of the political reality of the West, you have also worked with political mythology. I think, specifically, of your story "Phantom Silver," which is a remarkable handling of the Lone Ranger mythology.

Well, that story was really just an attempt to take that same imperialist mythology and tear it down. The reason for the incest story at the beginning is to humanize and break down that mythology immediately, and to try to make it personal, make it personal, make it personal. Until finally, you end up with this guy in San Francisco who suddenly takes off his mask, lays down his guns, and says, Well, okay, I'll just be a human being, instead of being a force for imperialism or a force for mythology or for whatever it is.

That story was published in the *Iowa Review*, originally. Coover wrote me a note and said he was editing a mythological issue of the *Iowa Review*, an idea that came out of that time when he was rewriting fairy tales and when everybody was redoing old stories. Again, I had taken a class from him called Exemplary Ancient Fictions, and we read Ovid and *Arabian Nights*, and we started thinking out innovative ways to tell our stories. What came out of that for me, five or six years later, was "Phantom Silver," which was an attempt at reinventing the Lone Ranger, turning the Lone Ranger story back on itself, and saying: this mythology, however useful it may have been fifty or hundred years ago to a people who were intent on conquering a part of the world, isn't even useful anymore, it's destructive. Whatever you may think about the takeover of the West, now *everybody's* suffering from this mythology; and, of course, the takeover of the West was pretty immoral in itself.

By having that ending there in San Francisco, the Lone Ranger laying down his guns and all, and joining that Chinese gang, you seem to be adding a twist, a commentary.

Well, I wanted to have all those people there, people from all kinds of cultures, and to take him out to the edge of the ocean and push it to the end of things: he walks out on the beach and – I can't remember whether I had him do it or not – he fires a shot off into the fog –

He does, yes.

And he's barefoot, he's got his horse stabled back in the Mission, and he goes out there and finally this is the end of it. He has no role anymore, it doesn't work anymore. He goes back and says, Okay, I'll act like somebody. The point is that the *culture* should do that, culture should stop trying to be the Lone Ranger. There's nothing left to conquer, there's nothing left to take over, there's nothing left to make subservient to us, and what we have to do is stop and figure out how to stay where we are, live where we are, and take care of what we've got. Bill Bevis pointed out to me that all the classical American novels are going-away novels – *Huck Finn* and all that – and that the classical list of Native American novels are coming-home novels –

Welch's novels and [Leslie] Silko's novel – all these books are about coming back and staying put and making peace with what you've got. *Winter in the Blood* is as good an example as any of this kind of novel, of somebody coming back and trying to find all of this stuff that was lost at *home,* rather than going off to Alaska or Australia, which is the current mythology all over the West: I'm getting out of here!

So anyway, all of that stuff in the Lone Ranger story is about that idea, that we've got this much world and this is what it is and we'd better take care of it because there isn't going to be any more of it.

Let me ask you another question about your use of Western mythology, this time in the Cord *novels. I have a student who's been reading your work – the serious fiction and the essays – and I recently gave him one of your* Cord *books to read. After a week, he came back and asked, What's he doing here? Is he selling out?*

Well, one of our ideas – Steve Krauzer and I wrote the novels together – one of our ideas was to make a buck. But the other idea was that we couldn't quite swallow exploiting the mythology in so bald a fashion. So we tried to figure out an alternative. We wanted these novels to cut subtly from within, and I think they did to some degree, but I don't think they were ever read that subtly. Except for one academic, who described the *Cord* novels as the first self-reflexive Westerns, as novels that commented back on the idea of the Western itself.

That's what I tried to convince my student, that they were an attempt to subvert the formula.

That's exactly what we were doing, or what we hoped we were doing, but I just don't think we ever did much. Somebody asked me, Who was the audience for those books? And I said, They're only read by people in jail. The idea, and possibly it was a lame one, was that these would be the first feminist westerns, and that we would slowly turn the series around like a TV show turns the characters' involvement.

I think that *The King of Colorado* was the best novel in the series; it was the book where we finally figured out how to do it, and weren't yet sick of doing it. Finally, though, it became so loathsome a job to write them – the novels were as thin as gauze – that we quit.

You comment in the jacket notes to The Van Gogh Field: *"I try to operate in the interface between myth and reality, sometimes overtly dealing with the mythological, at times trying to render life in a quiet, realistic manner."*

And you want to know if I believe it? I think I do believe it. Once again, it was an important story to tell myself at a certain point in my writing, because it gave me some idea of what I thought I was up to. Whether it was true or not, it allowed me to proceed. Whether I think that was an accurate representation of what I was doing or not, I really don't know. I don't think I'm real good at make-believe reality, in the sense of making up stories that ring real. Neither was Herman Melville, particularly, I don't think, and I don't think that that's a crippling defect. I would have to question that jacket copy a little bit, though; some of those stories are, in ways, very realistic. "Thirty-Four Seasons of Winter," for example, took a long, long time to write, but it seems real to me, I know those people – not literally, but there's a real world there. I think I could have written that story over and over in various ways, and probably gotten all the variations published and had a kind of career, but again that did not seem like an interesting thing to do.

It's a powerful story.

I guess it is, but I think you ought to try to do different things; it turned out that I could do that sort of stuff with some facility, but I'm real happy I didn't stick with it. I never seriously considered doing that at the time. I told myself, You don't want to write any more "Phantom Silvers," you don't want to write any more this or that – so that, for a while, I ended up with these stories that seemed like they were all over the place. I always envied somebody like Ray Carver, who seemed to find the kind of stories he should tell almost at once, and who told them. If you go way back in his career, to "A Student's Wife," which was written as an undergraduate – it was published in 1962 – it's just like his newest stories. It's not quite as good a story, but it's just like them, so he knew where he was and what he thought about storytelling almost from the very beginning. I admire that; Christ, I'm not sure I do yet, which is okay. It used to cause me trouble because I thought, Well, you're never going to amount to a shit. Finally, though, amounting to a shit grows less and less important as the years go by! I do think writers work for a long time, early in their career, in a *social* storytelling mode; at some point in their development, however, they begin telling more *religious* stories.

So do you see yourself moving in that direction?

I think that, in the long run, I probably am working in that direction; I don't think I'm *at* it right now – I think I'm *coming* at it. The impulses were always there, from the age of twenty-nine, from the time of my mental breakdown in 1961, on. The impulses finally are all metaphysical or religious or whatever, rather than social. That's why a story like "Thirty-Four Seasons of Winter," which I see as a social story, doesn't interest me that much anymore.

Actually, one of the things that's not done enough in our fiction is the mirroring of working-class society, of blue-collar society. Fred Pfiel had a review of Russell Banks's novel *Affliction*, in the *[Village] Voice*'s literary supplement, and in there he said that there aren't enough novels written well about the working class. I keep telling my students, Why doesn't anybody work for any money in this story? It's indicative of one of the holes in the way we think about fiction or storytelling right now, that stories have to be about relationships, *relationships*, that they can't be about these other things.

Though I think you do an interesting job with "Flight."

I guess I did. While I was in graduate school in Iowa City, I wrote a novel, and about three-fourths of it I don't think, at that time, was too bad a novel; but I fucked the ending up just completely. I love Dick Yates, but I wish he had just told me, Bill, do it this way, don't ever try to do it that way again; for once you wish your teacher had just taken you by the shirt-collar and given you a good shake. That novel was very autobiographical; it wasn't about leaving the ranch, but it was about getting a divorce which I did at the same time that I left the ranch. I was very close to it, having just gone through the experience a year or so before, and so a lot of these pieces, these stories came out of that novel, and they are quite autobiographical, though there's a lot of make-believe too. For instance, somebody gets shot in that story; I had to put in a shooting, because nobody got shot in my family in those days!

But that idea of ownership and relationships is something that works its way into the essays, doesn't it?

You bet! And "Balancing Water" is a story about a relationship and about owning things. It's about a guy in Montana working on a ranch where he grew up that's owned by a woman whom he's in love with and having an affair with, who lives in Seattle and who's married to another guy. She's always owned the property and he's *never* owned it, and he's content living there, essentially making this balancing act work for himself.

One of the most compelling images in any of your stories is that grizzly in your story "We Are Not in This Together." There, however, the protagonist literally confronts the bear, and tries to imagine the deaths of himself and of the woman who was mauled to death by a grizzly – you juxtapose that imaginative act with the image of the woman-friend training that rifle right back at him. That's a terrific ending.

That story was *very* difficult for me to find an ending for, because so much of the story is borrowed from "real life." Those girls really got mauled – Mary Beth Mahoney, who was a student at Montana – though I don't think she was ever a student of mine, she was somebody I knew, a barmaid in a bar I used to go to. She was nineteen or twenty. She had come out there, a real environmentalist from the East, and the first fucking thing she did was to go up there and get eaten by a grizzly bear.

Soon after that incident occurred, a woman who lives in Missoula named Deirdre McNamer, who's a wonderful writer, wrote a lead about this story that just horrified me – I almost cribbed it for the beginning of my story. Somehow I could not resolve that incident; I really was upset about it. For weeks I'd think about it, not in a compulsive way, but I'd think about it, it upset me. And I thought, if something bugs you this much you ought to write a story about it – that's what they always say, that's the standard advice. So I did. Then I got to the ending and I had no idea where I was; I must have written thirty endings to that story.

Stories worked that way for me for a long time; I think it's less the case now, after twenty or twenty-five years of writing. But for a long time I always would have stories going and never know how to end them, or there'd always be ten or eleven of them around and eventually one of them would get finished to the point where somebody would publish it. I'm a writer who really has to have good editors, because I tend to have a lot of wild ideas that don't work; I try them and see where they go, and a lot of times get myself so confused that I have to go see somebody who can say, No, no, do this. It helps.

Perhaps as a closing question, let me ask you about this distinction between the sacred and the profane, a distinction you emphasize in your essays –

Maybe I use it *too* much; I really try to find other language, but I say the same thing. That's what this book that I'm writing right now finally is about: using story to locate yourself and find what you think is sacred and worth preserving, and what you think is pernicious in the world, what you think is really a bad idea in the world. Like I said, pumping the Ogalalla Aquifer is a *bad* idea. I think it's a very simple notion; it goes right back to Aristotle – we use stories to come to a recognition, and we do it all day long in our lives. It finally is a very political idea; these are the things I'm willing to stand behind and these are the things I want to get rid of. I think that's what art is for; I really think art *does* have a purpose. While it can be entertaining and in-structive, I think that in the act of instructing it instructs us in what we think is valuable and what we think is bad.

So your work has a definite moral quality to it?

I think so, I hope so. The more those ideas come clear to me, the more I become clear about those ideas, the more my work becomes easier to do. By easier to do, I mean it becomes easier to shape the stories, I kind of know how the stories want to work. It may mean that they get more didactic and less convincing and less compelling – I hope not. But for me, there are some very simple paradigms that are enormously valuable, like the idea that in a story there has to be a discovery of what the problem is and a discovery of what the solution is, and probably some false solutions. It's a simple idea, but it will get you from one end of a long narrative to the other. And I didn't know those paradigms. A friend of mine told me, You should have taken Drama 101 – it would have saved you years!

But I really believe that you have to make some arbitrary decisions about what's valuable finally, and I think that life is valuable and I think that *human* life is valuable. There's a chapter in this new book called "Anti-distenasia," which is a made-up word that means the failure to take positive steps to preserve life. I think you must take positive steps. I really do believe that all human beings are interested in having some positive effect upon the world. Sure, a lot of people have some pretty peculiar ideas about what a positive effect would be – people like Hitler. Nevertheless, people make up these stories in which they convince themselves that some kind of idealized form of things would be the right thing to happen, would be good; and they try to make that actual, in lots of cases. When they *don't*, I think they become very disturbed, disoriented. What happened to me on the ranch when I had the breakdown, is that I lost track of what that "right thing" would be essentially.

One of the things about ownership in our society is that it cuts you off from so many things except selfishness. We're constantly told that it's okay to be selfish, that we should be selfish; that leads to anomie and great loneliness. I think that all this talk about lonely individuals who are causing such damage in the world is true, but maybe it's because they've been educated to be selfish and they've educated *themselves* to be selfish, and not because they've been educated to be self-reliant or to take care of themselves and the world too. I think you have to take care of yourself in order to take care of the world. Those are all pretty simple ideas, but I hope they're all true.

As I say, in the beginning I really didn't know what I was doing; the world seemed a series of apocalypses to me, and I was writing stories in which these apocalypses happened. Like in the story "Breaker of Horses" – that story is really about making a peace with that stuff, with death, and that's as typical a story of that time in my life as there ever was. There's an apocalypse, something bad happens that kills you, and you make some kind of peace with it as you die. If there's a theme that runs like a line through all of my work, it's probably that.

WORKS

With Steven M. Krauzer, under the pseudonym of Owen Rountree. The *Cord* series of westerns. New York: Ballantine, 1982–86.

Great Action Stories. Edited with Steven M. Krauzer. New York: New American Library, 1977. Short fiction.

The Great American Detective. Edited with Steven M. Krauzer. New York: New American Library, 1978. Short fiction and essays.

Hole in the Sky: A Memoir. New York: Knopf, 1992. Memoir.

The Last Best Place: A Montana Anthology. Edited with Annick Smith. Helena: Montana Historical Society, 1988. Fiction, poetry, nonfiction.

Montana Spaces: Essays and Photographs in Celebration of Montana. Edited by William Kittredge. Photographs by John Smart. New York: Nick Lyons Books, 1988. Essays and photographs.

Owning It All. St. Paul, Minn.: Graywolf Press, 1987. Essays.

Phantom Silver. Missoula, Mont.: Kutenai Press, 1988. Short fiction.

Stories into Film. Edited with Steven M. Krauzer. New York: Harper & Row, 1979. Short fiction and essays.

The Van Gogh Field & Other Stories. Columbia: University of Missouri, 1978. Short fiction.

We Are Not in This Together. Port Townsend, Wash.: Graywolf Press, 1984. Short fiction.

David Long

A short-fiction writer, David Long was born in Massachusetts in 1948. His stories have oft been anthologized, and his first collection of stories, *Home Fires,* was awarded the St. Lawrence Short Fiction Prize for 1982. Long came to Montana in the early 1970s – as a poet – studying with William Kittredge and Richard Hugo in the M.F.A. program at the University of Montana. He left that program a story writer.

Long now lives in Kalispell (where this interview took place in June 1990) and occasionally teaches fiction writing at the University of Montana in Missoula, when he is not playing in a blues band called Tut and the Uncommons. We met the morning of the interview at the Sky Jordan Restaurant on Kalispell's main street. Long, obviously a regular there, walked to the back of the restaurant and retrieved his white, nondescript coffee mug from a shelf of other such mugs and talked to the waitress Nadine ("One of the things that makes Kalispell livable"). Later in the day, as we talked in his house about his work, his sons Montana and Jackson broke into our conversation with questions about the computer and Little League. The beard that Long favored earlier in his career has given way to a mustache. He does not sound necessarily like the Massachusetts native that he is.

DAVID LONG

GREGORY MORRIS: *One of the things that happened to you when you came to Montana, I understand, is that you turned from a poet into a fiction writer. You have remained a committed story writer since that time. What attracted you to that form, and what keeps you at it? Why not try the novel?*

DAVID LONG: The advantage of being a novelist would be that you don't have to think of totally new material all the time – most of your writing is "middle" in a novel. John Gregory Dunne, I think, said that writing a novel is like laying pipe – most of the time you're just laying pipe. The *story* writer's problem is generating new situations constantly.

It's a form that's suited to the perfectionist mentality. Great short stories are things of incredible compaction and intricacy and beauty. It's simply a form I fell in love with – the way there must be musicians who have fallen in love with certain musical forms and not others. Originally, I didn't feel I had the endurance, I didn't know if I could keep myself writing on a project without knowing for sure I'd succeed. When I was younger, I thought, I can't put two or three years into a novel and have it flop – I couldn't stand it emotionally. So I thought I'd just write stories, and if they flop, well, there's always another story. I'm not sure I feel that way anymore, but it did help cement my attachment to the short story form.

I wouldn't rule out writing a novel, except that I'm very slow. My stories grow by accretion. I think if you're a novelist, you have to blurt all this stuff out page after page. My stories creep forward – it seems to take a long time to understand what's really at stake in them. Since I've begun working on a computer, there's really no sense of a draft process anymore; I'm constantly revising and composing all at the same time. I'm really a relentless sentence reviser, so every sentence that's finished has been tinkered with any number of times. Every time I sit down to write, I read what's been written before, and I end up changing something. So I don't know – it might be that I could write a novel that's like one of my short stories, only a little larger.

You seemed to be drifting that way with your story "The Oriental Limited."

I thought that that might be a novel when I started, but I didn't really define it. With that story, again, I was desperate for a new piece of material. I was up in the Glacier Park library, going through their archives – I was researching the building of Going-to-the-Sun Road. Well, it was an engineering marvel of the 1920s, building a road through this incredible mountain pass,

187

and I thought there'd be a story in there someplace. I read the oral histories, and they were interesting, but more from an engineering point of view; they're not stories of personal choice and so forth. I was all set to go home, kind of sheepishly, when I saw an index citation that said "Whitehead Brothers' Disappearance, 1924." So I said, Could I see *that* file, please? And they brought out these two huge manilla folders.

I sat with that material for weeks, made chronologies, tried to find out who knew what when; I didn't know what I was going to do with it. Nobody really knows what happened to these two brothers – so naturally I conceived of it originally as a mystery story. But I realized that if I told it that way, I'd have to *solve* it. It occurred to me that what I liked best was the mystery, and that if I solved it, it wouldn't be half as interesting as if I didn't. I mean, think of mystery stories – you have corpses all over the place. Two real-life boys who drown, or whatever, doesn't really pull the weight – you'd have to muck it up with lots of other business.

At that point, I realized it was a tale about survivors. In one of the letters, the mother mentions that she and her daughter, Edith Whitehead, had come out and visited the park the following year. So I took that simple mention of a sister and made a character out of her. Then I found myself telling the story in the first person, which seemed like a strange choice in a way, but step by step it was understandable.

I enjoyed working with that material. I found myself confronted with a lot of strange problems, like trying to reconstruct a neighborhood in Chicago in 1924 – I had no idea what the buildings looked like. You find yourself with lots of little problems when you work with historical material; for example, in another story, I didn't know if there was a radio in the car – what year did they start having radios in cars? What year did they stop having starter buttons?

If you're writing actual history, nonfiction, then you have to know *every-thing*. If you're writing a story, you do as much research as you feel is appropriate; you leave out what you want to leave out, you write around the problems. Many times you create the illusion of knowing the historical stuff; you put in as much detail as you have, and try not to violate anything you know to be true. In all of the history pieces I've done, I've tried to create a *sense* of place, and only changed things that really needed to be changed for the sake of the narrative, then just invented stuff around that.

As you did in "The Last Photograph of Lyle Pettibone," where you seem to make use of a lot of historical material?

That's an interesting case. Everything about the two brothers in "The Oriental Limited" is true (at least as true as I could determine), while everything about the sister is totally made up.

The "Lyle Pettibone" story was more a case of synthesizing activity that took place at a certain time. In Butte, during and just after the First World War, there was a great deal of union violence and political unrest. The union violence revolved around the Anaconda [copper-mining] Company, but there was also a fair amount of xenophobia here following the Revolution in Russia; in fact, in the early 1920s, Montana passed a Sedition Act which became the model for a national act enacted shortly thereafter. It was a nasty time.

Anyway, there was a guy named Frank Little, a union organizer and possibly something else – he may have been an informer – we don't know the whole story on him. But one night in 1917, Frank Little was hauled out of his rooming house, dragged through the streets of Butte, and hanged. Around the same time, there were strikes in the mines and in the woods, and a lot of tension between the general population and union organizers, especially the Wobblies. The Wobblies were looked on harshly by the general population, especially the conservative middle class whipped up by the local press. Much of the press in Montana was owned by the Anaconda Company until the 1950s. The Wobblies wanted to organize people who otherwise had no voice at all, people who worked in the lumber camps, migrant workers, and so on. They preached one big union.

So I read some six months' or so of our local paper, the *Daily Inter Lake*, on microfilm and made notes on any citation that said IWW. Then I simply sat with this material for a long time, thinking about it. At the same time, by chance, I went through a period of being enamored of the photographers who worked for the [Depression-era] Farm Security Administration – Walker Evans and all that crew; there's a remarkable body of literature around that period: biographies of people like Dorothea Lange, and critical books about the Roosevelt administration and about Roy Stryker, who ran the photography project for the FSA.

Finally, I conceived of a boy who grew up in this town of Stillwater who became a photojournalist, a documenter of social and political life. And I imagined him getting his start that summer of 1917. The story just emerged out of the research; I didn't have a person, or a personal dilemma, at the start, the way I would with most stories. I had a body of material I wanted to use, and eventually a story came out of it. Usually, it works the other way.

You mentioned the "illusion of history" — what about the "illusion of place"?
One of the things you've done in your fiction is to create a recurring imagined
landscape — the town of Stillwater, and Sperry County — a locale drawn directly
from your surrounding Flathead County.

I've been most comfortable making up a fictitious place, then using whatever real details of Flathead County I wanted to. It's almost as if I have a
circle, and everything in the circle is fictitious and everything outside is
authentic. There's no attempt to hide the fact that it's Flathead County; it is
just a psychological device to make myself feel comfortable about writing
about this place. There's an aesthetic distance that's necessary.

One trick I've used is to recycle names. Most of the place or people names
in the stories are common here; I just use them differently. Sperry, for instance — up in Glacier Park there's Sperry Glacier and Sperry Chalet, named
after Dr. Lyman Sperry who explored that country in the 1880s. The Stillwater River is a little river that runs through the Flathead Valley, so I
renamed the town of Whitefish, Stillwater. Most of my characters' names
come out of the phone book, or they're names I'm used to seeing on busi-
nesses. And I try to work my friends' names into stories — I named a lake in
"Clearance" after my friend Jim Clayborn. Names have a strange power,
though — until you get them right, you can't go forward. Something's out of
whack.

Insofar as I've established geography or names in one story, I'll reuse that
geography and those names in another story and maybe add to that material
each time. But in terms of reusing actual characters, what happens is this:
I'm writing what ought to be the most crucial moment of somebody's life —
I'm trying to find the moment at which their life becomes totally different;
and if I've already done that, there's no point in writing another story about
the same person.

In your essay "Straight to the Actual," you talk of the authorial necessity of
developing (in Wendell Berry's words) a "local intelligence." Is this something
you're trying to nurture in these Sperry County stories?

Berry was talking about animal husbandry — he's terribly concerned about
finding local solutions to things. "Local intelligence" has a great sound to
it — but in terms of stories, I'm not sure I know what it means exactly.

A reviewer of my second story collection, *The Flood of '64*, mentioned the book in the same breath as Faulkner's Yoknapatawpha County – I thought, Okay, it's nice to hear talk like that. But Faulkner had this incredible driving energy; I don't have anything like it. I don't have that huge confidence that allows you to fire out page after page after page. Again, my stories are constructions that come much more slowly, and it's been a workable thing for me to use this place in its fictitious guise, over again. Insofar as a story seems like it ought to be set here, I'll continue to call it Sperry and I'll continue to work with the vision I have of the place. I'd like to set more stories here, but in the *now*.

I think some of the stories in my first book, *Home Fires,* were a more romanticized version of Montana. I didn't know then what it was like to be an adult, or what it was like to be a Montanan, but I went ahead anyway and pretended that I knew. There's a little more romanticism in those stories, because of that.

Do you see a relationship between place and character? I'm thinking of "Border Crossing," where there seems both a spatial and an emotional relationship between place and character – specifically, the significance of border.

That story was based on a murder trial that took place in Kalispell a few years ago, so I can't take credit for the imagery. But there is probably a psychic sense that we're in a corner – it's not literally true, it's just all space. I do think it's different living in the valley; you have a discrete sense of where your space starts and stops, as opposed to living in southern Michigan, say, where the fields stretch out and if you drive far enough you get to the next major urban area. People ask, Well, how big is Kalispell? I never know. It doesn't really matter; what matters is how big the *valley* is – it's a unit.

This business of place, I'm not sure what it means. It's a very easy thing to latch onto as a critic. I don't know if place determines character – the relationship is complicated. It's probably close to what Wallace Stegner says: "There are saints and sinners everyplace." If you look at Montana history, you've also got to look at Montana myth and so you have this weird amalgam of the true and the untrue. Take the myth of the solitary frontiersman. I did a piece for *Montana: The Magazine of Western History* about a woman who was the prime mover in starting a rural electric co-op over in the northeast corner of Montana – a woman named Anna Dahl. If you study the history of Sheridan County, you find it's true that people had to be self-reliant in order to get through the tough times; but what's even more apparent is how much they cooperated. Everything was a co-op. These people were largely Scandinavian and German, they had a tradition in their own countries of cooperative ventures. So you have the myth of self-reliance, and the actual fact of intense cooperation: the truth is an amalgam.

I do think, after having lived here, that there was a Montana style that I came to appreciate – a friendliness, a trust, not sweating the small stuff, a lack of pretension. These were qualities that I admired, and they seemed to be part of the Montana myth – it just seemed different from the urban East. The twenty years that I've been here have been a time of terrific homogenization, so that Montana is a lot more like every place else now than it was twenty years ago. An awful lot of people have come into Montana. Of course, Montana's always been full of immigrants, but I do think the process has accelerated in the last twenty years. The other thing you need to understand is that Montana is really two states. There ought to be one state that starts at Spokane [Washington] and goes to Helena, another that starts there and goes east to North Dakota. Here we get the weather of the Pacific Northwest; out there they get the Canadian weather. Life over there is dominated by ranching; over here it's dominated by small towns, some manufacturing concerns, but mainly timber and small ranching.

While some of my fiction is set in Montana east of the mountains, it's the small-town Montana, the post-World War I Montana, the postfrontier Montana that I'm interested in. So my work might have more in common with somebody writing about small towns in Minnesota than with the work of, say, Gretel Ehrlich, who writes about ranching life in Wyoming.

Do you see yourself as part of any kind of Western tradition as a writer?

I really have no great passion for traditional Western writing. I don't think I've ever read a single pulp Western, even as a kid. But there have been some fine writers who have lived in the West and their works have illuminated Western history and Western politics. So I've read Bill Kittredge's essays and Bud Guthrie's books, and I've read around in the literature of the West – probably too scantily – some H. L. Davis and Wallace Stegner and Farley Mowat. More recently, I've been working through *The Last Best Place,* Bill Kittredge and Annick Smith's massive collection of Montana writing, and I try to keep up with what other contemporary Montana writers are up to. Some of this reading is essentially research, important for knowing how things came to be; other works are fascinating as literature and could have been about anything.

As for being a part of it: I've spent my adult life here, I've chosen to write from this point of view, and as long as I can stay here I'll stay here. To a degree, it's out of my control. I do shy away from feeling that I'm *representative.* I certainly grew up in a different place and time; I grew up in an aging New England mill town – Fitchburg, Massachusetts – a child of parents who were Midwesterners; they were part of the first wave of people who came into these old New England factory towns after World War II. Paper companies and steel companies, run by family dynasties, were everywhere. Everything changed. But my parents were not of that place, so I was not exactly of the people that I grew up with, either.

Let me ask you about some specific stories in your first collection, Home Fires. *Those stories seem often to dramatize the tension between* luck *and* nerve. *Characters are often victims of "bum luck" or the beneficiaries of good luck, of "miracles." Yet they also face tests of nerve and responsibility – they must act responsibly, act not "like a fool." Is this an accurate assessment?*

I think so. Bill Kittredge and I had a conversation years ago – we were talking about the most basic principle of fiction, which is that action reveals character. If that's true, then what happens in this constructed universe happens by virtue of who the people are; so it's unfair, in the contract you've made with the reader, to end a story with *chance* – you're violating that basic idea that lies at the heart of fiction, that there's a connection between action and character.

But, I thought, a story could start that way. What would happen if you started a story with an accident somebody survived, an accident that should have killed him? About that time, I overheard some people in a bar discussing the fate of a truck driver who'd disappeared after his truck crashed over an embankment in some remote country near here – they were speculating that he'd run off, that he'd staged the accident. I was reminded of my conversation with Kittredge; that was how "Home Fires" got going.

I also see that we witness things in our lives, and this idea of bearing witness and testifying I think is an important idea in my work. I also think that while you can't tie up the problems of narrative with a chance occurrence, that chance is a subject to deal with in fiction. One thing Dick Hugo used to say was that we write the same poem over and over all our lives. We have these obsessions. So I see that "Clearance" is another version of "Home Fires," as is a newer story, "Perfection." In "Clearance," it's not a question of the protagonist surviving the accident himself, it's a question of *witnessing* an accident. There are times when we're poised on the edge of some change in our lives, then something comes and triggers it, then that change is manifested in action. You don't change unless you're ready to be changed. So in "Clearance" you have a man off in the wilderness, testing himself a little bit, figuring out where he's going to go in his marriage; he witnesses a plane crash and pulls two people out of this light plane. (This idea grew out of a real plane crash here in the Swan Mountains. A friend of mine was hiking there months later and found some debris – the plane had come so close to making it over the ridge that the engine actually bounced over to the other side.) So the idea of "just making it" or "just *not* making it" was very intriguing to me, and the moment of awareness for the man in the story was that while he was feeling sorry for these people who had just died, he was suddenly filled with anger for the man who was piloting this plane because he realized that this guy had just barely cleared things all his life and had taken too many foolish risks. Then he realized that that's what *he'd* been doing: taking this foolish risk, just clearing it, just getting by. And in the last line in the story, after he's gone home, he calls his wife, who is down at her mother's ranch. The phone rings, his mother-in-law answers, and says, "*It's you* . . . you nearly missed us."

Which I thought was a beautiful ending. The endings of short stories are so determined by chance. You know how things have to be at the end, but not exactly what they look like. Syd Field, who's written about screenplay writing, talks about context and content. You can put your cups (context) in sequence without knowing what's in each cup. That's your problem, the day you're going to write the ending of the story. Sometimes you get lucky. I basically think that the writer makes his own luck, by working hard, by focusing his mind as hard as he can on the problem. Even so, words contain energy, and sometimes you stumble onto a word that contains all the energy of the story. There's a story in *Home Fires* called "Morning Practice": a woman and her father are looking for a cello that belonged to the mother, who has since died (the cello had been sent out to be repaired). They find it, finally, in a shop in Boston and this woman has a kind of catharsis where she recognizes that it's just a piece of wood – it doesn't mean anything, it's just a mangled cello. And the last line of the story reads: ". . . and they made their way out to the darkening street, unaccompanied." Somehow, by hanging around the ending of that story long enough, I stumbled onto the word – in this case, an actual pun. The same kind of thing happened with the ending of the Lyle Pettibone story, and in a very recent story, "Blue Spruce" – sometimes you just cry when it comes together like that.

Many of your stories deal with that problem of not taking action, of passivity.

Well, I'm a passive character myself, and I think it's a demon I've had to deal with. Somebody observed that in my stories people aren't doing things for themselves, don't crave things for themselves – they're just reacting. That must be a projection of my attitudes. So I'd have to agree that one of the stories I come back to is the one in which you encounter something that chastens you and makes you change.

One of the ways in which characters do act is through their imaginations – they "tamper with other people's stories." Is there a correct use of imagination and story by these characters? Is storytelling that important?

When I was in college I studied mythology – not so much classical mythology, but the nature of myth: Mircea Eliade and Lévi-Strauss and people like that. So I had a sense of how myths function in society. And Bill Kittredge has written rather eloquently on the nature of storytelling, so his ideas have really influenced me: simply that a myth is a story that tells us how to behave. They can be big myths or they can be personal myths. So I guess you could say that in a lot of my stories people are telling themselves a story about who they are.

I sometimes find myself wanting to write about storytelling directly. But my feeling is that a story writer should write about people in the real world; so I've tried, consciously, not to write about other writers. I just feel there's something closed about it, it's too solipsistic. Though I love certain books where the main character is a writer, [John Irving's] *The World According to Garp*, say, I just feel that *I'm* not going to do it, I'm not going to add to that literature.

But the notion of storytelling does enter in. There's a line in another fairly new story, "Lightning" – "If a story can ruin you, can a story save you?" – that becomes the text of that story. It's about the two sons of a rancher, one of whom is raised to be a rancher and the other who is raised to go to college. The son raised to be a rancher sees his wife eventually run off and his life gradually fall apart; the other son never really settles into any other work, so he and his wife come back and live on the ranch. There's this reversal. It's about how they were fed these stories about who they were.

The temptation is to write about art because that's the thing on your mind, so you find yourself trying to find analogues. I've tried a couple of times to write a story about a painter, because I thought that would be enough of an aesthetic distance that I wouldn't be writing about myself or my own dilemmas as an artist. Nobody wants to read about writer's block, or the process of your story; that's intensely interesting to yourself, and of no interest to anyone else.

It sounds like you have a fairly traditional aesthetic.

I do, I guess. I didn't think of myself as traditional when I was growing up; I liked to read everything. But I find, if I'm honest, that the things I admire are rather traditional. Some of my favorite writers are William Maxwell and Alice Munro and William Trevor and Updike and Cheever – and Mark Helprin. It doesn't mean that I don't also admire other, off-the-wall stuff. But that quiet work – William Maxwell's novel *So Long, See You Tomorrow,* for example – it's a short little thing that's just steeped with personal history and wisdom.

Many of the writers I've talked to seem to have a strong reaction against minimalist writing –

I have trouble with the term "minimalist" to begin with. First of all, you're a minimalist if you're writing in the short story form. In my work I try to cut back as much as I can. A novelist creates more of a world and fills it up; a short story writer uses much more suggestion. There's a wonderful line in an Annie Dillard essay recently where she says something like: "Have you ever ridden in a commercial airliner or eaten a cheeseburger? Don't describe it." So when I was teaching last winter, I told my students, Don't describe the cheeseburger – and that became a catchword. The point is that if you conceive of a scene, what very few details do you need to give to create that place and that action? Does that make you a minimalist? I don't think so. I think minimalism has to do with writing stories where nothing happens, where it's all gesture. There seemed to be, for a while, a kind of story that was very middle class, where people were all very low-affect, and I suppose that's what minimalism is about. But you have stories by other people like James Salter or Elizabeth Tallent, where there's an intense cutting back. It's not that you're leaving stuff out that *needs* to be there; you're just trusting in the power of the word. Every sentence is chiseled down; it doesn't have a syllable more than it needs. It has a good rhythm, it has shape, it has sound, and you leap from there to the next sentence. Whereas, often, a novelist puts every stepping-stone in. The short story writer leaves things out, but it's not done coyly.

I'd like to ask you one more question about Home Fires, *and the sense of "home" that seems to pervade the stories in that collection. I'm thinking of "Like Some Distant Crying," where Celestia comes to feel "at home" at the hot springs after having lost that sense; and of "Eclipse," where Jack returns "home to Montana"; and of "Home Fires," where Pack does return home, even when given the chance to start a completely new life, to leave home.*

I don't think it's anything peculiar to *my* stories. Someone once observed that there are only two plots: *Somebody goes on a journey,* and *A stranger rides into town.* So there's something primordial about home. It's always been important to me, that concept: having a center, a charmed space you can go from and come back to. I think maybe one reason I feel that way is that I've led a very stable life: I was the only child of older parents, and I didn't move much, I lived in the same house most of my life; I got married fairly young and have been married for twenty-one years. So I guess it's a natural out-growth of my life. On the other hand, you could talk to someone who's led a chaotic life and has a craving for home, because of *not* having that stability.

I would imagine that there's some kind of psychological projection onto my characters, but basically every story presents you with a certain aesthetic challenge: certain structural difficulties, certain conceptual difficulties of trying to figure out what is the crucial event in a story, what's ultimately at stake in a story. One problem you get to after you've written stories for a number of years is that the stories that were most available to you when you were younger, you've done. Now you have to do *other* stories, and you know a lot *more* about stories, so it's almost harder now to write stories than it was when you were younger: you didn't know what you were doing then, so in a way it was easier. So at this point there's this urge to *drive* a story, to find that one point that makes it different from any other story. The problem is that you start into a story and you can think of fifteen other stories just like it. We live in a very late era and we've all been exposed to hundreds of thousands of stories. Your mission is to find that one place, that one thing about the story that differentiates it, that one way of seeing the dilemma that's a new angle. Sometimes you find it, and other times you don't quite find it but other stuff in the story is interesting so you keep the story anyway.

I think Alice Munro's stories are so intriguing. They ramble, they go sideways beautifully – then out of all this material comes this one fine little place. In "Differently," for instance, two people who knew each other years ago under very different circumstances, have a brief visit. At the end of this, at the end of all this recounting of past history, the woman says, ". . . we never behave as if we believed we were going to die." And the guy says, "How should we behave?" And the woman responds, "Differently." Her stories often work this way, come down to this fine understanding. Other ones don't, quite – they're messier – but they just reek with lived life. She's the best.

Your story "Eclipse" seems to come down to this "fine understanding" that you describe – it's not a "messy story." You build up certain expectations on the reader's part, and you clarify the dilemma very nicely at the end. I'm curious about what you consider a "messy story" or a "neat story."

"Home Fires" is a clean story. A character survives an accident that should have killed him, and then is confronted with the problem of how he ought to live. It takes him a while to realize that that's what he's confronted with. He encounters two women who are running away from their bad lives, and he realizes by their example that he has a choice: he can go home, or he can go off and start a new life. That's the basic confrontation in the story, but as the story wrote itself out I realized that there was a third possibility, which is what he chooses in the story: to go *home* and start a new life. That was the moment of understanding, that fine point that I was talking about.

The story "The New World" is bigger, looser. The same themes of chance and choice come to play in it. The main character is a middle-aged guy named McCutcheon who grew up very much under the shadow of a boisterous father. His father built and ran the opera house in the town, and then he died suddenly; McCutcheon took it over and ran it for a while, until the Depression. All of this becomes a way of talking about the process of middle age where you're confronted with a world that you're overfamiliar with, that doesn't give you awe, and how you get beyond that point. At the end of that story, McCutcheon has a new relationship with a woman, he has patched his badly fractured relationship with his daughter, and he's just thinking back on his life, thinking about how things might have been different if he'd made different choices. Something in his character allowed him to be a little more open to the people around him, so he slowly dug his way out of this feeling of being closed and bitter. That's a messier story, and by messier I guess I mean that there's a lot of back-story, maybe more characters, more scenes. Some stories are just very straightforward – they may be one long episode, one long scene – and other stories just ramble around but do have a thread. I admire both kinds. Tom McGuane's story "Flight" is a good example of a wonderfully simple story.

Art has shape; life doesn't necessarily, so you try to find some way of giving it those qualities that people respond to in art: clarity, unity. You try to condense it so you get rid of the extraneous. If you think hard enough about your story, if you turn it another crank, you always can reach one more level of understanding, and maybe that's the point that nobody else has gotten to. There are no new stories – only new tellings – isn't that what they say? So how do you make it seem new? It means finding that one understanding of that one emotional vibration that strikes you as being something you haven't seen a trillion times. I think that's one of the problems with mid-career storywriting – you've read so much that your own ideas seem familiar to you; so that you're constantly discarding possibilities, unless you can get yourself beyond that. There's a lot of self-censorship going on. You may have an idea that's only fifteen seconds old in your mind, and already you've thought of twenty stories that it's like. So you've got to be able to hold it in mind without knowing anything about it, without judging it, until it can turn over a couple more permutations and become something interesting.

One dilemma I'm facing now is that good fiction is necessarily dramatic – to a degree – in the sense that internal choices are enacted publicly. So many of our stories are about the beginnings (coming-of-age) or the endings (the ends of marriages) – I'm trying to find ways of writing about the middles of things. How, for example, do you write about a marriage that's at its mid-point? We see a lot of marriages from the viewpoint of something that's already broken down, and the reason for that is that we need to show something in a moment of crisis. But there's something inherently non-dramatic about middles, and that's one of the private aesthetic dilemmas I'm working on now.

That's coupled with the theme of overcoming the weariness of the familiarity of life. There's a line in "Home Fires" that says: "But accidents happen, and sometimes a man or woman is lucky enough to see that all of it, from the first light kiss onward, could have gone another way." It has to do with still being capable of seeing the miraculousness of everything that transpires. At some point, you get this sense: The dead are out there in the cemetery for a long time, and you're up *here* for a real short time. That idea seems more obvious than ever at some point in your life, and that story becomes the only story that there is to tell. All this other stuff doesn't seem very important after that story.

But how do you write about constancy, except to show it being tested, and enduring? So you do that. Yet there tend to be rather stylized, familiar ways of doing that. How do we test a hero? There are only a few ways, and your job as an artist is to find new ways – I have one set of antennae out for that.

I'm not so interested in writing coming-of-age stories. I'm not so interested in mining my early life. My stories have less to do with self-expression than the urge to just build something.

Do you think that your fiction is informed by any sort of moral impulse?

I'm not a believer personally, but I'm a moralist in the sense that I believe in ethical behavior; I believe, in a kind of Buddhist sense, that there's a way of right being in the world, and you're either that way or you aren't, and that you should strive to be that way as much of the time as you can. You know in your heart that there's an ethical way to act. Sometimes it's complicated: What is the most ethical way to act among various choices? That's what you have to decide, and that's what my characters have to decide. It's a moral dilemma.

Some people criticize my stories for being depressing, but I feel that almost all my stories take a "hook" up at the end; you don't need to bring a character all the way up, in a short story, but you need to suggest where the movement is. So in a lot of my stories, you go down into the dilemma and then you hook up in the end, where you get resolution – compromise, or new ground, or new understanding.

That's interesting. I can't think of a story of yours that doesn't hook up at the end.

Well, there's one story called "Solstice" that's been misread by a lot of people. I see that as a very sarcastic story. The man in the story has been deserted by his wife, and the sympathy of the narrator's voice – you're down inside the main character's voice, in the third person – is with that man. But the reader should see that the *writer's* sympathy is with the woman who's taken off, because this guy is a jerk. That's one story that doesn't hook up: he's left cold, listening to the duct-work.

Even those stories that tend to be dark – "The Flood of '64" or "Compensation" or "Saving Grace" – hook up.

Well, you want to find the moment or image of resolution. I think I watched too many episodes of "The Waltons" in my formative years, probably at the same time that I was reading Camus. We do *root* for our characters; we do want them to solve their problems; we want to show strong sentiment without sentimentality. Sometimes we slip over to one side or the other side, but I always try for a happy ending. Like the ending of "The Oriental Limited" – it just kind of came to me: that sense of great joy mixed with apprehension when she gets on that train.

You seem very comfortable within the female presence or voice – in "The Oriental Limited," for example, or "V-E Day," or "Compensation." And yet with "Clearance" you write with equal ease the typical "man's story" – that sort of hunting-testing-proving male fiction that other Western writers have also written.

I really haven't had much to do with the "man's man" kind of life and the "man's man" kind of story. I've lived my whole adult life with a woman who is my best friend, and I've shared a great deal of her understanding of the world. Some people feel that a man can't write a woman's story, and vice versa, and that it's very presumptuous to do so. I don't feel that way, and I've gone ahead and done it. If there are some women who are offended by the fact that I've tried, then I'll just take that chance.

As a Western writer, do you feel obliged to incorporate a political impulse in your work?

My obligation is to write a short story that's never been written before. It's so easy to get into well-worn material when you get political, that you start becoming an essayist; as an essayist, I would feel much more comfortable writing about politics. But as a story writer it's much more difficult to work in that political material, aesthetically. That's not a good answer, but it's part of an answer. It's a question of priorities. You look at some people like

Wendell Berry, for instance – someone who's done a wonderful job of integrating his life. As a citizen I can be political, but not as a story writer. I wonder, if I played in a string quartet, would you be asking me the same question?

WORKS

Home Fires. Urbana: University of Illinois, 1982. Short fiction.
The Flood of '64. New York: Ecco Press, 1987. Short fiction.
Perfection. St. Paul, Minn.: Kutenai Press, 1993. Short story (chapbook).

Thomas McGuane

Tom McGuane is a writer whose work is marked by as much color and variety as is his life. He has succeeded as a fiction writer, as an essayist, as a screenwriter, and as a film director. At the same time, since his arrival in Montana in the early 1970s, McGuane has turned himself into a thriving cattle and horse rancher, as well as a champion cutting horse competitor. Born in Michigan in 1939, McGuane early in his career wrote with a dark exuberance of the Florida Keys and of his home state. Over the years, however, McGuane has gradually turned both his life and his fiction in a westward direction; indeed, his film *Rancho Deluxe* has become something of a cult classic in the region, providing the modern American West with an ironic and not-always-generous mythology.

McGuane now lives on a ranch outside the tiny town (a post office and general store, combined) of McLeod. Though this interview took place in writing (completed in late 1989), I did have the chance to meet with McGuane at his ranch – though only after an earlier missed connection when I ended up having a beer and a burger at the Road Kill Café in McLeod, served up by a bartender named Sam. (Sam was a woman who played out the almost archetypal Western story: a divorced mother working to complete a teaching degree, with plans to head for Alaska – plans, I learned later from McGuane, she had followed through on.) The day of my visit to the ranch, McGuane showed me first his office, in a small log building on the banks of the West Boulder River. Inside, the first item McGuane pointed out (clearly with great pride) is a recently received Trout Unlimited Award, for his efforts in promoting the trout population near his ranch. McGuane is a writer amazed and pleased at the durability of both his person and his work; he is also a rancher who has found full and comfortable accommodation in the lifestyles of the writing-and-ranching self that is Tom McGuane.

GREGORY MORRIS: *Do you still believe in the notion of "America as region," as undifferentiated space? Do you note any significant differences or changes in that "American space" you describe in your fiction?*

THOMAS MCGUANE: Yes, I do still believe in America as the basic region; I think we are, if anything, less and less segmented. It seems to me that we're entering the eerie new world of mono-space in America, a kind of vast media neighborhood, which may have some as yet undiscerned virtue.

In your work, you seem noticeably ambivalent about the American West, about both the Old West and the New West.

I certainly am ambivalent about the American West or any other region that attempts to bestow virtue through a kind of blessed nativity. I am a Meritocrat. The values of the "Old West" worth clinging to are the earlier American values worth clinging to and those are the systems and practices that derive from self-reliance. I do like to jar the complacency of the so-called New West. In my ranching, reading, conservation efforts, and writing, I would like to remind the West that the Golden Rule is still far superior to shooting first and asking questions later.

Do you feel you've replaced the Old Myth, the "Old Rugged," with a New Myth of the "New Rugged"? Do you think the New West capable of spawning new myths, new legends? Or are the Charlie Starkweathers the best we can do?

I do think that an area like this which retains a freshness of energy perhaps lost elsewhere has a chance to create if not new legends, at least new exemplary tales; but they will have to make sense within the very acute demands of current coexistence if they are not to be discarded immediately. The Code of the West, by current standards, is mere thuggishness.

Do you have any ideas on the resurgence in Western American writing, especially in its fiction? It seems that serious writers of the American West are enjoying a new popularity, a new visibility.

I don't know where this resurgence of Western writing is coming from. We are still in the frontier period here and this good new work is almost all the work of settlers. At bottom, writers nearly always work from optimism or the gaiety Yeats ascribes to tragedians. The West, generally, is a rather undepressing place to live. Maybe that's it.

Is Montana still your "adopted home," as you described it in your essay "Roping, from A to B"? Do you feel less of the adopted son after a few years there?

Yes, I feel settled here finally. I've been here a little over twenty years, raised four children here, voted and paid my taxes here. Sometime not so long ago it sank in that I've lived here far longer than where I grew up and it is certainly now home, I am happy to say: that was a lot of work.

Your vision seems to have grown less ironic, less satiric over time. Does the putting down of roots in Montana have anything to do with a greater affirmativeness in your fiction?

There are some areas from which I have lifted the pressures of satire through a kind of forgiveness. We do live in a time of a sort of furrowed-brow earnestness in which it is considered that irony is somehow a bad thing. I think irony is generally a good thing. Edmund Wilson once counseled people to cultivate a universal irony and he may have been right. Having said that, I do think that a tone of affirmation is definitely growing in my work from a variety of sources, like healthy children, happy marriage, love of the place in which I live.

When I speak of the "greater affirmativeness" in your writing, I'm thinking specifically of the stories in To Skin a Cat: *stories whose voices are generally sincere and unironic, whose characters are down-to-earth, whose visions are clear-eyed and sure. Yet the title story seems a throwback to your earlier fiction, seems an anachronism among the unironic kinds of stories.*

It's just a different story, though it is the oldest one in the collection, in my sort of Nathaniel West mode. I don't think it's important to produce a matched set, like china; and I often think of doing more sharply experimental work in the future.

Did your novel Keep the Change *fall into any sort of natural pattern, any sort of logical development of your fiction over time? Did that book differ, in any significant way, from previous novels?*

Keep the Change, in terms of its approach, is a perfectly evolutionary development of the books that preceded it. In fact, it is a key to the books that went before. It has some very systematic approaches to theme; and I'm amusing myself to see if anyone figures them out.

I'm pretty much going to duck your question as to how that book differs from early books. I don't think authors answer that one interestingly. Their strategies for preferment show through too clearly. I prefer seeing myself living and writing my way through life as a writer!

When envisioning the West, do you feel (as Patrick Fitzpatrick feels in Nobody's Angel*) that the Southwest was the "first part of the West with gangrene"? And has that gangrene spread farther north?*

I do think that a kind of corruption spreads across the country from the Sunbelt, a kind of hegemony of warmth promoters. Winter in the Northern Rockies has the same effect that tide has on the beach: it does tend to clean things up on a regular basis.

If America is, indeed, region, do you see yourself as a typically or particularly American author? Do you think your work travels well? Do you have to live in, or at least be familiar with "Hotcakesland" to understand what it is you're driving at?

I suppose I am typically American. I have had a fairly good reception overseas, especially France, Japan, and Holland. *Keep the Change* has been sold in ten countries and I am getting the feeling that something rather larger is happening for me out there. For a long time, I was told my work was "too American" for European consumption. This seems to be more of an English reservation than anything else, part of their ongoing fetish that we are screwing up the language.

We *all* live in Hotcakesland; it pours in through every opening: it is the absolute triumph of commerce over every other value; its effects range from the drug war to the hole in the ozone layer. Anyone who doesn't agree with me is wrong.

Thinking about some of the criticisms of your work, do you feel you're working toward a fairer portrayal of women in your fiction, toward some sort of sexual aesthetic? Do you see insuperable problems between the sexes, problems that render impossible any sort of reconciled, harmonious relationship?

I'm understanding women and other things which are not me better than I used to. The question implies a current political pressure rarely applied in the other direction. It is important to remember that I am a novelist, not a sociologist. Sure, the once-named "war between the sexes" may go on forever. Still, I raised my three well-adjusted daughters to be self-reliant and to apply the Golden Rule. That's about all you can do.

Perhaps as corollary to these concerns, it seems that the American family does not come off well in your fiction. Do you see the family as a casualty? Is the coherent family, too, a modern impossibility?

Without a chain of command – I don't care who is the captain – the nuclear family will have to go. As for the American family not coming off well in my fiction, where exactly does the American family come off well? Certainly not in statistics.

Could the failure of such relationships be in any way the result of the emphasis you place upon the individual, in that anyone external to that individual is viewed as secondary, as less than significant, as a nonsignificant other?

The modern deindividuated novel, the ensemble novel, the group portrait, the heroless novel is as incomprehensible to me as it would have been to the Greeks or to Shakespeare, or to Saul Bellow!

You seem, also, to dismiss religion as a source of belief and affirmation in your work; religion is, in fact, scarcely visible in your fiction. Characters seem to locate themselves and what little meaning and faith they can discover, in places other than institutionalized belief.

I do have an inchoate pining for religion. I see spirituality in the processes of natural renewal, in creation as it were. And I do think my vaguely Manichean worldview derives from my Irish Catholic heritage. In fact, I am very comfortable considering myself an Irish Catholic, implying, as it does to me, a superimposition of the life of Christ upon earth-worshipping pantheism. Like Flannery O'Connor, I frequently portray people in purgatory, hence the irreligious atmosphere.

Thomas Skelton says in Ninety-Two in the Shade: *"There are no great deaths anymore." Do you believe this to be true? Have we lost some basic, human capacity for the heroic, and for heroic loss?*

You must admit that the feeling that there are no great deaths any more is somewhat insistent. I do think that we have undermined the self to the degree that a long fall is inconceivable. I hope that is reversible. We go on pining for the Billy Sol Estes and Jim Bakkers and Richard Nixons to assure us that our national social life at least has some verticality. You need only to reflect on the death of Lincoln to sense the chasm between the trivialized present and the resonating individual lives of not so long ago.

You recently turned fifty. Does reaching that age seem in any way momentous to you? Are you surprised to have lasted that long, given the paths your earlier life often took?

Fifty. Yes, it seems momentous but I don't know just how. One is drawn to round figures. One remembers such a short time ago being eighteen and thinking fifty the last word in superannuated. I'm not surprised to have lasted this long and I haven't noticed any limitations yet based on age, except some tolerable morning aches.

Mailer said that a novelist at fifty is at the height of his powers, and I feel at the height of my powers. I don't know if I have matured, but I do know I have a more deeply layered sense of the human condition than I once had. Again, it is important to remember that literature is not sociology. Maturity may not have any particular merit in literature anyway. The greatest relief that has come my way, probably with age, is that I no longer feel as pained at being misunderstood as a writer as I once did. It doesn't hurt that I have numerous loyal readers who aren't having the same problems that some critics have and who have kept all of my books in print, nearly unheard-of in a writer of my generation working in the unfashionable backyard of the continent.

Do you still believe that "dropping six or seven good colts in the spring is just as satisfying as literature"? (Now that you're raising cattle, of course, the question should be about your calves.) Do you still feel — or perhaps feel even more strongly — that "art is no longer as important as life"?

I don't know about the life/literature split any more. They are both so absorbing and exclusive if given free rein. I still raise horses as well as cattle. The cattle business has taken me closer to the day-to-day actualities of Montana life, but the aesthete in me wonders about raising animals to kill. What has changed is that my family life seems so all-important. This is a little bit like wondering which is more important, gasoline or cars. The center of my life is writing; it is that without which I cannot be of much use to anyone or anything else.

You mention that you "grew up amidst an oral tradition." Do you feel that influence is present in your fiction?

I don't know about the influence of storytelling on my writing. I don't think of myself particularly as a storyteller. My passion is language and human perception, not necessarily in the form of stories.

You say elsewhere: "I'm trying to remove the tour de force *or superficially flashy side of my writing. I'm trying to write a cleaner, plainer kind of American English. . . . I feel I have considerably better balance than I have ever had in my life and I don't care to show off; I just want to get the job done." This remark was made at the beginning of the 1980s. Now that that decade has closed, how would you assess your success in this pursuit of an "American English"?*

I would still stand by this statement except to say that I think I am beginning to see possibilities for a new elegance in the American language. I am not so hellbent on plainness as I may have been recently. In fact, I've been thinking of gradually easing up on the old high horse once again, possibly in the form of a comic novel.

Your work in film seems to reflect your concern for the American West, a concern that spans both the Old and the New West. For instance, in Tom Horn *and* The Missouri Breaks, *you deal with the historical West, and in the former film with a specific historical figure of that West. In your screenplay for* Rancho Deluxe *you managed to create almost a myth of the New West, the film having attracted a cult following in some areas of the West today. Is this all just coincidence? Or have you found yourself becoming a chronicler (on film) of the American West by choice?*

It's a bit of coincidence, though it seemed to me that the West needed some revision; not just the corny cowboys-and-Indians West, but the pompous or backward-looking or nativist West of Wallace Stegner, Vardis Fisher, and even A. B. Guthrie.

Relatedly, you seem to write of that historical West only when you're writing for the screen. Do you ever feel the urge to write historical fiction for print?

I don't like historical fiction, ignoring for now the exceptions that prove the rule (Tolstoy, Stendahl et al.). I do love almost more than anything to read history, however.

Do you ever feel, then, the urge to create a particularly large work, something like McMurtry's Lonesome Dove? *You've said, for example, that your revision process often whittles down your work – work that originally might have been conceived upon a larger scale – into something more moderate, more contained.*

Writing historical fiction does seem to be one foolproof way to get large right now. I like McMurtry a lot, but *Lonesome Dove* is not a good book. I often wish I could write a long book, though few of the books I love are long. Having said that, I would note that the felt need to write "the big book" has injured more writers in mid-career than anything else. In our culture, a certain respect is paid to bigness without reference to anything else. Sharp careerists in postwar American letters have gone straight into the whopper business and stayed there, to their great benefit. A recent member of this school, John Irving, has shown in [*The World According to*] *Garp* that you can toss any damn thing into the stretched old hide of the American novel and thereafter have as your principal problem only the hauling of loot and medals and commendations. I've sometimes thought of writing a novel to my own taste and then have the family fatten it up over the winter by 75,000 to 100,000 words, as a sort of cottage-industry approach to literature, cutting them in fairly of course.

Unlike many other contemporary fiction writers, one thing you haven't had to do is to teach within the academy. Why?

I just think that teaching is a job itself, maybe even more on a collision course with writing than a more mainstream job. There is certainly something teachable about fiction writing; the trouble, though, is that students today are not often widely read, and they don't want to remedy that, which makes it sort of hopeless. Many writers work in the academy because it's a hell of a lot easier to be a writer-in-residence than to work for, say, Boeing or the Burlington Northern Railroad; and it's also a hell of a lot easier than subjecting yourself to the workplace brutality of the movie business.

I know you look for places, landscapes, that are the "ragged edges," the "blurred edges" of our American region. Are you still looking for those ragged edges of our continent, for those edges that cut, that are messy, that make your characters bleed so?

I think those ragged edges lie well within the world I know. No further searching required. A serious writer learns, sooner or later, that a sufficiency of material is always right at hand.

Lastly, it is well to remember that even Henry James, who thought out the obligations and systems of the novel more thoroughly than anyone else, concluded that the only real requirement of the novel is to be interesting.

WORKS

The Bushwhacked Piano. New York: Simon & Schuster, 1971. Novel.

Keep the Change. Boston: Houghton Mifflin, 1989. Novel.

Ninety-Two in the Shade. New York: Farrar, Straus & Giroux, 1973. Novel.

Nobody's Angel. New York: Random House, 1981. Novel.

Nothing but Blue Skies. Boston: Houghton Mifflin, 1992. Novel.

An Outside Chance: Classic and New Essays on Sport. Boston: Houghton Mifflin, 1990. Essays.

An Outside Chance: Essays on Sport. New York: Farrar, Straus & Giroux, 1980. Essays.

Panama. New York: Farrar, Straus & Giroux, 1978. Novel.

Something to Be Desired. New York: Random House, 1984. Novel.

The Sporting Club. New York: Simon & Schuster, 1969. Novel.

To Skin a Cat. New York: E. P. Dutton/Seymour Lawrence, 1986. Short fiction.

Amy Tan

Amy Tan was born in Oakland, California, in 1952, two and a half years after her parents immigrated from China to the United States. Upon leaving China, Tan's mother also left behind three children from an unfortunately arranged marriage; upon coming to America, Tan's father refused a scholarship to the Massachusetts Institute of Technology, electing instead to become a Baptist minister. These choices would have their effects upon Tan's nature and imagination.

Contrary to the hopes of her parents, who saw a neurosurgeon and concert pianist in their daughter, Tan pursued a master's degree in linguistics from San Jose State University and became a consultant to programs for disabled children. Later, she developed a successful career as a freelance writer for such companies as IBM and AT&T; when this career turned into a work addiction, Tan first sought psychiatric help, and when that proved fruitless she decided to write a novel. Attending the Squaw Valley Community of Writers workshops in California, Tan met fiction writer Molly Giles who, through those workshops and through later meetings of a writers group held by Giles in San Francisco, turned Tan toward the collection of stories that would eventually become *The Joy Luck Club*. Tan lives in San Francisco with her husband, and occasionally can be caught singing backup vocals for the Rock Bottom Remainders.

This interview took place in October 1992, in the old and elegant Edgeworth Club in the well-moneyed Pittsburgh suburb of Sewickley. Tan was in town to deliver a lecture and to autograph copies of her recently released children's book, *The Moon Lady*. As we talked, Tan smoked; her responses were often hushed, always careful and considered.

GREGORY MORRIS: *You live in and write of San Francisco, of course, and you were born in Oakland. I was wondering, then, if you are conscious of being what might be called a "Western writer"?*

AMY TAN: I have never been called a writer of the West, primarily because the critical focus is so much on the fact that I am Chinese-American, and that overrides any preoccupation with geographic residence. I do think the West has something to do with myself as a writer, though, in that the West to me is much more a place where immigrants come to. My background certainly has been one of living in a community that was primarily Chinese, and then moving gradually into the suburbs of California and seeing the changes that have gone on throughout the last thirty years. But I haven't really thought of myself as a Western writer; just as in some ways I don't identify myself as a writer of Chinese-American stories, so I don't identify myself as a writer of Western stories.

So that particular landscape of California and of San Francisco has no significant resonance for you as a writer?

Oh, it certainly has resonance for me. As I travel around, I am struck by how different my environment is from the rest of the world. I'm used to hills and cement and no seasons and the same clothes that I wear year-round. I also take for granted being in a city where everyone is different, and I don't mean just culturally different but different in various ways, so that I never feel that I stand out that much. When I go to China, I realize that I'm very much rooted not just in the United States but very specifically in San Francisco. If I had to choose a geography that is my sensibility, I would say it is San Francisco, very specifically. I wouldn't call it California.

You see San Francisco as being distinct from the rest of that geography which is California?

I think it's certainly different in its look, being a very small city on hills and right next to water and close to the mountains. But I think it's more the tone of the city, the feelings of the city, and the fact that you take for granted that people are not simply tolerant of other lifestyles but that they are interested in them.

Do you feel you have followed a typical pattern of assimilation? Or are you of "two minds" – of Chinese and American? What is the difficulty of being a woman artist who combines "American circumstances with Chinese character," as one of your characters puts it; or of putting "Western thoughts into a Chinese mind, causing everything to ferment," as another character puts it? Is this fermentation good for you as a writer?

Yes, I think a certain amount of confusion is valuable, and that a certain amount of contradiction is valuable to a writer, because I write out of a sense of conflict and not knowing answers and feeling that there are no truisms in the world, no generalizations that can be made. So that what I have to do is express a form of truth through the story; that, to me, is the closest I can come to finding *a* truth, but including all the circumstances that surround that truth, the entire concatenation of events which led up to that particular truth.

When I was growing up I was exposed to two different forms of belief, though I certainly wasn't aware of them as being in conflict with one another. My father was a Baptist minister, and my mother took on the outward appearances of being a minister's wife who embraced the same beliefs as her husband. But after my father became ill when I was fourteen, I saw these other beliefs emerge that I realized had always been there, but that came out in full force at that time. They were things having to do with a combination of beliefs that I think are part of Chinese culture. It's not really Buddhism and it's not really superstition; it's a combination of almost all possibilities. I always think of it as being pragmatism in its broadest sense, for economic and political and spiritual purposes. That, more than anything, has been important to me as a writer, the fact that there are all possibilities and it's up to me to determine which ones I embrace as my own set of beliefs – and that those beliefs are not fixed but change over time. It's not just saying that I'm wishy-washy on things; it's more a realization that life changes and that I bring different considerations into that life over time. If I believe anything, it's that there's no one answer to any one question; there are many answers. That, I think, is an outgrowth of my background.

One of the tensions in your fiction seems to be that between the impulse to tell stories and the impulse toward reticence and secretiveness. Your characters – particularly the mothers – tell stories to "save" their daughters, to save their lives and their spirits. At the same time, those characters keep secrets and seem reluctant to tell their "truths." How do these impulses reconcile themselves?

Well, I think what was always a part of my life, as well as my mother's and father's, was a quality of storytelling *and* of keeping secrets, and those qualities became, consciously or subconsciously, part of my writing. My mother had a secret about her life for many years that I didn't know about, and there were things about my father's life that I didn't know about. Basically, their life – pre-1949 – was unknown to me. My father, as a minister, was a storyteller; his sermons were very much like stories of the fantastic coupled with a personal sense of where he fit into the story. There was always a reason why he had to tell that story, just as there was a reason why my mother had to tell me something about her past. I think that element of there being a reason behind the story is very much a part of what I do in my fiction. As you probably have noticed, with basically everything I've written, I have a frame around the story, and the frame is the reason why the story must be told. As I find myself writing my third book, I don't yet have a frame to place around that story. It's an impulse I have: I must have this reason why the story must be told at this particular moment. That, to me, is almost as important as the story itself. The story may be the longer part of the work, but what motivates it to be told colors the way the story is told.

And that frame determines the number of voices required to tell that story?

In a way, because I often think of stories as having an interaction: a listener and a teller, or perhaps two people in a dialogue. It could be an internal sort of dialogue with oneself, but to me it's more powerful if there's another person who needs to hear the story, and that it's rooted in some *other* story related to *that* person.

The fact that there were so many voices in *The Joy Luck Club*, though, had more to do with the way that the whole book was shaped from the beginning. It was not a conscious effort – I did not start off saying to myself, Gee, I'm going to write this book and it will have these multiple voices and that will create this complexity having to do with the confusion in our lives as to where stories come from, and so forth. It was, instead, the fact that I was writing short stories, and I wrote one and then another, and they all had different character names. Then somebody, at one point when I had written three of them, said, Why don't you write a book of these; and I thought, Hmm, that's an interesting idea. By then I had all these characters, so I decided to make it a community of different people who had their stories to tell. I suppose I could have looked at the conscious choices that I made when

I included so many voices, could have gone back and done repair, could have given it a more cohesive and traditional narrative structure. But I also was aware of a freedom which allowed so many different characters to tell so many different types of stories. Too, I was a new writer and I didn't know what I was doing or what my voice really was, so for me it was a chance to try a lot of different voices and see if any of them would settle in as *the* voice.

As a writer, are you haunted by past lives? Does there come a point in the career of a writer of mixed heritage when she begins to write of the new world and not of the old world? Is it necessary to understand the old-world past before writing of the new-world present?

My motivations are not to write historical novels or to chronicle a kind of history. I'm fascinated by the past, mostly because I'm a storyteller who thinks that she has a free ticket to go anywhere in the world, at any time in the world, and why would I stay here? I would go somewhere else. The questions that I ask, though, are very contemporary ones, so I think of myself as writing a contemporary story but one that may be based on the past. What I learn from the past has a lot of relevance to my life or to whatever situation I have created that happens to be in the present. On the other hand, I do have an interest in the history of Chinese people because that's my family history, and for such a long time I didn't know anything about it. I didn't know that there was a war in China that happened in World War II; I thought, like Pearl in *The Kitchen God's Wife*, that World War II was something that had nothing to do with China and Japan. I understand a lot more about myself and what was given to me because of what my parents went through in their lives. For instance, these warnings that my mother always used to give me when I was growing up – so many of them were rooted in experiences she had gone through, and until I had gone through them myself in a story, I didn't fully understand what she was talking about.

I'm writing a story now that has nothing to do with my family in one sense; the history is in Shandong Province a hundred years ago, and my family never – well, they lived in Yentai for awhile doing some trade there – but the story is not about the events and details of their actual lives. It has more to do with questions that are in my family that I can find during that period in history. Not just religious questions – for example, my father's family was converted by missionaries sometime around the turn of the century – but different questions relating to responsibilities that were always a part of my upbringing. I think that by writing with those questions in my mind, I can go back to an interesting period of history and find a story, any kind of story, and approach that question from many different angles that will surprise me, simply because it is fiction. It will surprise me, and I will learn something that is true about what I think about these questions.

Seiwoong Oh has commented that your novels "signal the beginning of a new phase in Asian American writing, the shift from an aggressive and desperate search for identity, as in Frank Chin and Maxine Hong Kingston, to the proclamation of pride and reconciliation." Do you feel that this is true? Do you feel that the Asian-American self has been pretty well established in the fiction of Asian-American writers?

It's always curious to me how other people analyze one's work; they seem to have a much clearer perspective on how it compares to other work. I don't necessarily even want to compare my work to that of other Asian-American writers, as if that is the category that our literature should be placed in and that that should become the basis for the comparison. I don't think of myself as having an agenda or a theme that has to do with culture so much; I write stories about human nature – the same sorts of stories anybody would write about. I'm not reacting, I guess, to anything. My stories come from a much more personal sense of what I want to write stories about. Part of that might also be because when I started writing fiction I was largely unaware of what was going on in the literature, so I had no assumptions to kick off of. So when I hear these remarks about a shift or something, I think, Well, that's very interesting; but I take neither credit nor blame for it because it never was my intention to do one or the other.

I have thought about this issue of people's expectations for a writer who happens to be of (as you call it) "mixed heritage." It's almost as if people place this mantle on you and say, Your responsibility is to write about culture and to demystify culture, to talk about identity, to assert that this is not the stereotype that we want and then to create a new image for your people. I think it's a very dangerous assumption – that writers who happen to be not of the typical mainstream are supposed to create models. It limits what the work can be. The critical perception of the work immediately is: Why aren't you writing more positive role models of Chinese men? Are you going to do fathers and sons? It's a *strange* question to me. When you think about it, it's not a question posed to other American writers: Annie Dillard, would you start writing about urban America and industrialization, since you've written so much about nature? John Updike, don't you think your role models of disaffected men in Pennsylvania should change to something else? It's a curious question. It goes back to thinking about the reasons why writers write. I know there are writers who write for political reasons and who want to change the world and hit upon great political themes. But I write from what is of specific interest to me – and that may be selfish. I sometimes wonder if I'm just a very selfish writer, but maybe that's the wrong term. A writer's sphere of influence varies from writer to writer, and I see mine as being a very small one; and if it affects people in a larger forum, well that's what they have put on the writing afterward, that's what literature does. I write fiction, and people take it and that becomes the literature and what they do with it – that's *their* literature, that's not *my* literature. When I take it back for myself, it's fiction and it's very personal.

So you feel no real political responsibility as a writer?

That's not to say that I'm unaware of it; it certainly has been thrust at me as something I'm supposed to do or somehow it's perceived that that's something I'm doing. I could say that I'm a political writer but that the politics I'm writing about are very personal to me. I think of my next book as being very political, and I think of *The Kitchen God's Wife* on some level as being political: beyond the basic storyline of a woman who goes through a terrible life, it's a story about beliefs and where they come from and all the different forms through which beliefs are thrust upon us, whether through propaganda or old wives' tales.

You talked of men earlier, and I'm reminded of a remark made by Pearl in The Kitchen God's Wife: *"But that was how I was raised – never to criticize men or the society they ruled, or Confucius, that awful man who made that society. I could blame only other women who were more afraid than I." To what degree is this true? To what degree were Chinese women subordinated to men and to the teachings of Confucius?*

My father was a great believer of Confucius in terms of his philosophy, and I think that his writings are wonderful. But along with all of those writings, Confucius created a social structure for how you meet your responsibilities to one's self and to society; that structure placed different people in different hierarchies of authority, and women were at the bottom basically. My mother is not that schooled in Confucianism, but what she felt as a result of how society was set up for her is that Confucius was the source of a lot of women's suffering. That line is actually a quote from my mother; I just loved it when I heard her say that, and I thought, I'm going to put that in the book.

This character also ends up blaming women for believing those things, for believing they were the ones who were wrong, that if anything went wrong in their lives they had to look to themselves for the cause. And yet they had no recourse for changing anything. Basically, in a Confucian society (which is similar to the society now in China, only layered with a Communist government), the Emperor (or the head of the Communist party) is the ultimate authority from which all thoughts of how you lead your life come. It's up to these different orders within the society to keep that overall order in the universe. Men – fathers – were the ones within family units to keep that order, and their sons would be the next to pass that role along. Yet at the same time, women were very strong and upheld family values in their own ways, but they didn't have the power for the most part. I don't think that was true of every family; it's like saying in the United States, here's your traditional family, here's how the structure works, women always are the caretakers, men are traditionally seen as the breadwinners, then you have your two-income families but still the women end up washing the dishes and taking out the garbage. It's just a generalized perception. I think that in China, especially before 1949, the idea that there was always someone lower than you was part of the general thinking; you were always looking for someone who was lower than you were.

Do the women in your fiction find a form of empowerment through economic gain and enterprise? I'm thinking of the women who form the lending society in The Joy Luck Club *and of the two women who co-own the flower shop in* The Kitchen God's Wife. *Do these women find a source of power in these ventures, power denied them in China?*

I don't consider the Joy Luck Club as a credit society; it is a social club and the members invest money, but the money stays with the society. People don't actively lend money one to another unless it is out of friendship, like sending June to China. Associations like these exist primarily in the Cantonese communities – they have a long history of associations that not only lent money but also intervened in family matters, for example, when sons or daughters got into trouble or a new relative came over and needed help in finding housing or finding a job. The people who came from China to the United States after 1949 were from a different part of China, by and large they were educated people or political people who were leaving because they had worked for the Kuomintang as opposed to the Communists; and they came from such different areas of China that they didn't really form family or clan associations in the same ways as those long-time associations that you find in Chinatowns in the United States: they formed social clubs where they could meet one another. My family, for instance, lived in Oakland for a number of years. Oakland didn't have the same kind of Chinatown community as San Francisco, but they would all get together and all our family social gatherings were with Chinese people. It was a chance to invest and to get to learn the "American rules" together – how things work, how you make money in this country – but it wasn't their primary source of investment. They all had their own lives and jobs.

I would say that empowerment is an interest of mine, but it's not a concern of mine in my writing. Again, I'm not setting out to write about the empowerment of women; I'm writing stories, and maybe they happen to be about women because I'm a woman and the concerns I have naturally lend themselves to such stories. But I don't start off consciously deciding to write about the empowerment of women, of how they have been disenfranchised from the world and the economy, and of how they're making a change for themselves. I don't set out with those agendas.

Your work certainly has been concerned with the construction *of the individual identity, with the difficulties of establishing identity amid the web of family. What special pressures are placed upon the emerging, individual, Chinese-American self by the familial, Chinese-American self?*

Are you asking about how I think about things or about how things are portrayed in my fiction?

I guess I'm asking about your fictional world.

It's funny: when you ask these questions, I know they're a part of my work but it's not the way I think of my work. Again, it's a matter of people deconstructing your work, and when they deconstruct your work they deconstruct your life.

Is that because there's such a strong autobiographical impulse in your work?

No, it's because when I write a story I'm not conscious of the themes people tend to talk about outside of writing fiction. The approach is so different; in a story all of a sudden you have all of these things that you've done, and then people come back and say this is what went into your story, and you say, Oh, that's interesting. The grossest example of that, one that surprised me early on, was what my editor said to me after I turned in the manuscript of *The Joy Luck Club*. There was one story in there that was not about a mother and daughter, it was about a relationship between a husband and wife – and my editor said, You know, I see this book as being a book about mothers and daughters. And I looked at her and said, Really, you do? You would think I had started off saying: I'm going to write a book about mothers and daughters. I just wrote stories, and they kept turning *up* mothers and daughters. I could just as easily have written a story that could have come out to be about relationships, but at the time the stories just came out that other way. I didn't see it until after she pointed it out to me. So when you ask me even more delineated questions about the emergence of identity, I know it's in the story but I don't know how to explain it, I don't know how to explain it from a sociological point of view. I could tell you a story. If you want to hear a story about identity, I can tell you a story.

I suppose that's the route that you take – the act of storytelling is the act of explaining.

Yes, we're starting from different ends of it. I start off with something that moves me and puzzles me and I start writing, and in the end it emerges perhaps as a story about identity, but I don't know that until the end of that process. I never go back and analyze my stories; I see it in reviews and I've stopped reading reviews because I get very confused about what it is I'm writing. I don't want it to color my writing, but it's as if I'm supposed to shape my stories around knowing ahead of time the overall construct of an idea and how the story fits into the construct. A story is very organic and it creates its own context; at the end there is a construct, but it's after the fact.

Identity. Self. Hmm. Well, these characters all have identities apart from their families. I think what happens when people look at cultures and bicultural upbringings is that they think there's either this amalgam that happens and you know what the amalgam is, or there's a duality, there's a split, and it's 50 percent this and it's 50 percent this, or it exists at this point and the other's in conflict with it. I think that part of that identity, whether you're talking about daughter versus individual or Chinese versus American, is not that clear; it's in flux all the time, and we never know what the interaction is except in the particular moment. We become aware of things that are comfortable or not comfortable, of things that are familiar or not familiar. When I'm with my friends shopping, I'm certainly not thinking, Am I a daughter or an individual, am I a Chinese or an American? If I'm in China with my family, and my sister is scolding me and telling me not to do certain things, I'll think, Geez, this is really a Chinese family here! But I don't think of my stories or of myself in those psychological terms, because such thinking assumes that there's a whole set of parameters about what it all means: what goes into identity and selfhood and family webs.

But do your own stories grow out of that tension? I guess I'm interested in your storytelling technique, in the pressures that exert themselves on that technique and shape it.

My storytelling technique is probably undefined. It often starts with a question about life; coupled with that is an image of something, or of several images, that are interesting to me. I don't know how the image is related to the question, and I start to write a story from that. The question and the image can both fall away and be replaced by other things when I start writing the story and other things emerge. I'll give you an example – I can only tell you how it happens for each book.

With *The Joy Luck Club*, it was just in the beginning a desire to write a story. I didn't know what a story was or what voice was, but I knew that fiction was things that were not true – that's what I thought fiction was at the time. So, in the beginning I wrote stories about rich girls whose families lived near M.I.T.; that never was my experience, so that was fiction. And things came out sounding really silly. Then I wrote a story about a young girl who was a chess player; now I had read a story in *Life* magazine about a chess prodigy who happened to be Chinese, and I wondered what kind of mental attitude this woman would have toward life now that she was grown up. I decided to write a story about that because I don't play chess, but I would make her Chinese-American because perhaps I'd be able to put in detail that I was familiar with. The story for some reason had to do with this strength that she had, this way of looking at the world, and with who her adversaries were. But this story kept veering off toward being not so much about chess as about this relationship with her mother. Well, this is very strange, I thought; I'd keep trying to yank the story back and put it in the context of this chess game, because in my mind there was an image of this chessboard and pieces and darks and lights. But in the end I had this story that was more about a girl and her mother, and that was when I found that fiction is a form of truth because you can start off writing something that is not true and you come up with a form of truth. What I discovered was something about my own life, and the feelings I had about my own mother, knowing that she had given me a certain kind of strength *and* at the same time wanting to separate myself and claim that whatever strengths I had came from me, they didn't come from her – but finding out that they in fact did. And finding that in some other way when she denied herself to me, that I lost that strength, and that was very mysterious. But I couldn't explain to you why it is we lose that strength at that particular point; I have no psychological reference for that. I'm just writing a story about what I have found to be true.

With each story it was the same thing. I might have a question about, well, what would it be like to lose hope? What if you had someone in a situation where hope was just the stupidest thing in the world? And I started writing a story about that, but the story kept veering back to things that related to my life and my mother's life and situations about hope.

So the story comes with a very amorphous question, then it shapes itself with a couple of images, and then it becomes its own thing. The next story that I'm writing is about responsibility, but I suppose I could say that one day I was watching television when the Gulf War [in 1991] was being broadcast as if it were some kind of football game, and people all around me were saying that we have to be the police to the world. I started thinking about the responsibilities we have within small groups of people or within families or within communities, and how those responsibilities extend out to country and then globally. I had no clear answers. I was very uncomfortable that I had no clear answers to this question. I wanted to define things almost as in a mathematical equation: you have intentions, you have actions that you take as a result of your intentions, you have consequences of your actions, and in the end you have responsibilities that you take in respect to all of that. The values of that equation aren't absolute; you change them and fiddle with them, you so warp the equation that the formula doesn't work. It just goes askew in different ways.

So I started talking to different people about areas in their life that related to this question of intentions and responsibilities, and found out that none of these people had any idea how this problem related to their lives, and this bothered me a whole lot. I thought I should have a moral position on how I feel about the Gulf War or about how I feel about children starving in Africa or about how I should feel about taking care of my mother or about how I should feel about taking care of relatives in China who are strangers to me in some respects. So I thought I'd write a story and I'd discover all the contradictions that I feel about this question – not to find the answer to the question, but to find all the permutations to the problem. And that's how my stories start.

WORKS

The Joy Luck Club. New York: G. P. Putnam's Sons, 1989. Novel.
The Kitchen God's Wife. New York: G. P. Putnam's Sons, 1991. Novel.
The Moon Lady. New York: Macmillan, 1992. Children's story.

Douglas Unger

Douglas Unger was born in Moscow, Idaho, in 1952 and, despite early travels in the eastern United States and in Latin America, grew up an intimate of ranch life. That knowledge and that experience Unger has turned into the stuff of much of his fiction. In particular, Unger works with the landscape of western South Dakota and with its sometimes bleak agrarian history. During the farm troubles that began in the late 1980s, Unger also turned into something of a spokesman for the beleaguered farmer, and he continues to labor for the recovery of the American farm to its place in U.S. culture. A graduate of the University of Iowa Writers Workshop, Unger long taught in the creative writing program at Syracuse University. At present, however, he directs the international writing program at the University of Nevada-Las Vegas, a program he himself developed. His novel *Leaving the Land* (which, with *The Turkey War*, forms part of what Unger laughingly calls his intended "turkey trilogy") was a finalist for the 1985 Pulitzer Prize and the 1985 Robert F. Kennedy Award, and received the Society of Midland Authors Award in 1984.

This interview with Unger is one of only two interviews in the collection that took place east of the Mississippi River. Unger and I talked in 1988, while he was still teaching in Syracuse; we sat at his dining room table. In the living room were photos of family members – generations of family members – as well as photos of Raymond Carver, whose first marriage was to the sister of Unger's wife Amy. As he talks, Unger gestures with long and expressive hands.

GREGORY MORRIS: *Your work is known for its concern with place, and one of the places you write so eloquently of is the American West. Your familiarity with this region came, I believe, from your childhood experience there, with your family's roaming through that region?*

DOUGLAS UNGER: My father had three different ranches: the first in Steamboat Springs, Colorado; the second in Craig, Colorado; the third in Newell, South Dakota. So we kind of hopped from place to place. Land values were part of the incentive to buy bigger and better farms in those days. Steamboat Springs became a ski resort in the 1960s, and that's about the time my father sold out. It was also the time that he divorced my mother, so that was part of it. Then he bought a place north of Craig, Colorado, about 30 miles south of the Wyoming border; he sold that place around 1971, and bought a big place in Newell, South Dakota, which we were on for only a few years – we sold that in 1978.

I had kind of a dual childhood, actually, because after my mother divorced my father, she moved back East, to Long Island. I spent some school years there and some with my father in Colorado, so I went back and forth. I guess you'd say I'm from a *partly* farming family. In a sense, it's not a traditionally oriented family-farming family, because my father originally was a lawyer and an Easterner, but he always had this dream coming out of World War II that he would go West and get a place. He taught at the University of Idaho when I was born, and did really strange Western things – for example, he was rodeo coach at the University of Idaho.

But he didn't grow up with that sort of experience?

No, he came from the East; he was born on Long Island, but he watched a lot of rodeo, spent several summers following the circuit and talking to the cowboys. I suppose that like many newcomers encountering a particular style of life, he embraced it with more passion than even the natives did. He started dressing in Day-Glo cowboy suits and sunburst Mexican handmade boots, and cultivating a sort of Richard Boone, rugged aspect about him. So I have both of these backgrounds. It's strange how whenever I turn around, it seems that despite this East-West dichotomy that exists in my background, there's always a farm somewhere, including the one my wife Amy and I are managing, trying to figure out what to do with.

You've said that you listened to a lot of your mother's stories at the kitchen table, out West, and that those stories were a source for the voice of Marge Hogan in Leaving the Land.

Actually, those were my father's second wife's stories. The origins for *Leaving the Land* really came from her. She was from Gillette, Wyoming, originally, and was a very tough Western woman. She grew up raising turkeys, pretty much like the character in the book. That was during the Craig, Colorado, period, when I was living with my father and his mother and his second wife. I would listen to her, and to her talking to neighbor women a lot, and that generated much of the story. She also taught us how to ride, and how to deal with horses; she could cold-cock a horse, literally. She just had no fear. Her stories of growing up in the late 1930s, pre-World War II, on a place outside of Gillette, Wyoming, and how much she hated it in childhood, what it was like – these were sources for the novel. And her stories of her romantic problems of the time, these were stories that stuck with me and became a genesis of the book.

I believe, too, that you and your two brothers ran a ranch for a while?

That was a sheep ranch in South Dakota. My father basically left it up to my brothers and me to manage; my older brother and my younger brother were there pretty much full time, but I was there during college vacations and all summer long providing labor and a lot of other things.

Actually, "managed" was probably not the right word – *mis*managed would probably be a better word, but there was a lot of work to do, and we did our best. My father, at that point, was hoping that we would go on with it, but in the end none of us really did. My younger brother saw how hard it was, that it was bigger than any of us could manage, so he bailed out and joined the Navy. And I sort of bailed out and became a writer and went to graduate school.

So none of the brothers stayed?

None of the brothers really stayed, though we keep rebounding back. My younger brother, who's an Alaska fisherman, just bought a place, 20 acres, up very close to where Amy and I have a farm in Washington State. So I guess we're all becoming part-time, long-distance farmers.

Keeping a tie to the land?

Keeping some sort of tie, I suppose. Legitimate, big-business farmers would scoff at us and call us part of the problem, no doubt.

So when you write in El Yanqui *of the high school years, those high school years were in South Dakota?*

I went to several different high schools; basically my high school career is very checkered, has a lot of missing parts to it. Until I got to Argentina. I doubt if I ever, in fact, would have graduated from high school in any traditional way if I hadn't gotten the American Field Service scholarship.

Were you politically active while you were down there, in 1969–70?

I was politically active, in terms of the chaos of the times and what a high school student could do. We went out wall painting; we joined in the demonstrations when there were national strikes, and there were *regular* national strikes. But it was a kind of youthful, completely unaligned political activity. It was more like teenage vandalism with a cause, going out and wall painting with my Argentine brothers. Flirting with leftist ideas, flirting with leftist Peronist ideas in particular – which of course infuriated the parents at that time. It was their way of rebelling, and maybe in a more serious way than we rebelled in this country in the 1960s. I was very active when I came back in the 1960s, to the University of Chicago, in the antiwar movement.

And it was at Chicago that your own development as a fiction writer began?

The years at Chicago – 1970 to 1973 – were interesting times for me; I got to know Wayne Booth, Norman Maclean, Saul Bellow – well, I'm not sure any student got to know Saul Bellow. Most important, though, was Richard Stern. He has consistently been a big help to me.

While I was there I wrote a novel called *Fevertree*, which was my bachelor's thesis at Chicago; it's such a scattered undergraduate book that it has elements of everything I've ever written in it: the farm is in Colorado, and there's an Argentina section, and there's a crazy brother in it who's just gotten back from Vietnam. Plus there's a lot of urban stuff in Chicago. Still,

Random House optioned the novel, and I was flown to New York by Jason Epstein – I thought I had it made.

That's a heady experience.

It *was* a heady experience. In fact, he met me at the Plaza Hotel's Palm Room; it was the first time I'd ever been there, and I was in a borrowed corduroy jacket and seated there and drinking wine. Jason was chomping on an Havana cigar and saying, Well, what are you going to do with yourself? Why don't you come to New York? We'll rewrite this book. I said, What am I going to do here? And he said, Don't worry about that; we'll help you get work. So I abandoned my graduate studies at the University of Chicago, dropped my scholarship, came to New York in January and rented a garret. I earned my living doing ghost-writing, and occasionally would drive my roommate's cab at night.

Meanwhile, I rewrote the book *three* times from January through July, and we kept having huge fights about it – Epstein just didn't think it was coming together right, and I was very full of myself and thought it was perfect. Finally, he just said, Look, forget it. And he threw a big double issue of *Antaeus* at me – hit me in the face – and said, Here, read this. Model yourself after these writers; go out and make a name for yourself, kid. And that was it. Bang!

So you left New York?

I left New York and, with the help of Richard Stern, got into the University of Iowa Writers Workshop. I spent two great years at Iowa. I got a teaching-writing fellowship in the second year and read fiction manuscripts every day for the *Iowa Review;* T. Coraghessan Boyle and I would sit side by side and read just tons of manuscripts.

As a student there, I worked with Leonard Michaels and John Irving. Irving was a good teacher, a really strong influence, and helped me out a great deal. He also directed me into writing about rural places; I was doing all kinds of stories then, some urban, some South American, some set in these odd farm worlds – I think the first real Newell [later to become Nowell] stories I wrote were written then – and John sort of pointed out these stories and said, This is your strongest material – why don't you focus on that?

So you were writing short fiction then?

Well, I was sort of experimenting with short pieces, and I've never really gone back to them. Irving helped me decide that I should write about that world. As I said earlier, every summer, every vacation I was going back and working the sheep ranch with my brothers; even when I was admitted to Iowa I didn't go directly to Iowa – I spent a month on the sheep ranch and drove from South Dakota in a broken-down GMC panel truck, smelling of lanolin and sheep shit.

It sounds as though you maintained that "in-transit" lifestyle that marked your childhood – a lot of time spent moving from here to there?

I suppose that's true. After Iowa (where Amy and I met), we went out to California and spent a year there. It was probably the drunkest, craziest time in my life. In fact, most people involved either ended up in detox centers or mental hospitals.

Then from there, we went back to New York and I managed the East Side Bookstore for almost a year. I was still working on *Leaving the Land* all this time, the original parts of it, and it was being rejected everywhere. It had this metafictional baggage behind it – I had a Japanese firm turn up in Nowell, South Dakota, with a way to raise turkeys on reprocessed automobile tires. I was still playing around with those Pynchonesque kinds of ideas and having a great deal of fun with it. I had Karl Marx turning up, literally – it was his reincarnation – passing through town, affecting the town and disappearing like a Marquezian character, never to return again. Doing crazy things, ripping off a lot of effects, and writing the wrong way.

Our life came to a kind of halt in New York, and after a short stop in Iowa City, we went back west to Washington State. Actually, at one point – from 1978 through 1980 – I didn't work on fiction at all. I felt like it was all over; the big book I was working on would never go anywhere. So in Washington I got a job as a commercial fisherman, which was an ideal life, really: you'd start work on a boat around June 1 and fish all summer and on through the middle of November, and then you'd get to collect unemployment the rest of the year.

The first year I was on a purse-seine boat, and we did so well in fact that I was able to buy my own little boat and ran my own operation for the next three years. Then I had a bad year; that last season, I had horrible luck fishing – there's no other way to explain it, really. I was also deep into redoing the book then, too; I just couldn't stop. I was back into writing fiction again. I figured out that those two novellas could go together and become a book, and I sent them off to Ted Solotaroff [at Harper & Row].

After I sold the boat (which I really hated to do), we moved on to Amy's aunt's farm – the original homestead of Amy's family – and used some of the profit from the boat to develop the farm, putting in a good well, then a drainfield.

And it was on this farm that you did much of the writing of Leaving the Land?

Well, a lot of it.

Do you think that your own experience on that farm – with the tax burden that came with it – contributed in any way to the darkness that seems to prevail in Leaving the Land? *I know that students and other readers continually remark on the bleakness of the book, on its darkness. They keep waiting, they say, for something good to happen to someone – and nothing good, they argue, ever does happen.*

I think a lot of people react that way to it, and it is a dark book. I see great darkness there, and I still see it despite the fact that the *New York Times* and the prevailing media have declared that the farm crisis is over – it's not over. You know, I was writing *Leaving the Land* constantly from 1976 through 1983, and I saw what was happening in South Dakota. First of all there was a big drought there in the early 1970s – my father bailed out of his farm during that period. Then Amy and I went to the Pacific Northwest to her family farm, which had been abandoned for nearly twenty years, was in ruins, and which was a lot like the dark farm at the end of the novel. (Yes, I did a lot of the writing and rewriting, especially of the second half of the book, also facing the dark heritage of my wife's farm, and it did affect the coloring of the novel.) And I do feel the whole disappearance of that particular mode of doing things as a particularly dark phenomenon.

So that while people talk about Douglas Unger as an agrarian writer, they shouldn't talk about you as a romantic *agrarian writer?*

Right. I think I'm basically on the dark side of things. As a writer, I find that's my impulse. I know it's hard to take, I know it's not popular – and I've had the same experience of facing groups of young people who say, Come on, where's the light, where's the hope? I think that I'm very pessimistic, especially about that particular subject; I *feel* a great deal of pessimism at times, and I don't know if I'll be able to turn that around. It would be nice to be able to write comedy; I'm not sure that I'm able to. I think I can write ironic humor, but I don't think I can write a completely comic structure with a happy ending. It's never been something I could do and feel convinced was right.

I think if you look at the agrarian writers closely, you'll not see much brightness in their work. Look at [Frank Norris's] *The Octopus;* what a dark ending that book has. Look at *A Deal in Wheat,* or look at *The Pit.* Those are all dark, dark novels in which these overwhelming economic forces overcome individuals and destroy them. [Steinbeck's] *The Grapes of Wrath* – I don't think that could be very much darker than it is. And the same is true of contemporary writers in this tradition. I don't think Louise Erdrich's work is any brighter, and I don't really think Janet Kauffman is much lighter in tone either, although *Collaborators* has many bright, wonderful moments. Larry McMurtry's *The Last Picture Show* is a dark, dark book. Carol Bly is extremely dark in her stories about the future of farmlands, the future of small-town sociologies and what's going to happen to them. So I think the tradition itself is pretty darn bleak if you look at it closely. I find very few novels I pick up out of the agrarian tradition that are really speaking in a hopeful way.

Getting back to Leaving the Land *for a moment, one of the striking things about that book certainly is the split narrative voice, with Marge Hogan as the focus of the third-person narrative of the first half of the book, and her son Kurt narrating the second half. How did that rather radical technical approach grow from the original concept for the book?*

Originally, the book was five related novellas. One of those novellas was about the German prisoners of war in the United States; I've turned that into a very straightforward narrative and into a short novel, *The Turkey War.* I took two of the remaining novellas and put them together, began to play with their echoes back and forth, until the book finally jelled.

One of the natural questions is why not give Marge her own voice in the first section?

I tried that, but I couldn't do it. It was too hard to work from inside that character; I had to stay just outside her. The androgynous work of writing from another gender became overwhelming in the first person. So I had to do it just very close to her point of view.

Originally I wanted to do a romantic kind of narrative in one novella, an historical narrative in another, a very surrealist kind of narrative in a third, and a first-person, antiheroic narrative in another; then I wanted to do an omniscient third person in which all members of that town, in which the whole consciousness of the place exists all at once – like William Gass's *In the Heart of the Heart of the Country*. This was the concept behind the five novellas that I was thinking of as one book. So I took the romantic narrative and linked it with that alienating, antiheroic voice and organized it around that one character, because she is at the center of both narratives, as is the land. And those two centers come together. It was a kind of organic process.

I tell writing students that in order to be sure about a book, you've got to try every different combination you possibly can. Don't accept the way it's written the first time through; try it again, try changing your narrative point of view, try changing the point of view character. Try a lot of different ways of working out a book until you've got several different alternatives, and then decide which is the best one and begin to work on that. That's very much the way I work on a book: going back to old ideas I've written one way, and then trying them a completely different way and seeing how it works, and then putting that aside and working on a different idea, and so forth. Things go through transformations while they're sitting in a drawer; you pull them out, and the words really have changed, they're not the same words.

And what has happened to the stories in these other novellas and to the many stories you once said you could tell of this region and this period? Do you find yourself ever tempted to build any sort of community in your fiction, as Faulkner and Wendell Berry have done?

Sometimes, but I also have a tremendous desire to get out of there and move elsewhere, because I think it's been done. I think it's been done in a Faulknerian sense. I know one of the dangers that Louise Erdrich faces – and I admire her work a great deal – is getting trapped up there in North Dakota. I think she has a much broader vision than that, and that she should in some way write her way out of that.

Are you trying to write yourself out of that sort of trap? Considering that your latest novel, The Turkey War, *returns to that same Nowell community described in* Leaving the Land *– aren't you, in a sense, writing yourself back into it?*

The Turkey War is an industrial story, though, and not an agrarian story. *Leaving the Land* is about, or takes place around, a farm; there's a center to the book, that one character and that one farm that we follow. In *The Turkey War*, the center of the book is the machinery of the process itself inside that plant, that factory, and how a man devotes his whole life to that process. It's a different view of that same world.

Certainly, turkeys are the same as farms in an economic sense; they're equally manipulated as metaphors, as economic metaphors. That's what intrigues me, really, about the idea of working with an economic metaphor like that. I was amazed at how comfortably points could be made, at how I could still do new and different things with it, specifically within the context of World War II and that particular product. What an American thing it is! Imagine our soldiers at Monte Cassino on Thanksgiving, with these turkeys from the Midwest being delivered! In some ways it's very absurd, and yet in some ways it's very American. To me it's a metaphor for that kind of profit. I was also very fascinated – perhaps *too* fascinated – with the inside of the factory; perhaps the problem with the book is that it's so involved with the actual machinery of the production itself.

But of course, it is a book about a factory, about a meat-packing plant, and I'm very moved by what's happening in that industry right now. I followed the Hormel strike in Austin, Minnesota, very closely, and I followed Iowa Beef's problems. It's also happening in the eastern part of South Dakota, though that's not the particular area of the state that I'm writing about; wages have dropped tremendously, from $9 an hour down to $4.50 and $5 an hour. Most people have no idea what that world is like, and so I decided that would be one of the justifications for going back into it.

You mentioned earlier that you consider the style in The Turkey War *to be more straightforward, more lean?*

Yes, stylistically it's very minimal compared to the first two books. Minimal in terms of flatter sentences and a less elaborate prose, mainly because the narrative follows a blue-collar character and it would be hard to wax lyrical in his imagination or from his point of view. I don't know what the world is going to think, but it was just a book that was there, and I decided to do it. I decided to do it partly because I felt it was incomplete, and partly because I wanted to try the subject again.

And you use the same locale and some of the same characters who appear in Leaving the Land.

Yes, the book is set in the same sort of fictive world, and a couple of the minor characters in *Leaving the Land* are major characters in this book. Mose Johnson is the major point of view character, whom Ben Hogan dislikes intensely because he works for the company; he in fact ridicules him for being not too bright, and the fact is he's *not* too bright. He's manipulated by the system in a great way. The novel also picks up on that little side story about the German prisoners of war, so it all takes place during three and a half years of the war, basically from 1942 through 1946.

Does this novel exhaust that supply of stories, or at least the supply of significant stories of that area?

Well, you asked earlier about my keeping in that world and creating a sort of Faulknerian idea out of that world and so forth – there's actually one more book that I have in mind that goes in that world. I don't know when I'll ever write it, but it has to do with – I forget Wendell Berry's exact term for it – but it has to do with reviving land, with reviving an abandoned farm. So that will sort of complete "The Turkey Trilogy," as my friends are calling it.

Do you ever feel the urge to break out and do something like Lonesome Dove, *something completely out of our time?*

Oh, I'd love to be able to at some point. I love Larry McMurtry's work; I find my impulse to be closer, in fact, to what he's doing. I got a lot from him, reading him as a young man; I got a lot out of his landscapes, and from his way of treating characters.

I have thought about a few things. I think a good idea for a novel, for example, would be the Carlin hunting party of the 1880s – they were just this group of Easterners who decided they'd go out to Idaho and have a great time. They went up into the mountains and of course immediately got sick, and they all just panicked and left this sick cook behind, thinking he would die. When the Army went in to try and find them, they found the five survivors and gave the cook up for dead; but the next spring they found the cook only 15 miles from where the others had been picked up. The guy had made it, terribly ill, all that way down the mountain on his own. What a great irony! There was a big press stink about it all, about what these cowards had done by leaving the man behind. There are a lot of old Western stories that would make a great book, a book more in the traditional Western vein.

Oddly enough, in fact, in Finland *Leaving the Land* did extremely well partly because the bookstores sold it right alongside the Westerns. They put it right next to the Louis L'Amour novels, and all these Finnish fans of the American Western bought it and really liked it. I'm not sure what that says about the Western, about me – or about Finland!

WORKS

El Yanqui. New York: Harper & Row, 1986. Novel.
Leaving the Land. New York: Harper & Row, 1984. Novel.
The Turkey War. New York: Harper & Row, 1988. Novel.

INDEX